Fishing Maine

by
Tom Seymour

FALCON™
HELENA, MONTANA

Falcon Press® is continually expanding its list of recreational guidebooks using the same general format as this book. All books include detailed descriptions, accurate maps, and all information necessary for enjoyable trips. You can order extra copies of this book and get information and prices for other Falcon books by writing Falcon Press, P.O. Box 1718, Helena, MT 59624. Call toll-free 1-800-582-2665. Also, please ask for a free copy of our current catalog. Our e-mail address is: falconbk@ix.netcom.com.

Front cover photo: Richard V. Procopio
Back cover photo: Richard V. Procopio
All inside photos by Tom Seymour
Illustration by Ashley A. Dean

Printed in the United States of America

Library of Congress Cataloging-in-Publication Data

Seymour, Tom.
    Fishing Maine / by Tom Seymour.
        p. cm.
    ISBN 1-56044-514-9
    1. Fishing—Maine—Guidebooks. 2. Maine—Guidebooks. I. Title.
SH503.S48   1997
799.1'09741—dc21

 Text pages printed on recycled paper.

CAUTION
    Outdoor recreational activities are by their very nature potentially hazardous. All participants in such activities must assume the responsibility for their own actions and safety. The information contained in this guidebook cannot replace sound judgment and good decision-making skills, which help reduce risk exposure, nor does the scope of this book allow for disclosure of all the potential hazards and risks involved in such activities.
    Learn as much as possible about the outdoor recreational activities you participate in, prepare for the unexpected, and be cautious. The reward will be a safer and more enjoyable experience.

*This book is dedicated to my father,
Robert Seymour, and my grandfather, Tom White.
Both of these anglers always went out of their way
to take a boy fishing as often as possible.*

CONTENTS

Preface vi
Introduction 1
Tips and Advice 12
How to Use This Guide 18
Maine's Game Fish
   Bluefish 20
   Atlantic Mackerel 22
   Striped Bass 25
   Brook Trout 28
   Brown Trout 32
   Lake Trout 36
   Rainbow Trout 40
   Landlocked Salmon 42
   Splake 48
   Largemouth Bass 50
   Smallmouth Bass 53
   Pickerel 57
   Northern Pike 60
   White Perch 63
   Other Species 66
Maine's Record Game Fish 68
Map Legend 69
Map of Maine's Top Fishing Spots 70
Southern Maine
   1. Mousam Lake 72
   2. Little Ossipee River 73
   3. Portland Shoreline 74
   4. Pleasant River 75
   5. Presumpscot River 77
   6. Sebago Lake 79
   7. Popham Beach 80
Western Mountains
   8. Lake Auburn 83
   9. Nezinscot River 84
   10. Cobbosseecontee Lake 85
   11. Great Pond and Long Pond 86
   12. North Pond 87
   13. Wild River 89
   14. Rangeley Lake 90
   15. Wyman Dam on Kennebec River 91
Midcoast
   16. Kennebec River, Bath 94
   17. Damariscotta Lake 97
   18. St. George River, Thomaston 98
   19. Rockland Breakwater 98

20. Oyster River 100
21. Seven Tree Pond 102
22. Medomak River 103
23. Sheepscot Pond.. 104
24. St. George Lake 105
25. St. George River Headwaters........................ 107
26. Megunticook Lake 109
27. Belfast Shoreline 110
28. Belfast Footbridge 112
29. Goose River 114
30. Passagassawaukeag River 115
31. Swan Lake... 116
32. Fort Point State Park Fishing Pier 117
33. Sandy Point Flowage 119
34. Verona Island 120

Central Maine

35. Kennebec River, Hallowell to Augusta 123
36. China Lake 124
37. Kennebec River, Waterville 125
38. Kennebec River, Shawmut Dam..................... 127
39. The Great Eddy 128
40. Sebasticook River, Burnham 129
41. Unity Pond 130
42. Sebasticook Lake 132
43. Brewer Lake 133
44. Piscataquis River 134
45. Piper Pond 135
46. Penobscot River, Lincoln to Costigan 137

Downeast

47. Beech Hill Pond 139
48. Fox Pond 140
49. Bog Lake 141
50. Rocky Lake 142
51. Gardner Lake 143
52. Patrick Lake 144
53. Cathance Lake 145
54. Meddybemps Lake 146
55. Crawford Lake 147
56. St. Croix River 148
57. Big Lake 149
58. West Grand Lake 150
59. Lower Oxbrook Lake 152
60. Junior Lake 153

Mount Desert Island

61. Eagle Lake 157
62. Bubble Pond 158
63. Jordan Pond 158

64. Upper Hadlock Pond 159
65. Echo Lake 160

Northern Maine

66. Lake Hebron 163
67. Indian Pond 164
68. Moose River 165
69. Holeb Pond 167
70. Canada Falls Lake 169
71. South Branch Penobscot River 169
72. Moosehead Lake 170
73. West Branch Penobscot River, Ripogenus Dam to Abol Falls 173
74. Chesuncook Lake 176
75. Baxter State Park 179
76. Millinocket Lake 180
77. South Branch Lake 181
78. Sebec Lake 182

Aroostook County

79. East Grand Lake 185
80. Prestile Stream 186
81. Aroostook River 187

Savoring the Results 189
Appendix: Sources for More Information 192

PREFACE

The information in this book has been gleaned from a lifetime of fishing and from time spent listening to other anglers. As with any avocation, one's sum total of fishing knowledge comes only partially from observation and hands-on experience. The rest is gained vicariously, through the experiences of others. It is a wise angler who seeks such advice and then goes out and puts it to use. The tips and suggestions given here are designed, therefore, to better acquaint you with Maine's fish species and to illustrate proven angling techniques for those species.

The sites listed here are only a representative sample of what this majestic state has to offer. It could not be otherwise, since Maine contains more waters in which to fish than you could cover in a lifetime. Some of us do spend lifetimes trying!

INTRODUCTION

Maine, a Unique Place

Maine is unique among the eastern states in preserving large areas of relatively unspoiled woods and waters. Ninety percent of Maine is forested, a higher percentage than any other state. Within Maine's borders are 30,000 miles of flowing water and 2,500 lakes and ponds, a total of one million acres. For the angler, Maine offers an abundance of natural resources and a great variety of places to fish and fish to catch.

Maine is known as the last frontier for native eastern brook trout. Except for the extreme southern part of the state, most of Maine's brooks and streams hold populations of these brilliantly colored native trout, a genetically distinct species that has occupied these waters since the end of the last glacial period. For some anglers, native eastern brook trout are an almost mythical prize, well worth the time and effort required to seek them out.

Maine is also a stronghold for other species of fish. Landlocked salmon, lake trout, brown trout, and rainbow trout are all found here. Nor are trout and salmon the only species worthy of the Maine angler's attention. Black bass abound, and smallmouth bass are so numerous that Maine is said to offer the best smallmouth fishing in the world. Pike, a new introduction to Maine waters, are prospering. Saltwater species are available all along the coast. Bluefish, striped bass, and mackerel invade Maine's saltwater environs each summer, providing countless hours of fishing for shorebound anglers and for those fishing from boats.

Maine's fishing areas are never very far out of reach. Even in Maine's cities, anglers have only to go to the nearest river to find excellent fishing. In Waterville and Augusta, for example, you can fish for brown trout and other species within the city limits. Many of Maine's rivers, lakes, and coastal areas are also within easy driving distance of the urban areas that make the East Coast one of the most congested and industrialized parts of the country. Anglers bent on pristine fishing in perfect solitude will find what they seek in Maine, as will family groups who need easy access to productive waters.

Water Safety

Maine is a safe and friendly place in which to enjoy the outdoors. Most accidents occur because people fail to observe basic rules of safety. Anglers using boats and canoes must be aware that an unexpected dip in our frigid water can lead to hypothermia or even drowning.

Maine has laws that require boaters to carry one U.S. Coast Guard-approved, wearable personal flotation device (PFD) for each person on board. Children 10 years old and under must wear a PFD at all times. Unfortunately, adults do not always wear a PFD and that is when tragedies are most likely to occur. Play it safe and wear a PFD at all times. You should get a copy of the Maine boating laws. Ask for a copy when you buy your fishing license.

An angler holds his fly rod high as he works a scrappy smallmouth bass toward shore. Spring and fall are prime times to fish the rocky shorelines for smallmouths.

No law can make up for a lack of common sense. Some Maine lakes are so large that waves can develop to the point where navigation is foolhardy. Always keep an eye on the weather, especially in the summer. Dark-looking cumulus clouds often indicate an approaching thunderstorm, as do sudden squalls and distant thunder. At any hint of a thunderstorm, make for land immediately.

Once, during a violent windstorm, the author and friends were safe inside a lakeside camp. A canoe, loaded to the hilt with camping gear, passed within sight of the camp. The two men in the canoe were obviously in desperate peril. We tried to rescue them with a motorboat, but were unable to reach them. The canoe finally swamped, but the men managed to hold on to it and reach a distant point of the shore. They spent a wretched night on that barren beach in a cold rain. Had they not kept hold of the canoe, they would probably have died. These incidents need not happen. The men should never have gone out during that storm. Only luck and quick thinking saved their lives.

You must also keep an eye on the antics of other users of Maine waters. Drivers of personal watercraft and power boats pulling water skiers do not always pay attention to other boaters. The wake from a large powerboat can upset a canoe, especially one that lacks a keel. Do not trust the other person to watch out for your safety; you must do that yourself.

Finally, do not forget to insert the drain plug before you launch your boat. Nothing is more embarrassing than to have your boat fill up with water in front of other anglers at the launching ramp. It can be dangerous as well.

Respect Rising Water

Many Maine rivers and streams are subject to sudden rises in water le[vel]. Hydroelectric dams release water at regular intervals. Whitewater rafters r[ely] upon these releases so they can take advantage of artificially high water. Fish ermen need to be constantly alert for their own safety. If you notice bits of debris coming downstream, even though there has been no rain, expect the water level to rise. Some dams have alarms that sound when water is released. If you hear a siren or horn, get to a place where you can go ashore fast, be cause the water is going to come up in a hurry.

Some Maine rivers have sections that are simply too dangerous to wade. Others have slippery bottoms and sudden dropoffs. Always wear felts or some other device to increase your traction when wading. And always wear a belt around the waist of your waders so they don't fill up with water, just in case you take a spill.

Maine Wildlife

Maine wildlife is generally inoffensive. Maine has no poisonous snakes, although timber rattlers did inhabit western Maine many years ago. Still, big game animals such as black bear and moose need to be treated with respect.

Many veteran Maine woodsmen have never seen a black bear. Conversely, some first time campers have. Bears are attracted to food, and the worst mis take you can make while in bear country is to keep uncovered food in your tent. Always make sure you keep your food in a separate location, in an air tight container.

Moose are found throughout the state. While it is a great thrill to see one of these massive animals for the first time, resist the urge to see one up close. A bull moose can be a mean customer at certain times, and a cow moose with a calf is something to view from a distance. Use a telephoto or zoom lens for your moose photos.

The possibility of encountering a rabid animal is always present. Small animals such as raccoons and skunks are the most likely to carry rabies, but any animal, wild or domestic, is at risk. If you see any wild animal that is not afraid of you, or that exhibits unusual behavior, get away as quickly as you can. You should report any suspected rabies sighting to the nearest Maine game warden or police officer. Once again, common sense is the key to pro tecting yourself from harm in the Maine wilds.

If you fish any Maine lake or pond during the open-water season, you will probably hear or see a loon. To many, loons symbolize Maine wilderness. Their haunting, raucous cries echo the length and breadth of the state. A quiet evening spent paddling a canoe on most any Maine lake is made even more memorable by the plaintive cry of the common loon.

Unfortunately, man is the loon's chief enemy. Loons nest on the edge of the water and the prop wash from a speeding powerboat can destroy the nest. Approaching too close to a nesting loon may cause the parent to abandon the nest. Always travel at a slow speed when you are near the shore. Enjoy Maine's loons, but allow them to keep their own distance. Maybe, after a deep dive, a

3

Loons are a common sight on Maine's lakes and ponds. Their eerie, laughing cries are a hallmark of the north country. Adult loons usually travel in pairs, as shown here.

loon will emerge within feet of your boat. Perhaps you will be lucky enough to see a mother loon with her young riding pickaback. Respect and enjoy this magnificent embodiment of the last and greatest wilderness area left in the northeastern United States.

Insect Pests

Fly fishers eagerly await the emergence of various mayfly species, but the joy of matching the hatch can be overpowered by the return of the blackfly. Beginning in late April or early May, swarms of these biting gnats appear, causing extreme discomfort to man and beast alike.

Blackflies inject their victims with a local anesthetic before biting and extracting blood. People can suffer numerous bites without their knowledge; the only defense is to take precautions against being bitten.

Old-timers know the best way to thwart blackflies is to keep as much skin covered as possible. To wear shorts and short-sleeved shirts is to ask for trouble. Long pants, long-sleeved shirts, and a hat are the minimum needed to protect yourself from blackflies. Unfortunately, these diabolical creatures have the habit of crawling up pant legs and inside stockings. You can put rubber bands around your pant cuffs to prevent this from happening.

Blackflies do have a few virtues. They provide food for untold swallows and bats, an example of even the most lowly and unloved creature occupying an important place in nature's grand scheme. By the time summer arrives, blackflies have all but disappeared from most of the state.

Mosquitoes begin to be a nuisance shortly after the blackflies have stopped hatching. Thick woods, wetlands, and coastal marshes are prime areas for mosquitoes.

No-see-ums are sometimes described as being all teeth and no wings. These minuscule insects, capable of passing through most window screens, are primarily nocturnal. If you awaken during the wee hours with a burning, itching sensation, you are probably suffering from no-see-um bites.

Ticks are present in Maine, and with them, the possibility of lyme disease. The best way to keep ticks off you is to stay on trails instead of bushwhacking. Since ticks stick to the brush, in wait for passing animals, you should walk in the open as much as you can. Be sure to check your clothing for ticks after each day's outing. Tick populations are localized in Maine, but even in tick-free areas, it pays to take precautions.

Deerflies are the ubiquitous summertime nemesis of animals and people. These biting flies will swarm about your head, finally landing on your neck to inflict a large, painful bite. Some anglers use deerfly strips, sticky rectangles of paper that attach to the back of your hat. Deerflies land on this strip and are trapped. Deer and moose are sometimes driven to distraction by deerflies. The frenzied animals are often struck on Maine highways after running out on the road to escape deerflies.

Maine's coastal residents are familiar with the pesky greenhead fly. These look like houseflies, but are decked out in a shiny, emerald green. Greenheads, like deerflies, inflict nasty bites. In fact, greenheads can bite through some clothing. Greenheads are found along beaches and in salt marshes, and will often follow boats over the open ocean.

All of Maine's insect pests can be thwarted by applying insect repellent containing diethyl toluamide (DEET). Different brands contain varying percentages of DEET. The stronger the concentration, the more long-lasting the effect. DEET does have a few drawbacks. It is harmful to some finishes, especially those found on fishing rods and fly lines. Additionally, DEET can eat into some plastics. Make it a practice to wash your hands with soap and water after applying insect repellent, especially before handling your fishing tackle.

Some persons are fearful of the chemicals in standard insect repellents, so they choose natural repellents. These usually contain oil of citronella and pennyroyal. Others choose to protect themselves in a different way. Two-piece mesh suits will give full body protection. Sometimes, an insect headnet is all you need to keep bothersome bugs at bay. The choice is yours.

Children and Angling

One fishing tackle manufacturer used to print the following line on its products: Take A Boy Fishing Today. The advice is still sound, although girls should be included as well. Most youngsters are fascinated by every aspect of fishing. The small, magical things that surround a fishing trip are not lost on kids. The song of the red-winged blackbird, the little whirlpools that float behind the boat after each stroke of an oar or paddle, the morning mist on a shaded stream, all have important lessons to impart to wide-eyed youngsters on their first fishing trip.

One of the most valuable things you can give children is a love of fishing, a fondness for the myriad aspects of nature that can be found in every lake, pond, or tidal river. If you take the time to introduce children to the art of angling, you may be giving them something they can cherish for the rest of their lives.

It may be best to limit children's first few trips to panfish rather than the more difficult game species. Experienced anglers need not catch buckets of fish in order to have a quality experience, but youngsters need a tangible reward, at least the first few times out. Let children learn how to use the tackle, how to play a fish, how to release a fish, and how to respect the resource. Then it is time to go for the glamour species.

Some adults make the mistake of paying too much attention to their own fishing, leaving the youngsters to figure things out by themselves. It is better to give children all your attention at first. Kids are fast learners, so this should not take much time.

Maine's *Hooked on Fishing* program, begun in 1996, is designed to instill a love of fishing in children. Volunteers are always welcome to participate. No matter what your skill or talent, you can help make a difference. For more information on this and other volunteer projects, call the Maine Department of Inland Fisheries & Wildlife at 207-287-8069.

Fish for Fun

More and more anglers are realizing that in order to have good fishing tomorrow, we cannot kill all the fish we catch today. In Maine, this particularly applies to coldwater game fish and black bass. Catch-and-release is a practical approach to fishing, in more ways than one. Even if you could keep all the trout and salmon you wanted, you would soon tire of eating them. Even the finest foods lose their luster when they are served up in endless profusion. Better to keep a limited number for the pan and release the remainder to fight again another day. Practically speaking, a competent angler can catch dozens of fish in a single day. What could anyone possibly do with all those fish, except keep a few for the pan, savor the moment, and release the rest?

Catch-and-release requires special care on your part, in order to be effective. You simply cannot play a fish until it is belly-up, then tear the hook out, throw it back in the water, and expect it to survive. You need to play a fish as quickly as possible, within the limitations of your tackle. If you can easily remove the hook without taking the fish from the water, so much the better. A pair of forceps is an indispensable aid in hook removal. If the fish is deeply hooked, you must cut the line as close to the hook as possible. Acids in the fish's system will soon dissolve a standard wire hook, but gold-plated or stainless steel hooks will not dissolve, so stay away from them.

If your fish is sluggish, you may have to hold it in the water and slowly move it forward and backward, forcing oxygen-bearing water through its gills. This may require some time, but it does work.

Fish taken from deep water, such as lake trout, will often have an expanded air bladder. Using your thumb, press along the fish's stomach, beginning near the vent and sliding it forward a few times. This will remove the excess air.

Finally, barbless hooks may be cheaper than you imagined. Any hook can be rendered barbless by filing the barb, or bending it down with needle-nose pliers.

Clothing

No matter if you are wading a river or trolling from a boat on a lake or bay, you need to be prepared for foul weather. Even in summer, temperatures can drop to the point that you will be uncomfortable without a jacket or sweater. A poncho or waterproof windbreaker is standard fare for all Maine anglers. The author takes a Gore-Tex lined windbreaker on all fishing trips. Gore-Tex allows the garment to shed external water while allowing inside moisture from perspiration to escape, thus keeping you truly dry.

Early spring fishing can seem colder than a day spent on the ice. Temperatures of 45 to 50 degrees, coupled with drizzle and a strong wind, can reduce an angler to a shivering hulk. Even your fingers can become numb, if exposed to wind and rain. Make it a point to bring along several pairs of cotton gloves. Flexible rubber gloves will keep your hands dry and therefore warm.

A wool jacket or overcoat can be a welcome item when a cold spray is flying from the tips of curling waves. Wool has the ability to absorb water and yet remain warm.

If you fish from a boat, footwear selection is not too important, as long as you have non-slip soles. If your destination is a remote area, a comfortable pair of hiking boots is recommended.

A baseball-type cap is another valuable addition to the Maine angler's wardrobe. The visor helps to shade your face from the sun's rays, and deerflies are prevented from biting you on the scalp. A pair of polarized sunglasses will round out your outfit. Polarized glasses will help protect your eyes, as well as enable you to see beneath the surface glare.

Protection from the Sun

Protection from the sun's harmful ultraviolet rays is an important concern for anglers. Not only are you exposed to direct rays, but you can easily suffer harm from rays that are reflected from the water's surface. Ultraviolet rays are present on cloudy days too, so you need to be vigilant.

Your best protection, given that you are wearing protective clothing, is to apply sunblock lotion at intervals recommended by the manufacturer. Sunblock lotions come in different strengths, but for the best protection, choose a factor of at least 15.

Clothing for Ice Fishing

Those who go ice fishing are obliged to pay strict attention to their clothing. It is possible to spend a balmy day on the ice, especially on a sunny day with a southwest breeze, but such chinooks do not happen frequently. You can always take off extra clothing, but you cannot put it on if you did not bring it.

A warm cap, with ear protection, is absolutely necessary when ice fishing. With wind chills down in the minus numbers, your ears are subject to frostbite. Some anglers use a balaclava cap for full face protection.

Layers of clothing are suggested, rather than a single heavy jacket and single pair of trousers. A down vest under a wool shirt, coupled with a tightly knit windbreaker or canvas jacket, makes a good outfit. A heavy parka with a sweater beneath it is useful, as long as you remember to unzip the parka when you begin to perspire.

Blue jeans and insulated underwear are barely adequate for a truly cold day on Maine's frozen lakes or ponds. Flannel-lined jeans and insulated underwear work better, but a pair of solid-wool pants over your jeans or other trousers are best.

Your choice of footwear can make or break your day. Most Maine anglers use pac-style boots, the kind with leather uppers, rubber bottoms, and a removable felt insole. Make sure your boots are rated for at least zero degrees.

If you drive to the frozen lake in your vehicle with your heater on, your feet may sweat, in which case they will become chilled after a short time on the ice. It makes sense to wear light footwear on the way to the lake and put on your pacs just before you venture out on the ice.

While not strictly an article of clothing, a handwarmer can be invaluable while ice fishing or even in early spring fishing. You have a choice of the refillable kind, or the disposable style. Both work well enough to bring the circulation back to stiff digits.

This angler is dressed for the cold; down-lined parka and insulated hat with ear protection. The wind-chill factor on Maine's frozen lakes often reaches minus 50.

8

Responsible Behavior on the Ice

You will probably notice other anglers driving their vehicles out on the ice. This is not yet illegal, but it is irresponsible and dangerous. Nobody has the moral or ethical right to take the chance of fouling Maine's waters with gasoline, motor oil, and other engine fluids. Individuals who do drive on the ice are responsible for the removal of their vehicle should it break through, as well as any environmental damage that might occur. Walk to your fishing spot. Do not drive.

Fish Consumption Advisories

Small amounts of dioxin have been found in fish tissue from the Androscoggin River, the Kennebec River below Skowhegan, and the Penobscot River below Lincoln. Dioxin is a by-product of the papermaking process and is discharged into these rivers in minute quantities. The Maine Department of Inland Fisheries & Wildlife has posted health advisories for these rivers. These advisories do not necessarily preclude eating fish; they simply give recommendations as to how many meals per month different individuals might safely consume.

Mercury contamination has been found in some Maine lakes and ponds. The Maine Department of Inland Fisheries & Wildlife has issued a statewide fish consumption advisory. Note that Maine's mercury guideline for human consumption is well above the U.S. Food and Drug Administration's guideline of one part mercury per million parts fish, by weight. Additionally, not all fish species contain similar mercury levels. Generally, trout and salmon have the lowest mercury content, and warmwater fish such as pickerel, bass, and perch have a higher content.

One private study found that ponds and lakes situated in lowlands, especially those surrounded by bogs and swamps, were more likely to contain fish with high mercury counts. Conversely, high-altitude lakes and ponds showed little mercury contamination. Interestingly, larger fish were found to have higher mercury levels than smaller specimens. It is safer, therefore, to release the larger fish and keep the smaller ones for eating, if you wish. For total peace of mind, follow the Maine Department of Inland Fisheries & Wildlife fish consumption advisory for mercury.

Fishing Regulations

Maine publishes two sets of fishing regulations, one for open water and one for ice fishing. No one should fish any body of water in Maine without consulting these regulations first. Special regulations apply to various locations, so what may be legal on one lake may be prohibited on another.

Admittedly, Maine's regulations are complex. Efforts are under way to simplify them but even simplified versions will be lengthy. You will need to study the regulations carefully before fishing any body of water in Maine.

Some of these special regulations are a comprehensive part of the Maine Department of Inland Fisheries & Wildlife Quality Fishing Initiative (QFI), which goes into effect in 1996. This program is designed to provide high catch

Special fishing regulations are designed to ensure high-quality fishing and trophy-sized fish for years to come. As this sign indicates, fishing is a family affair.

rates for mature fish. Essentially, the regulations allow game fish to grow to large sizes by keeping them in the water until they become adults. The regulations vary from artificial-lures-only to no-live-fish-as-bait and fly-fishing-only. Some waters are listed as no-kill and others have slot limits for game species.

Maine Governor Angus King, discussing the QFI at a 1995 sportsman's congress, said, "We have the resources that are the envy of the nation. We can absolutely have world-class fishing." Department of Inland Fisheries & Wildlife Commissioner Ray B. Owen, addressing the same gathering, said the initial purpose of the QFI is "to increase size class of fish, mostly brook trout, bass, brown trout, and landlocked salmon." According to Owen, one percent of Maine's ponds and between one and two percent of its rivers and streams will fall under the QFI.

Maine's fisheries managers are breaking new ground in enacting these historic regulations. With such progressive management techniques, Maine's angling opportunities are limitless.

The One That Didn't Get Away Club

The Maine Sportsman, a monthly where-to-go-in-Maine outdoor publication, sponsors The One That Didn't Get Away Club, which recognizes anglers who have caught trophy freshwater fish in Maine waters. A few Maine sporting goods stores carry club application cards. Otherwise, you can write or call *The Maine Sportsman* directly (P.O. Box 910, Yarmouth, ME 04096-0910, telephone 207-846-9501 or toll-free in Maine 1-800-698-9501) to obtain application cards and a list of minimum weights for the different species. Qualifying anglers are awarded a membership card and jacket patch, and gain the satisfaction of belonging to the select group of anglers who have taken trophy fish. *The Maine Sportsman* also sponsors the Tacklebusters Club for saltwater species. The same address and phone numbers apply.

Boat Ramps

For a complete listing of state-owned and assisted boat-launching ramps, write to: Bureau of Parks and Recreation, Department of Conservation, State House Station 22, Augusta, ME 04333-0022, or call 207-287-3821. Boat ramps, as well as campgrounds and other noteworthy sites, are shown in DeLorme's *The Maine Atlas and Gazetteer*, published by DeLorme Mapping, P.O. Box 298, Freeport, ME 04032, telephone 207-865-4171.

Stocking Reports

Maine issues an annual summary of all waters stocked, with numbers and species of fish, dates, and locations. This list can be valuable when planning a fishing trip. For a current copy, send two dollars to: Maine Department of Inland Fisheries and Wildlife, 284 State Street, 41 State House Station, Augusta, ME 04333-0041.

Fly Fishing Hot Line

L.L. Bean, Inc., of Freeport, Maine, offers a fly fishing hot line. You may speak to one of their fly fishing specialists any day from 8 A.M. through 10 P.M., by calling 1-800-347-4552.

Wilderness Areas

Wilderness, when mentioned in this book, does not always refer to designated wilderness areas; it refers to the complete tranquility of Maine's wild and remote areas. Wilderness is a state of mind, and Maine has more than its share of places where that state of mind is a reality, not just a concept.

Campgrounds

For a complete list of private campgrounds in Maine, call the Maine Campground Owners Association at 207-782-5874.

Dealing with Maine Weather

Weather can make or break your fishing trip. Wind, rain, prolonged spells of hot or cold temperatures, the whims of the Gulf Stream, and approaching fronts all create unique conditions that must be dealt with if you are to be successful.

Maine is not so much a producer of storm fronts and varying weather patterns as it is a receiver. Typically, systems approach Maine from the south and west in summer and from the north and east in winter. Constantly changing barometric pressures from arriving or departing fronts can turn fish on or off at a moment's notice.

When fishing during an approaching low-pressure system, you should persevere even if the fish are not biting because a major feeding spree may occur. On one occasion, we were trolling for brown trout in a Midcoast lake, and the total take was two trout in seven hours of fishing. Low clouds scudded over the distant hills and cold drizzle fell from a leaden sky. The nasty weather had arrived that morning and although fishing had been good until then, the changing air pressure had made the fish reluctant to bite. Assuming that it was only a matter of time until the trout would put on the feedbag, we trolled over areas that had produced earlier in the week. Suddenly, large trout began to hit our streamer flies with reckless abandon. No sooner did we unhook one fish and get the fly back in the water than another would strike. Some of the fish hit within a few feet of the boat, as the line was being payed out. The action lasted only 20 minutes, but those were the 20 minutes we had been dreaming of all winter.

High pressure generally has a negative effect on Maine freshwater fish, though it has little bearing on saltwater species. It takes several days for fish to adjust to newly arrived high pressure. Such changes in fish behavior are more notable in ponds and lakes than streams and rivers. If you have a flexible schedule, it is better to fish before, during, or immediately after a low-pressure system passes through than during an approaching or newly arrived high-pressure system. Inevitably, gusty winds accompany high air pressure, adding another factor to the equation. On the other hand, the best time to go fishing is every chance you get, but don't expect too much during an approaching high.

Wind is probably the biggest bugaboo for Maine anglers fishing ponds, lakes, and rivers. Depending on what you are fishing for, wind can be your friend or your enemy. Trolling for landlocked salmon or brown trout is best if accompanied by at least a light breeze to stir the water. On the other hand, casting for bass or trout is made difficult when gusts of wind impede boat handling. Sometimes the only way you can conveniently fish during windy weather is to anchor at every spot.

Wind can be a blessing or a curse for fly fishers. High wind can blow mayflies away from the stream as soon as they hatch, leaving trout nothing to come to the surface for. In summer, wind can actually be beneficial because terrestrial insects are swept into streams from the riparian habitat, stirring otherwise lethargic trout to activity.

A great many of Maine's lakes and ponds are situated in a north-south direction, courtesy of the last glacier to pass through the region. If you want to go fishing during periods of moderately high wind, take into consideration which direction the wind is coming from. If, for instance, you want to fish a north-south oriented lake and the wind is from the north, you will have little chance of finding a lee where the wind is not an issue. In this case, you would be better off to consider a lake that heads east and west. The north shore would likely offer some relatively calm areas.

Moon Phases

Full moon is a good time to fish for mackerel, bluefish, and striped bass. Conversely, the full of the moon is not a good time to seek freshwater bass, bullheads, white perch, or pickerel.

If you have the option, try to plan your freshwater fishing trip to coincide with the week before or after the new moon.

Bait for Freshwater Species

Maine laws concerning the use and gathering of minnows and other fish to be used as bait are complex and often illogical.

For example, spiny-rayed fish may not be used as bait in Maine. The intent here is to prevent accidental introduction of unwanted species. The law does not allow you to use any part of any spiny-rayed fish, even in waters where they already exist. Since this regulation pretty much precludes the use of strip or chunk bait, you must resort to other alternatives.

American eels are allowed for use as bait, as are suckers, so it would pay to freeze strips of sucker or eel flesh. Large golden shiners are quite common in many of Maine's warmwater lakes and ponds and they can be easily taken on a small bit of worm or even a dry fly. Cut the minnows into strips and refrigerate or freeze.

Also effective on such species as perch and pickerel are the old-fashioned pork rind strips. Even strips of cut squid will take freshwater fish. You can buy fresh or frozen squid in almost any Maine supermarket.

If you want to catch your own bait fish, you are limited to using a bait trap. Note that you must possess a fishing license before trapping minnows because this is considered a form of fishing. You may get a free permit to take bait from waters not currently open to fishing by writing to the Maine Department of Inland Fisheries & Wildlife.

Finally, before using any fish as bait on any Maine water, study the regulations carefully.

Maine has lots of other natural baits and most of them are easy to procure. Crayfish come immediately to mind. Dragonfly nymphs make dynamite bait for most freshwater fish, but few anglers are aware of their potential. Dragonfly nymphs, the juvenile form of the dragonfly, are commonly found on the bottom of most warmwater lakes and ponds. They are easily taken with a hard-toothed garden rake. Simply rake the muck from the bottom of the pond and pick up the nymphs as they struggle free of the debris and begin to crawl back to the water.

Keep the nymphs in a well-ventilated container. Be sure the container is in a cool, shady spot, or you might find your nymphs turning into full-grown dragonflies.

Tides

Maine's tides are among the highest in the world. Such powerful forces can create unique situations for the angler. A moving tide can create a rip near any point of land or sand spit. Such areas are particularly good spots to seek striped bass. Do be aware that smaller motors may not be able to make much headway against a fast-moving tide, so gauge your travels accordingly.

Generally, an outgoing tide is best for fishing from shore on tidal rivers but an incoming is nearly as good. Dead low tide is a good time to sort your tackle or rest in the shade. High tide can be productive but you have to cruise around to find schools of fish.

Boaters lacking a tilt-trailer should plan to hit the launch before dead low tide.

Freshwater anglers can benefit from following the tide clock too. Fish in lakes and ponds in Maine seem to be most active from one hour before high tide to one hour after high tide. Schooling fish such as white perch are especially sensitive to tidal influence, even though the tide in a lake or pond is negligible. Tide tables are printed in all coastal newspapers and are also available in *The Old Farmer's Almanac*. Select the tide schedule for the coastal area nearest the body of fresh water you plan to fish.

Record Keeping

If you do any amount of fishing in Maine it will pay you to keep records. Although the Maine climate is unpredictable, it is still possible to establish general trends.

Include any pertinent information in your records, including type and numbers of fish taken, air and water temperatures, types of insects present, wind direction and speed, phase of the moon, and state of growth of local flora. This last bit of information can be particularly useful, because even though a wild cherry tree may not bloom on the same date each year, it will bloom when the temperature has been constant for a certain period of time. Sheep laurel, a wetland shrub with magenta-colored blossoms, is the author's favorite indicator of the best time to fish for native brook trout. You can develop your own set of indicators.

There is no need to buy an expensive record book for this task. Simply pick up an extra wall calendar and jot your notes down after each fishing trip. Several year's worth of calendars can be used to establish general patterns, thus making it easier for you to plan your trip for the best time for whatever species you seek.

New Products

Advancements in fishing line technology have given modern anglers a decided advantage over their predecessors. Nylon monofilament line has been superseded by high-tech material that is vastly superior. New lines are thinner and have less stretch. This means that you can fill a lightweight spinning reel with 10-pound test line that has the diameter of yesterday's 4-pound test material.

Some of the new lines have a few drawbacks, the braided variety being the most difficult to use. Such lines are strong and durable but have a tendency to knot up when used for casting. It is better to stick to the single-strand stuff for casting and use the braided material for trolling or jigging.

Modern leader material has the advantage of being thinner, stronger, and—in some cases—invisible to fish. This gives the fly-fisher the opportunity to use a small-diameter tippet that is capable of steering a big fish away from snags without breaking.

Rods have come down in price and up in quality. Modern graphite or graphite composite rods are affordable and responsive. Nobody need invest large sums of money in ultra-expensive fishing tackle when high-quality rods are available for 50 dollars or less.

Scents

Commercial scents can be highly effective on Maine fish. All saltwater fish and most freshwater fish will respond to an artificial lure that has been treated with scent.

The best application for scents is on soft plastic baits. These lifelike baits feel like something from nature and when treated with a scent, the deception is made even more convincing. Metal and hard-plastic lures don't hold scent long enough to warrant its use.

The Fall Flurry

Trout fishing and salmon fishing are at their best during spring and drop off as summer's heat raises water temperatures. September frosts quickly lower water temperatures, making a brief but productive second season possible. In fact, some of the biggest fish of the season are taken in the fall. If you can't find time to sample Maine's spring fishing, you have a second chance in September.

Saltwater fishing is good in September too. Striped bass, while fewer in numbers, tend to run larger. The same goes for mackerel and bluefish.

The Ant Hatch

In late May and early September, you may find the surface of a lake or stream covered with winged ants. This most often occurs where white pine trees line the shore. Trout, bass, salmon, and white perch all feed on the ants, to the exclusion of other forage species.

For most purposes, a size 14 floating ant pattern will suffice. The specific pattern is not important; you will get results with deer-hair ants, fur-bodied ants, and cork-bodied ants. Even a scraggly dry fly will take fish at this time.

Since the ant hatch is short-lived, usually no more than three or four days, fish take advantage of it to the fullest, feeding around the clock. If you have the stamina, you could go on a fish-catching marathon, catching fish on floating ants 24 hours a day.

Anyone can easily make terrestrial imitations like ants, bees, and beetles. A hook, some thread, a scrap of balsa wood, and some model enamel are all you need to create high-floating flies to catch Maine gamefish.

A Handy Cooler

Have you ever stopped to fish on the spur of the moment and caught a beauty that you would have taken home if only you had a cooler to preserve your catch? As long as you have a wool jacket or shirt, you have no problem. My favorite method is to stick the fish in one of the sleeves of a wet wool jacket and then wrap the rest of the jacket around the sleeve. A variation of this trick once kept a salmon frozen for 10 hours. As wet wool dries, evaporation cools it down and if you wrap a fish thoroughly in wool and dunk the whole thing, it will remain cool for hours. Just be sure to keep it out of direct sunlight. Dry wool is also a good insulator and can keep frozen objects hard for extended periods. Fortunately, fish odor is easily removed in the washing machine.

Warmer Water

If you go trout fishing in a brook or stream in the early season, try to get out as early as possible. Snowmelt, which occurs when the sun gets high in mid-morning, drastically lowers the water temperature, making already lethargic trout even more sluggish. Hit the streams before the sun gets high. The water will be warmer and the trout more active.

Shadow Warning

When fishing a stream or brook, always keep the sun to your face, even if that means crossing the stream and fishing on the brush-filled side. If the sun is at your back, you will cast shadows, alerting wary trout of your presence, and causing them to dart off and hide.

Vibrations and Noise

Despite what you might have heard, you can talk as loud as you want when fishing. You could hold a hog-calling contest on the banks of a pond and not bother the fish in the least. Underwater vibrations are another story. Dropping a tackle box on the bottom of an aluminum boat will instantly alert any fish because water is an excellent transmitter of vibrations. Likewise, when walking along a stream step gingerly; fish can feel the vibrations from heavy footfalls.

Stealth Pays

When fly fishing in a stream or river, try to get as close as possible to a rising trout before casting. A shorter cast is a more accurate cast, and pinpoint accuracy is more valuable in the end than a long, fancy cast. By working your way to a trout from downstream, you should be able to get to within 15 feet or less. Just make sure not to cast directly over the trout; the shadow of the line or even the leader will spook it.

Fish Deep

When trolling for mackerel, stripers, or bluefish, you should carry a spare rod and reel filled with lead-core line or a fly outfit with fast-sinking fly line. Sometimes the smaller fish stay on top while the larger specimens remain 10 to 20 feet deeper.

Terminal Gear

No matter what species you are fishing for, resist the temptation to use swivels, snelled hooks, and excess weight. Use only enough weight to get your hook down where you want it. Swivels are not really effective against line twist and their presence can alert a wary fish. Snelled hooks are fine for bottom feeders such as eels and bullheads but are worthless for trout. The line used on commercially made snelled hooks is usually too thick and stiff for trout fishing. Better to tie a hook directly to your line.

HOW TO USE THIS GUIDE ─────────────

The **Species** section will give you a solid working knowledge of Maine's various species of game fish. The more you know about the habits, habitats, favorite forage species, and biology of any fish species, the better your chance of being a successful angler. This basic information appears at the beginning of each species listing.

The species section also provides a list of techniques used to fish for each species. This section is broken down according to the different types of tackle commonly used for these species. Again, nothing is carved in stone. Even if a certain kind of gear is not mentioned (for instance, bait casting tackle is not listed in some sections because it is rarely used for those species), it does not mean you cannot catch that particular species on any kind of tackle you like. The guidelines are only intended to acquaint you with the popular methods used in Maine.

A **Best bet** section appears at the end of each species section. Each site in this section has been selected because it is a popular and reliable spot, or because it is a lesser-known spot that the author has found productive. It is important to understand that the sites listed here are not necessarily the only places in Maine where you can find good fishing for these species.

Sites

Each site listing provides the following at-a-glance information: The key species found in this particular body of water, the best way to fish it, the best time to fish it, and DeLorme's The Maine Atlas and Gazetteer (MAG) references. (DeLorme's MAG available in stores throughout the state or by contacting DeLorme Mapping, P.O. Box 298, Freeport, ME 04032; 207-865-4171.) Note the example below:

2. LITTLE OSSIPPEE RIVER

> **Key Species:** *brown trout, brook trout, landlocked salmon*
> **Best Way to Fish:** *wading*
> **Best Time to Fish:** *May and June*
> **MAG:** *2, A-2*

After reading the above at-a-glance information, you can see that the Little Ossippee River contains brown trout, brook trout, and landlocked salmon, that it is best fished by wading, that the best times to go there are from May through June, and that it can be seen on Map 2 of the MAG. Note that the MAG references are often approximate. Not all sites fall on the confluence lines between the numbers and letters given.

The **Description** contains general information about the site and will include special features and interesting local attractions. More in-depth information on how a site may best be fished will be listed in this section, including if a canoe is better for the site, if a motorboat is needed, if any navigational hazards are present, if wading is possible, and so on. Campgrounds and primitive campsites are often found at or near the site and these will be listed in this section.

The **Fishing index** is designed to impart the information you will need in order to be successful at any given site. If any special technique or method is recommended in addition to that contained in the technique and tackle sections of the Species descriptions, it will be noted. Best times to fish for certain species will be given as well as safety tips (for instance, some lakes are prone to high winds and unsafe boating conditions). The best times, as suggested here, are always subject to change because of unusual climatic conditions. For instance, a late spring might mean that a stream that is usually good around the beginning of May might not be fishable until the end of the month.

The fishing index also suggests the best places to begin fishing. These are only suggestions and are certainly not the only places where you can expect success. If the fish are not biting, you must be willing to do some exploring yourself. The more familiar you become with Maine lakes, streams, and ponds, the better able you will be to read the water and anticipate where the fish will be holding at any particular time.

Directions are given from the nearest major highway or population center. In cases where the site is in a remote area, a map is provided. When possible, directions are given to a Maine Department of Inland Fisheries & Wildlife boat ramp. If other boat ramps are present, they will be mentioned as well.

Site maps are included for sites that are remote and difficult to find and for sites where the text requires the support of a visual aid in order to be more easily understood.

The locator maps are broken down into regions and are intended to give you an idea of where the various sites are in relation to each other and in relation to major highways and population centers. You should use the locator maps in conjunction with other reference material, such as the MAG.

The state map shows all sites on a statewide basis.

For more information. This section provides additional sources of information about the site. Addresses and phone numbers for these sources are listed in the appendix. Some sites are miles from any population center, and seasonal or specific information is scanty. Some sites are far away from any tackle or outdoor stores. In these cases, you can always write the Maine Department of Inland Fisheries & Wildlife, at 284 State Street, 41 State House Station, Augusta, ME 04333-0041, or call the regional headquarters at the numbers listed in the back of the Open Water Fishing Regulations booklet.

Bluefish

Bluefish, *Pomatomus salatrix,* sometimes invade the Maine coast in vast numbers, with individual specimens occasionally reaching the Canadian Maritimes, the extreme northern range for the species. The bluefish run usually begins in mid-July in southern Maine and may not reach eastern Maine until sometime in August. In an average year, Penobscot Bay is the northernmost point for large schools of bluefish, although individuals often turn up farther north and east. Bluefish are so popular in Maine that an annual bluefish tournament, the New England Bluefish Open, is held in Bath, with a variety of big-ticket prizes for the largest fish in varying categories and for taking a tagged bluefish.

Maine anglers seek bluefish with every conceivable kind of tackle, from fly gear to tarred handlines. It is not difficult to understand the bluefish's popularity, since they fight like demons, will strike at anything, and are extremely flavorful when grilled.

Bluefish, like striped bass, are school fish. Individuals range in size from diminutive "snapper" blues weighing 2 to 5 pounds, to huge "chopper" blues, which can weigh up to 20 pounds.

While bluefish will attack anything that crosses their path (hands and feet of careless swimmers are subject to bluefish bites), their favorite prey in Maine is menhaden, an oily bait fish. Consequently, menhaden are a popular bait.

After boating a bluefish, be extremely careful when handling it. A bluefish will do everything in its power to lunge at you, and can inflict a serious wound. A live bluefish is a dangerous bluefish.

The newfound popularity of bluefish and striped bass has spurred a sizeable industry. Party boats take anglers out throughout the season. If you don't own any tackle, you can usually rent rods and reels from the boat for a nominal fee. For a list of Maine party boats, write to the Maine Department of Marine Resources, Station 21, Augusta, ME 04333.

As of 1996, the possession limit on bluefish is 10 fish. It would be unwise to kill that many, however, since bluefish quickly lose their flavor when frozen. It is better to keep only what you can eat fresh and let the rest go to fight another day.

Techniques

Spin fishing - Spinning tackle is universally popular with bluefish anglers. Medium-weight tackle is adequate for casting from a boat, but for surf casting, heavier gear is recommended. Lines should be at least 12-pound test. A 3-foot steel leader is a must, because bluefish can literally "walk up the line" when they attack a bait or lure from behind.

Bluefish anglers must pay strict attention to drag settings. In order to set the hook, you must have a fairly heavy setting. Things quickly change after the fish is hooked. Bluefish make powerful, line-sizzling runs, so when you have your fish solidly hooked, turn your drag down a few clicks so your line does not break or the hook pull out. Be especially careful about drag settings when the fish is ready to be netted. A "whipped" bluefish will often summon up enough energy to make a last line-popping run. Adjust your drag as needed and you won't lose a fish because of human error.

Just because bluefish are strong fighters does not mean you cannot land one on medium or even light tackle. It will take you longer but it can be done!

Anglers casting for bluefish from shore use large-sized Rebels and similar lures, as well as large poppers. When the big lures fail, bluefish will often respond to the fluttering action of a .25-ounce gold-and-orange spoon.

Anglers fishing from boats usually carry two spinning rods, one to troll with, and another at the ready in case a school of bluefish shows near the surface.

Trolling - Any rod can be used to troll for bluefish, although most anglers use spinning rods. The author is fond of using a 9-foot, 6-weight fly rod, and either a streamer or a small gold spoon. Even bluefish of 12 to 15 pounds will ultimately succumb to the steady pressure of the long rod.

Vertical jigging - Few anglers are aware of this deadly method. Use the heaviest diamond-type jig your tackle will bear. Drop your jig to the bottom and reel it in as quickly as you can. Keep repeating the process. A fast-retrieve spinning reel is perfect for this specialized type of angling.

Fly casting - Anglers with fly rods are fond of working schools of bluefish, either from a boat or from shore. Large streamers and poppers are effective. Fly-rodding for bluefish is one of angling's greatest thrills, because of the terrific aerial displays. Flies are ideally suited to bluefish, since they are light and not easily thrown when the fish jumps.

Use at least a 9-foot rod, since you need the extra length in order to apply the most leverage you can. A 10-foot rod is even better. Leaders can be nothing more than level 12-pound test monofilament, but instead of a wire leader at the end, most anglers use a shock tippet of at least 50-pound test monofilament. A weight-forward, floating fly line will suit most purposes.

When schools of "snapper" bluefish come into the small coves and river mouths, fly fishers can find fast action. You can keep the school near if you occasionally drop some chum in the water. See the section on bait fishing for more about chum. Carry the largest landing net you can find and never try to land a bluefish by hand.

Some anglers keep a fly rod at the ready when trolling with spinning gear. If you get a bluefish on the spinning gear, it will often be accompanied by one or more others. All you need to do is net the fish taken on spinning gear and cast a fly to its companion.

Bait fishing - Any tackle can be used when bait fishing for bluefish, as long as a large hook and long, steel leader are at the terminal end. It is not necessary, but it does help to have a chum line. If you catch a number of menhaden, or even mackerel, cut them up into small bits and drop them overboard at regular intervals. If you are unable to find fresh fish for use as chum, buy several cans of inexpensive, oily cat food and ladle out a tablespoon at a time. This works best on a moving tide. Bluefish can be attracted to a chum line from considerable distances.

When bait fishing for bluefish, cut a menhaden or mackerel in half and hook it once. Extra weight is usually not needed. While your boat is drifting, lower the bait into the chum line and let line out so the bait floats freely with the tide. When enough line is out, the bait will come to the surface because of the pull of the current, so you will need to reel in and repeat the process. When a bluefish bites, strike as hard as you can and then strike again.

Best bets for Maine bluefish: Portland Shoreline, Site 3; Kennebec River, Bath, Site 16; and St. George River, Thomaston, Site 18.

Atlantic Mackerel

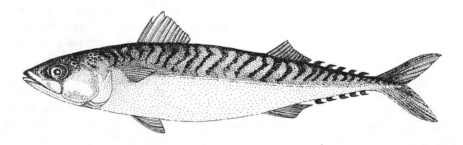

Atlantic mackerel, *Scomber scombrus*, are an important food and sport fish in Maine. Mackerel are pelagic, or fish of the midwater. They spend the winter on the Middle Atlantic shelf and migrate north and inshore as spring progresses, reaching Maine coastal waters in early summer. Mackerel are underutilized as commercial fish, resulting in large numbers being available for recreational use.

Schools of mackerel consist of fish of a similar age-class. These range from diminutive "tinker mackerel" of 8 to 10 inches to so-called horse mackerel weighing more than 3 pounds.

In summer, schools of mackerel are found off the entire coast of Maine. These fish are sought by anglers trolling from boats and by those casting from shore. Mackerel are not selective and can be taken on any natural bait or artificial lure. Each year, anglers eagerly await the cry, "the mackerel are in." With this news, hundreds of boats are launched and each breakwater, float, and pier is jammed with anglers anxious to get that first mess of tasty mackerel.

Techniques

Fly casting - Few anglers fly-cast for mackerel, but those that do have great sport. The best way to achieve success is to use a boat to locate schools. Action can be fast for a short while, until the school moves, in which case you must find it again or look for another school. Use any small bucktail. The best colors are white, red, and yellow. You can make your own mackerel flies without any special equipment; just tie some colored deer hair or calf tail hair to the shank of a size 6 hook. No body is needed. Trim the hair even with the bend of the hook. Any fly rod is suitable, but lighter outfits provide more sport. Remember to rinse your reel off after use, since saltwater is highly corrosive.

Spin fishing - Anglers fishing from shore rely on spinning tackle. Small spoons and jigs are cast as far out as possible and reeled in with constant twitches of the rod. Any rod and reel combination is acceptable, but as with fly casting, lighter outfits provide more fun. You will have the most fun with ultralight tackle. If you fish from a bridge or pier, you may want to use a medium-weight outfit, because you may have to reel your mackerel up for a considerable distance, depending on the stage of the tide.

If mackerel are present but are not hitting your lures, try reeling as fast as you can. Mackerel are a fast fish and are used to chasing forage species at high speeds.

Trolling - Most Maine mackerel are taken by trolling. This is a relaxed and enjoyable way to get a supply of mackerel. Rod holders are preferred, since mackerel have soft mouths and can easily hook themselves.

In earlier times, Maine anglers used a stout rod with a jig on the end and any number of simple bucktails above the jig. The idea was to hook one mackerel and wait until other fish, attracted to the struggle, became hooked. While this was an easy way to catch lots of fish at one time, more anglers are turning to light rods with a single lure or fly. This allows the scrappy mackerel to make the best possible show. A 20-inch mackerel on the end of a light rod can temporarily fool you into believing you are fast to a bluefish or striped bass.

Any rod is sufficient for trolling for mackerel, but fly rods provide the most sport with the least trouble. Spinning lines tend to twist, even with the use of a rudder. A fly rod, reel, and line, equipped with a 10-foot leader, is supremely efficient as a mackerel outfit. For flies, any streamer or bucktail will do, but small spoons or jigs are also effective.

Mackerel usually hold fairly close to the surface. As long as your lure or fly remains beneath the surface, you will catch mackerel. Be sure to watch for floating bits of aquatic weeds and other debris. Even a small bit of seaweed on your hook can cause your fly or lure to ride on the surface, rendering it ineffective.

Some savvy Maine anglers like to troll around working lobster boats. Any bait discarded by the lobsterman will attract mackerel.

You do not need to go far from shore to find schools of mackerel, although in places like Penobscot Bay, Blue Hill Bay, Englishman Bay, Machias Bay, and Cobscook Bay, schools of mackerel can be found cruising in the middle of the bay as well as near the shoreline.

Bait fishing - Anglers fishing in protected harbors, as well as those fishing from bridges and piers, often take good messes of mackerel on bait. Use light spinning gear, a small amount of weight, and a size 6 hook. Frozen shrimp, small strips of mackerel flesh with the skin on, mussels, marine worms, and even earthworms are all good bait. Let your bait sink to the bottom and keep a tight finger on your line, since mackerel are notorious bait stealers. Some anglers choose to employ a small bobber a few feet above the baited hook. This is most useful when fishing with frozen shrimp, since the shrimp is easily dislodged from the hook and the bobber will indicate the slightest nibble.

Care of mackerel - Of all Maine fish, mackerel are the most likely to spoil quickly unless properly taken care of as soon as they are caught. Some anglers keep mackerel in a bucket of salt water, changing the water frequently to keep the fish cool. This is a troublesome method and although it keeps the mackerel from spoiling, it makes them soft. A better method is to carry an ice chest full of ice. Unhook the mackerel and immediately place it on ice; it will remain firm and fresh for several days. You might want to use a separate cooler for your beverages and snacks.

Best bets for Maine mackerel: If you use a boat, you can catch mackerel anywhere along the coast during the months of July, August, and September, with bays and coves being the most productive places. The largest mackerel can be found in Downeast Maine, especially the waters off Eastport. If you are casting from shore, try Rockland Breakwater, Site 19; Belfast Footbridge, Site 28; and the State Pier at Fort Point, Site 32.

Striped Bass

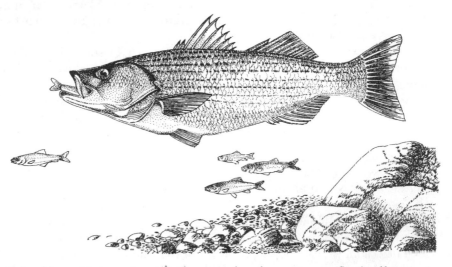

Striped bass, *Morone saxatilis*, have made a dramatic comeback off Maine's rugged, 3,500-mile-long coast. Special regulations, in the form of a 36-inch minimum length limit, a virtual catch-and-release, artificials-only law for certain areas during part of the year, and a ban on the use of gaffs, have combined to make Maine a premier striped bass location. For details on Maine's striped bass regulations, write to the Maine Department of Marine Resources, Station 21, Augusta, ME 04333 or call 207-624-6550. Regulations are always subject to change, so it is best to keep up with the current laws.

School stripers, averaging from 2 to 15 pounds, make up the bulk of the catch, but fish weighing up to 50 pounds are taken each year, especially by anglers using bait.

Stripers move inshore with the coming and going tides. Dead high and low tides are not good times to fish unless you can locate a deep hole in a tidal river where bass are holding.

Striped bass are voracious feeders, gorging themselves as they slash into schools of bait fish. Herring, menhaden, silversides, sand lances, and eels are favorite forage species. Sand lances have the peculiar habit of burying themselves in the sand as the tide retreats, and emerging with the incoming tide. Striped bass, attracted by the emerging sand lances, will often be seen searching the bottom of tidal rivers on an incoming tide. Marine worms are yet another inducement for striped bass to enter shallow water. Clam diggers, while turning over the tidal flats, leave countless marine worms exposed. When the tide comes in, the bass have a feast on the helpless worms.

Stripers are nocturnal, providing action 24 hours a day, as long as the tide is moving.

Anglers searching for striped bass rely upon their eyes as much as anything else, since stripers are easily visible as they feed. Also, sea birds are attracted to striper activity. Swirling herring gulls often signal a striped bass feeding frenzy.

Regarding the striper's future in Maine, Governor Angus King has promised that as long as he is in office, there will be no commercial fishing for striped bass in Maine. The immense economic value of Maine's recreational striped bass fishery is certainly worth protecting, and it is hoped that future lawmakers will follow King's lead.

Most of the Maine striped bass you will catch will be somewhat below the minimum length limit, but the potential is always there to take a legal fish, a trophy in anyone's book. Perhaps that hope is part of the glamour of this new and popular fishery.

Techniques

Spin fishing - You don't have to invest in specialized tackle to be successful at striped bass fishing. Standard spinning gear will suffice. You should always rinse your tackle off with fresh water after each use, to nullify the corrosive effects of salt water.

Spinning gear allows you to cast from shore or from a boat. Most Maine striped bass anglers use spinning tackle. Use at least a medium-weight rod and reel. Lines should test at least 12 pounds, with 15-pound test being more practical.

Stripers respond to a wide variety of artificial lures, both surface and subsurface. If you are geared up for freshwater bass fishing, any of your surface lures will work for stripers. If you want to stock up on saltwater lures, get a few of the new cigar-shaped sinking poppers. These lures are made to sink slowly, so you need to constantly work them to keep them at the surface. Stripers love them.

Trolling with Rapalas and other sinking minnow imitations is an effective method. Tube-style lures, made of surgical tubing, can be trolled as well. These imitate eels and are quite effective.

Shore-based anglers can do well with metal jigs and spoons. These need to be retrieved quickly for the best results. Stripers can swim at speeds of up to 40 miles per hour and often hit that speed when pursuing baitfish.

The new breed of plastic lures are deadly on striped bass. These lures have the feel of natural bait and the fish do not reject them as quickly as harder imitations. Using a plastic eel or baitfish imitation, allow the lure to sink and then apply a forceful twitch. Allow the bait to sink again and then bring the rod back. Repeat this process until it is time to recast. This is a productive and enjoyable method. When you feel a hit, strike with as much force as your tackle will allow. You might even strike several times to ensure a positive hookup.

Surf casting - Most anglers use heavy-duty spinning outfits for surf casting for stripers, but fly rodders have learned that they can get in on the sport too. When the tide is moving, bait fish are found near the breakers, and stripers are often there after the bait fish.

Cast your lure or fly as far as you can and fish it all the way in, even through the curling waves. Given the extreme clarity of Maine's salt water, you may even get to see the striper as it strikes your lure. This is one of the best methods for fly-fishers to take truly large striped bass.

Fly patterns designed for striped bass fishing are becoming common. Large wet flies, tied on hook sizes 1/0 to 3/0, represent a variety of sea creatures, including sand lances, herring, squid, and mackerel. Popular patterns include Catherwood's eel, Catherwood's herring, Catherwood's pogy, Whitlock's sheep streamer, McNally smelt, Lefty's deceiver, and a wide range of popping bugs. In the days before established patterns, some hard-core fly anglers used simple streamers tied with a silver tinsel body and a long, white hairwing. These primitive flies worked then and will work today.

Surf casting with a fly rod requires that you use a commercial or homemade casting basket to hold your loose fly line. Without a basket, your line will become hopelessly tangled and may pick up sand, which could damage your reel.

Fly rods should be at least 8-weight, with 9- and 10-weight preferred. Heavy freshwater fly reels will suffice, but saltwater reels are better, since they have the most powerful drag systems and are resistant to corrosion. Fly reels should have at least 100 yards of 18-pound test backing.

Spinning tackle should be medium-heavy, with 15- to 20-pound test line preferred. Plastic and metal minnow imitations work well, as do a wide range of poppers.

Fishing from a boat - A boat allows you to go to the fish, rather than hoping they come to you. You can tell when a school of stripers is working the bait fish, because of whirling sea birds. Sometimes you can even see plumes of water, the result of a striper "blowing up" on a bunch of bait fish. When you see this, get within casting range as quickly as possible. Any tackle can be used when casting to a school of striped bass from a boat. Take advantage of these feeding binges while they last, because they can end as quickly as they began.

If you don't see any overt signs of activity, try trolling around points and river mouths, using large streamer flies or diving bait fish imitations.

Bait fishing - The largest striped bass are usually taken on bait. The use of bait does have a drawback. Mortality rates are high on released fish, something that doesn't hold true for artificial lures and flies. Live eels are the favorite bait for striped bass, followed by mackerel and sandworms. Eels are difficult to handle, so you should keep them on ice to keep them dormant. Once you pick them up to hook them through the snout, they come to life in a hurry, covering you with slime.

Eels, mackerel, and sandworms are fished on the bottom during a moving tide. A sliding sinker rig is favored by many, but if you can get by without a sinker, so much the better. If a small striper is deeply hooked, take care to cut the line close to the hook. Stay away from non-corrosive hooks when fishing with bait.

Best bets for Maine striped bass: Popham Beach, Site 7; Kennebec River, from Bath to Popham Beach, Site 16; St George River, Site 18; the shoreline along Belfast, Site 27; and the Penobscot River near Verona Island, Site 34.

Brook Trout

Maine has more brook trout waters than any other state. *Salvelinus fontinalis,* or brook trout, are fish of cold, well-oxygenated waters. Because so much of Maine is rural, and so many lakes, rivers, and streams are in near-pristine condition, Maine represents the last frontier for native brook trout. In all but the southern sections of Maine, most streams and brooks that do not run dry in summer hold populations of native brook trout.

Brook trout vary in size according to the waters in which they live. A mature fish from a large lake may be 18 inches long, while another fish of the same age living in a tiny brook may be only 8 inches long. The largest brook trout taken in Maine weighed 8.5 pounds, but specimens half that size are considered trophies. Many small streams hold populations of stunted trout, with 8-inch fish considered a good size and fish of 12 or more inches giants. The largest brook trout come from lakes and ponds, where 3- and 4-pound fish cruise rocky shorelines in search of minnows. Anglers intent upon taking trophy fish should take notice of those ponds that are strictly regulated as part of the Quality Fishing Initiative, because these will produce the largest brook trout. Check the current Maine open water fishing regulations for the locations of these waters.

Brook trout are dogged battlers. Unlike brown trout or landlocked salmon, brook trout seldom jump, although they do splash on the surface when hooked. Brookies make short but spirited runs and then settle down to slug it out in deep water. Most brook trout spend their entire lives in fresh water but will migrate to salt water if allowed the opportunity. Anadromous or sea-run brook trout usually ascend brooks, rivers, and streams in early spring. In fact, sea-run brook trout provide Maine's earliest open water fishing.

Streams and rivers that are not dammed usually host runs of anadromous brookies. Even the tiniest brooks, the kind that all but dry up in summer, will see a run of brilliantly colored brook trout in early- to mid-April.

Fishing these tiny brooks is sometimes difficult. Alders and raspberry bushes line the banks and casting is almost impossible. Although sea-run brook trout will hit flies and other artificials, the easiest way to go about it is to use an ultralight spinning outfit and worms as bait.

These little trout can be skittery to the extreme, so the brook fisher must sometimes creep about on hands and knees in order to prevent a shadow from spooking the fish. Sometimes the only way to get a bait into a pool is to stick your rod through an opening in the bushes and drop your line straight down. Even if you do hook a fish, it can be difficult to guide it through the ever-present tangle of the brush and limbs.

Sometimes patches of snow still spot the ground in the shady glen where the little sea-run brookies are found. The author has kept his catch fresh by placing a few handfuls of granular snow in his creel and placing the just-caught fish on ice. Fishing for Maine sea-run brook trout in April presents some interesting paradoxes. Where else can you catch brook trout while standing in the snow, within earshot of the surf? Sea-run brook trout can be found in rivers that also hold Atlantic salmon smolt. Because newly arrived sea-run brookies are iridescent, they are sometimes mistaken for salmon smolt. If you are not sure what you have caught, remember that all brook trout have vermiculations on the back and all brook trout have a square tail. Salmon have a forked tail and no vermiculations.

Beaver flowages

Beavers are ubiquitous in Maine. Though sometimes cursed by landowners, the busy rodents are responsible for creating some fantastic, albeit short-lived brook trout fishing. When beavers dam a stream or brook, the resulting impoundment is called a "beaver flowage." Any native brook trout living in the newly created pond is suddenly faced with an abundance of food and plenty of room to grow. Eventually, tannin leaching from decaying plants renders the water infertile, forcing the trout to move on.

Most beaver flowages are small, usually much less than 10 acres. The fish are easily caught and heavy fishing pressure can wipe out the population in a short time. That is why beaver flowages are such well-kept secrets. Ardent brook trout anglers search far and wide for new flowages, always hoping to strike it rich. And they never, never divulge the location of a prime flowage.

You can find your own personal brook trout haven if you are willing to expend enough time and energy. The hours of tramping through alder jungles will be forgotten when you first behold wild brook trout dimpling the surface of some remote flowage and realize that you are the only person who knows of its existence. Treat such flowages with respect, for they are special places. Penobscot, Piscataquis, Aroostook, and Washington counties are all worth exploring for flowages.

Techniques

Spin fishing - An ultralight spinning outfit is perfect for brook trout fishing. Use from 2-to 4-pound test lines, since the light line will not scare the fish as would a heavier line and you will be able to make longer casts. Most Maine anglers favor a one-piece rod simply because it is usually shorter than the two-piece types, making it easier to tote along brushy streams and brooks.

One of the best spinning lures for brook trout is shaped like a small minnow and is called a goldfish by several manufacturers. This lure is of a simple, basic design, but it is a real brook trout killer. Use this lure in streams or ponds. If fishing a stream, cast upstream and reel slowly as the spoon is carried downstream with the current. When fishing ponds, cast out as far as you can and let the spoon settle to the bottom. Reel in slowly, imparting action with the tip of your rod. This lure is especially good early in the season.

Small spinners such as the Mepps series are effective on brook trout. These are best used in streams and rivers. As with the goldfish lure, reel in slowly, allowing the current to take your spinner where it may. You may want to bend the barbs down on the hooks of your spinning lures to make it easier to release fish.

The Super-Duper is another old-time favorite of Maine brook trout anglers. This odd-shaped lure is good for ponds, streams, and especially beaver flowages. Use the smallest, lightest Super-Duper you can find and fish it slowly.

Fly casting - Fly casting for brook trout is the most enjoyable and rewarding method of all. Unless you are fishing a big lake on a windy day, use the lightest rod you can find. A 7.5- or 8-foot, 3- to 5-weight rod is a pleasure to use and provides the most sport.

Brook trout are not terribly leader-shy, so a 9-foot leader with a 3-pound test tippet is about right for most situations. Brook trout are not usually as selective as brown trout, although at times they can drive you to the brink of frustration. While most brook trout are taken on underwater offerings, brookies do feed on the surface. Brook trout can also be "pounded up" with attractor patterns such as the royal coachman and Adams. You should stock some caddis patterns, as well as dun variants and blue-winged olives in a variety of sizes. The best time to take brookies on dry flies is in the morning and evening hours. Brook trout sometimes feed on the surface during the day, especially in shaded sections of ponds and streams and on overcast or rainy days. If you are fishing with bucktails or nymphs from a boat or canoe, always keep a separate fly rod strung up with a dry-fly attractor pattern. That way, you will be ready to present a surface offering should surface activity commence.

Nymph fishers take their share of brookies too. Again, pattern is not especially important. The author has pared his nymph fishing down to one pattern, the soft-hackle fly. These simple flies, in various shades and sizes, are very effective on not only brook trout, but all salmonids. A sinking fly line, long leader, and 2- to 3-pound test tippet will round out your outfit.

Bucktails and streamers are popular brook-trout flies, with bucktails taking the edge in fish appeal. Bucktails, hair-wing flies tied on size 6, 8, and 10 hooks, are realistic minnow imitations. Popular patterns include red-and-white, Edson tiger light, Edson tiger dark, gray ghost, Jerry's Smelt, any of the Thunder

Creek series, and muddler minnows.

Just after ice-out, bucktails can be used to take brook trout by trolling. Troll in a zig-zag pattern, not more than 50 feet from the shore. It is important that you go slow and impart plenty of action to your fly. Bucktails can be used in conjunction with dodgers to take brook trout. Use a 5- or 6-inch leader between the fly and the dodger.

Bait fishing - In early spring a can of earthworms, an ultralight spinning outfit, and a small stream spell brook trout fishing for many Maine anglers. At this time of year, trout are sluggish because of the influx of super-chilled water from snowmelt. Spring freshets wash earthworms and other land-based food forms into the trout's habitat so the fish are attuned to feeding on worms. A meal of fresh brook trout, coupled with a plate of steamed fiddleheads (the immature fronds of the ostrich fern) is a rite of spring for Maine folk.

Using a size 8 or 10 barbless hook, lightly impale one or two earthworms so they dangle. Do not ball the worm up on the hook. If you must use a sinker, use only one size b.b. split shot, about 10 inches above the hook. Do not use a swivel or any other terminal gear. You want your offering to appear as natural as possible. If fishing a brook or stream, cast upstream and let your offering float downstream. Keep your line tight enough to detect a take but don't impart any artificial action.

You can fish ponds from the shore, using worms. Cast out and let your bait sink to the bottom. Slowly retrieve it in short increments. You might use two rods, letting one worm sit on the bottom while you slowly retrieve the other. In early spring, search for sandy bottom on the south side of a pond or lake. The trout will be here now, taking advantage of the warm mini-climate created by the sun's rays.

Ice fishing - Brook trout are willing feeders in winter. Tip-ups, baited with small minnows or earthworms, are standard fare. Brook trout bite so well through the ice that many trout ponds are closed to ice-fishing. In general, trout bite best in the early part of the season.

Set your tip-ups out in no more than 20 feet of water. When you get a flag, make haste to attend your tip-up. Carefully watch the underwater spool for signs of movement but don't pick it up until you are sure the fish has a solid hold on the bait. Any undue pressure before the fish is ready to be hooked will cause the fish to drop the bait and depart.

Best bets for Maine brook trout: Prestile Stream, Site 80; Moose River, Site 68; Rangeley Lake, Site 14; and Swan Lake, Site 31.

Brown Trout

Brown trout, *Salmo trutta,* are not new to Maine waters, but until about 25 years ago, few Maine anglers knew how to catch them and even fewer cared to learn. Brook trout, the undisputed king of Maine salmonids, received top billing. Relegated to a few rivers and a handful of lakes, brown trout lived and died without fanfare. But today, brown trout are a favorite game fish.

Maine has an immense number of lakes, ponds, rivers, and streams that are not suitable for brook trout because of warm temperatures and the presence of predators. Many of these waters are suitable for brown trout, however, and are being managed for this species.

Maine brown trout represent the fishing challenge of the modern age. Plentiful and inclined to grow much larger than the native species, browns are currently being stocked in all Maine counties except Penobscot County.

Brown trout are not pushovers like native brook trout. The angler who does not use stealth will often fail to interest even one brown trout during a day's fishing. Another angler, fishing the same water but schooled in the ways of brown trout, may have the best fishing of his life.

Maine brown trout can be divided into two categories: stream or river fish and flatwater fish. Flatwater brown trout fishing in a placid section of a slow-moving stream is essentially the same as fishing a pond or lake. One further division may be added: anadromous brown trout. Some Maine rivers host runs of sea-run brown trout. These runs occur in the fall and early winter and techniques for these fish are the same as for any other brown trout.

Brown trout, especially the sea-run variety, can be mistaken for landlocked or Atlantic salmon. There are several ways to tell the difference between the two species. The tail of a young salmon is more deeply forked than that of a brown trout. The caudal peduncle, that area between the adipose fin and tail, is thin and tapered on a salmon. Brown trout have thick, stocky caudal peduncles. The best and most positive way to tell salmon from adult brown trout is by checking the vomerine teeth, that row of teeth in the center of the roof of the mouth. Adult brown trout have a crooked double row of vomerine teeth, while salmon have a rather straight, single row.

The Maine record, a 23-pound, 8-ounce brown trout, was taken from 910-acre Square Pond in Acton in 1996. This pond has no boat landing, nor has it been stocked with brown trout in recent years. The previous Maine record brown trout weighed 19 pounds, 7 ounces, and was taken from Sebago Lake in 1958. Compare these weights with the all-time world record of 35 pounds, 15 ounces, and you will see that Maine has the potential to produce a world-record brown trout.

Techniques

Spin fishing - Lightweight or medium-weight spinning rods and reels are best for Maine brown trout. Load your reel with 4- to 6-pound test line.

Most anglers who fish for brown trout with spinning tackle do so in rivers rather than lakes. Diving minnow imitations such as Rapalas and Rebels are used by the wide majority of anglers.

Gold spoons are highly effective on brown trout. These should be fished slowly, near the bottom.

A good way to fish the larger rivers is to select a prime part of shoreline and cast toward it as you float past. Keep returning to your starting point if you have strikes but miss the fish.

Fly casting - Of all fishing techniques, none is more suited for Maine's brown trout than fly fishing. Maine's rivers and streams offer superlative fly fishing. Even near southern Maine's densest population centers, you can find idyllic settings with fast brown trout fishing.

Southern and coastal Maine fly hatches often correspond with the timing of the hatches on New York's Schoharie River. The emergence tables in Art Flick's classic book, *The New Streamside Guide*, can be used as a general guide to when the major hatches will occur in southern and coastal Maine. An extremely cold spring will disrupt this general rule.

Except for small stream and brook fishing, anglers should choose a 9-foot fly rod. Weight is a matter of choice, but a 6-weight can usually supply the power for distance casting and is light enough so even a 10-inch trout can put up a respectable battle. Anglers on the bigger rivers might want to take along an 8-weight rod just in case.

A 9- or even 10-foot rod is ideally suited for fishing from a canoe. A shorter rod does not have the power to drive a line from the sitting position. Your casting arm will not be as tired at the end of the day with the longer rod.

Red quill hatch - Red quills, *E. subvaria,* are eagerly anticipated by Maine brown-trout anglers. These flies usually start showing up around the end of April in the south and can last well into June in northern regions.

Red quill duns usually don't come off before noontime, and there's no sense in expecting to see them any sooner. The beginning of the hatch can be a spectacular event. Trout begin rising sporadically, picking off a struggling dun here and there. As insect numbers increase, the stream seems to explode with trout. Your biggest problem may be deciding which fish to cast to first.

Other insects - Most of the common mayflies found in the eastern United States are found in Maine, but other insects are worth considering as well. Stone fly nymphs are good early-season offerings. Finally, the author wouldn't think of leaving home without at least a few soft-hackle flies in his box. Soft hackles may represent a number of food sources to a trout. These simple flies have a floss body and woodcock or grouse hackles. Fished quartering downstream, with a slack line, these flies can bring strikes when nothing else will. When browns are in shallow, riffly water, a dead-drifted soft hackle will often bring a strike.

If you plan to fish during the warm summer months, be sure to include a variety of terrestrial patterns. Black and red ant patterns are extremely effective, as are cork-bodied flies. The author makes his own generic terrestrials from nothing more than a toy balsa-wood glider and model enamel. Cork-bodied beetle patterns, tied on a size 14 hook and painted red, are extremely effective. Round out your terrestrial assortment with a few Letort hopper grasshopper patterns in sizes 10 and 12.

Flatwater fly casting - Brown trout in small ponds are by far the most intimidating fish in Maine. The best way to fish these ponds is from a canoe, although shore-based fly casting can be effective. During an insect hatch, browns will cruise the surface, taking insects seemingly at random. You need to anticipate the direction in which the trout is moving and place your fly where it will be noticed. If a brown rises within casting distance, quickly dropping your fly inside the rise form may elicit a strike. It may also put the fish down.

Flatwater browns lose some of their native wariness during a mayfly hatch. The correct imitation of the same size as the naturals will usually take browns at this time.

Caddis flies are probably more common than mayflies on Maine ponds, and the astute angler will carry a good assortment of caddis patterns. The Henryville is a good caddis imitation for Maine waters. Carry a variety of sizes.

May and early June are the best times for dry-fly fishing in Maine ponds, but even in summer, dawn and dusk fishing can be rewarding. The fish become active again during the last week of September.

Trolling - Most trollers use spinning gear, but to avoid line twist, more anglers are turning to the fly rod and sinking line. If you don't have a sinking line, a 20-foot leader with several split shot will get your lure down to where the browns are waiting. Even if your leader becomes twisted, the fly line will remain straight. To untwist, simply remove your lure and pull the leader behind the boat.

Some fishermen troll with a live minnow or smelt, but you can catch as many and more brown trout on artificials. Besides, the fish you release on artificials have a greater chance of surviving.

The traditional Maine way of taking landlocked salmon by trolling with a fly rod and single or tandem-hook streamers can be easily adapted to brown trout fishing. Browns, like salmon, are active after ice-out, chasing schools of smelt and other minnows that cruise just under the surface. Some of the biggest brown trout in the lake can be taken by this method in early spring. The combination of a well-used fly rod, comfortable boat, and feisty brown trout tearing into traditional streamer patterns is enough to conjure up images of pine trees along a rocky shore and thin wisps of wood smoke curling up from a cabin's chimney.

When trolling with streamers, be sure to vary your course every once in awhile. Browns, like salmon, often hit when the fly is completing a swing. And don't be afraid to go too fast. The majority of anglers simply putt-putt along, giving the trout a chance to examine the streamer fly close-up. It's better to go a bit faster and allow your streamer to create the illusion of a speeding smelt about to dart out of range. You will definitely elicit more strikes at faster speeds.

As with landlocked salmon, brown trout in ponds seem to have a preference for lures trolled in a certain direction. You can troll a shoreline in one direction and not get a strike. Reverse the order and the fish begin to bite. The reason for this behavior is subject to debate, but it's true all the same.

Lake fishermen, used to trolling for salmon and lake trout with lead lines and huge revolving spoons, have adapted their time-honored techniques to brown trout fishing. A gold or copper set of spoons is usually more productive than chrome-colored sets. Deep trolling is made easier by the use of a fish locator. In summer, when deep trolling is most effective, the trout are somewhere near the bottom of the lake. Anglers using fish locators can often anticipate a strike. Deep-trolling usually accounts for the largest brown trout of the year, specimens of 8 and 10 pounds. Carry the largest landing net you can find!

Night fishing - The biggest brown trout in a stream or river are often nocturnal feeders. During the dry months of July through September, night fishing can be rewarding.

Night fishing is best when the water is warm and low. This is when the big brownies come to the shallows to feed. Use large wet flies and don't be concerned about presentation. You want to attract the fish to your fly and a splashy presentation is the way to do it in the nighttime. Leaders should be stout, capable of turning a brown weighing 5 pounds or more.

Woolly buggers, zonkers, and black muddler minnows are all good choices, but any large and bushy fly should work. You can also take fish on small poppers, such as you would use for panfish.

Always check the stream out in the daytime before going out at night. Learn where the deep holes are and get acquainted with the stream bottom.

Don't go night fishing on a moonlit night. Wait for a new moon or an overcast night. And don't shine a flashlight on the water. That will put the fish down for the duration.

Sea-run brown trout - Sea-run brown trout can be taken by the same methods you would use for landlocked browns. However, if you are fishing in tidal water, the best way to locate these fish is to search at low tide. That is when brown trout will be schooled up in tidal pools. Use caution when casting, since these fish are extremely wary. Sea-run brown trout are usually taken on artificials—either streamers or bucktails—or lightweight spinning lures.

Ice fishing - Ice fishing for brown trout has become a favorite pastime for Maine anglers. Browns can be taken on either bait or artificials. Most anglers use tip-ups and a medium-to-small live minnow for bait. Others prefer night crawlers. Most of your strikes will come when your bait is suspended only a few feet under the ice. Fish near rocky points or similar structures. Browns have the unusual habit of cruising very near the shore, so be sure to set one line close to shore in no more than 2 feet of water.

You can usually tell when a brown trout takes a bait. A brown may run as far as 50 feet before slowing down to turn the bait and swallow it. Resist the urge to strike as soon as the flag goes up.

If you decide to use worms or night crawlers instead of minnows, look for a muddy bottom, preferably along the edge of a weed bed. Let your bait crawl on the bottom in 8 to 10 feet of water. Browns frequent these areas in search of insect larvae and freshwater snails.

Jigging for brown trout has its advantages over bait fishing. Browns often go on feeding sprees and hit jigs with reckless abandon. A jig rod is easier to carry than a set of tip-ups and when jigging, you don't have to carry bait. Try using a small- to medium-size Swedish Pimple jig. Some anglers combine tip-up fishing with jigging, placing a few baited tip-ups out and jigging other holes at the same time.

Best bets for Maine brown trout: St. George River, Site 25; Piscataquis River, Site 44; Kennebec River, Sites 16, 35, 37, and 38; and China Lake, Site 36.

Lake Trout ─────────────────────────

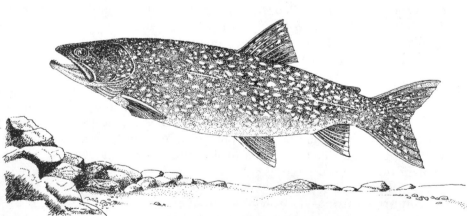

Lake trout, *Salvelinus namaycush,* are called togue in Maine. The state record weighed 31.5 pounds and individuals up to 20 pounds are taken regularly, although specimens weighing 3 to 8 pounds are more common. Except for a short time in very early spring, when they are drawn to shallow water by spawning smelt, lake trout are fish of cold, deep water.

By and large, lake trout are fish of lakes, preferring a water temperature of about 50 degrees. For this reason, lake trout are found in deep water, the only place they can find suitable temperatures in summer.

Even if water temperatures are suitable, lakers will not go in shallow water on a bright day because their eyes are light-sensitive. This fact is often overlooked by eager fishers, but it will pay off in dividends if you stay away from the shallows on bright days. By following the same strategy, you can expect lakers to be in more shallow water around dawn; they will move to deeper water when the sun becomes bright.

Lake trout do not jump when hooked and rarely make any kind of fuss on the surface. They do put up a powerful, dogged battle. Anyone who has caught a laker of 7 or 8 pounds or more will agree that you just don't reel them in like an old boot.

Lake trout feed almost exclusively on other fish, including other trout.

Techniques

Spin fishing - Spinning lures can be used to good effect for lake trout. Immediately after ice-out, lake trout are in relatively shallow water and can be taken on spoon-type lures such as Mooselook Wobblers and Dardevles. This can be done either from a boat or from the shore. Cast, allow your lure to sink to the bottom, and slowly reel, giving an occasional twitch of the rod tip to impart action. When the water warms, usually a month or so after ice-out, lake trout head for the cool depths and spinning techniques are no longer effective.

Use a medium-weight rod and reel and the largest lures your outfit can handle. Your rod should have plenty of backbone in order to set the hook in the toothy maw of a lake trout. Use at least 8-pound test line.

Bait fishing - Smelt are a prime source of bait, especially during the smelt runs. Large golden shiners up to 5 inches long and white suckers of a similar size are also good choices. Because lake trout are reluctant to go too far from the bottom after food, keep your bait on the bottom for the best results.

Still fishing, casting a baited hook and letting it lie motionless on the bottom, is the most effective way to employ bait. Still fishing can be tedious; sometimes you can go for hours or even an entire day without a bite. At other times, you can catch two or three fish in an afternoon. A boat with a fish locator helps to even the odds because you can at least be certain you are fishing in a spot that contains fish.

Use baitholder-style hooks in size 4 or 6 and above all, do not add any more weight to your line than is needed to keep the bait down on the bottom. Bell sinkers, rubber-core sinkers, and the like will only cause the lake trout to drop your bait. You want it to appear as natural as possible. If you have trouble with your minnow swimming to the surface, kill it. Lake trout will take a dead bait as well as a live one. You might even get more bites on a dead bait.

Fill your reel with at least 100 yards of 8-pound test monofilament, but beware of anything over 10-pound test. Lake trout will avoid your bait if it is attached to a thick, stiff line.

Trolling - During open water fishing, most lake trout are taken by deep trolling techniques. The tackle used for lakers is the same as that used for land-locked salmon, except that lake trout prefer trolling spoons with copper or gold blades, not the chrome blades used for salmon. Lake trout anglers also use a single-blade spoon with a few red beads strung above it. These spoons are often as much as 8 inches long and 5 inches wide.

Size of bait is important. When trolling for salmon, a 3-inch minnow is about right, but lake trout like larger bait, even minnows 6 inches long and more. It would be difficult to find a minnow too large for lake trout.

Slow is the key to trolling for lake trout. A motor capable of smooth operation at the slowest trolling speeds is a must. Many anglers prefer electric motors because of the infinite number of speed adjustments. Go just fast enough so that your trolling spoon blades barely turn. At speeds this slow, your outfit will sometimes touch bottom and you will need to reel in and remove any debris. Remember that you need to be within a foot of the bottom anyway. If you do not bump bottom once in a while, you are not deep enough.

When a lake trout takes a trolled bait, you need to strike with all the force your tackle can stand. Lake trout have tough, bony mouths, and it requires considerable force to set the hook properly.

Some anglers use medium-weight spinning or bait casting gear along with a downrigger, rather than heavy tackle and lead-core line. You might use a dodger a few feet ahead of your bait. The bait should gently sway from side to side as you troll for lake trout, so check the action alongside your boat before you begin fishing. This is one of the few instances where you would not want the lure or bait too close to the dodger. The dodger should be used as an attractor only, not to impart action to your bait or lure. If you are fishing with a partner, have that partner bring the downrigger up as soon as you hook a fish so you can enjoy the battle without fear of your prize getting wound around your downrigger cable.

Lake trout are sometimes taken by anglers fishing for landlocked salmon with streamer flies. When conditions are right (proper water temperatures and overcast skies), lake trout can be found near the mouths of streams during a smelt run. This happy circumstance does not occur frequently, and when it does, it is of short duration. If you want to up your chances of taking a lake trout on a streamer with your fly rod, use a high-density sinking line. Don't expect to take many lake trout this way, but be aware that the possibility exists.

Vertical jigging - This tactic was once widely known, but fell into disuse; it is only now regaining its popularity. Jigging with artificial lures, bait, or a combination of the two is an efficient and enjoyable way to fish for lake trout during the open water season or through the ice. Jigging can be done with any tackle, but most anglers prefer heavy spinning gear.

In days past, anglers jigged with a 12-inch-long strip of white flesh from the belly of a sucker. Sucker skin is tough, so the bait stays on the hook a long time. If you want to try this old method, use a thin strip of sucker belly and hook it at one end, making sure the hook point protrudes. Allow it to reach bottom and lift your rod about one foot, then drop it. The sucker belly will flutter on its way back down, attracting any lake trout that may be near.

Modern ice-fishing lures are ideally suited to summertime jigging, and are all solid producers of summertime lake trout. Some anglers add a bit of minnow or even a small strip of sucker belly to the jig hook, but you can still take fish without adding bait. If you can find an ice jig with glow-in-the-dark paint, buy it. If not, you might apply some glow paint to your existing jigs. When fishing in 60 or so feet of water, you need to do everything you can to make your jig visible.

Most anglers use a fish finder to locate groups of lake trout and then slowly drift over the schools. This eliminates all guesswork, but does not guarantee results. Lake trout are never pushovers.

Ice fishing - Ice fishing is probably the most popular method of fishing for lake trout. The fish tend to congregate under the ice, so a spot that produces one fish will usually be good for a few more. As the winter wears on, lake trout seek progressively deeper water; if they are in 45 feet of water in January, they may be in more than 100 feet of water at the end of February.

Tip-ups and live or dead minnows are standard fare for lake trout. No matter how deep the water is, always set your bait on the bottom. Veteran lake trout anglers will use the largest golden shiner they can find and kill it so it rests on the bottom where the trout can find it. Other good anglers insist on live smelt, but in fact both will take lake trout if they are fished on the bottom.

Anglers usually match their tackle to their quarry, but in lake trout fishing this is often a mistake. Your line must be relatively thin and very supple. If the line has been on the spool for a season, be sure to stretch it or even pull it through a bit of rubber to remove any tendency to coil. Stick to 8- or 10-pound test monofilament.

Use no additional weight if you can help it. It may take some time for your dead minnow to reach bottom without weight, but lake trout can detect the presence of sinkers and will reject a bait if they are the least bit suspicious. The use of a good, straight line and no weight are the two most important considerations when ice fishing for lake trout.

If you get a flag, don't rush to the tip-up and begin pulling line. Lake trout sometimes take a long time to ingest a bait. Typically, a fish will run with the bait, drop it, and pick it up again before turning the bait to swallow it headfirst. Lake trout may run as much as 100 feet with a bait, so don't set your lines any closer to each other than that or you may wind up with a tangled mess beneath the ice.

Best bets for Maine lake trout: Sebago Lake, Site 6; Beech Hill Pond, Site 47; Indian Pond, Site 67; and Millinocket Lake, Site 76.

Rainbow Trout

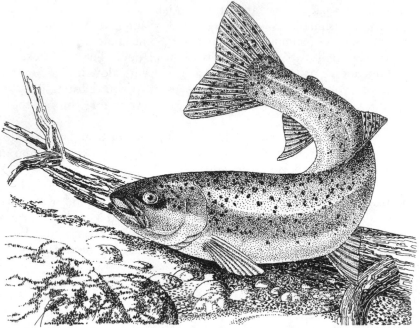

Rainbow trout, *Salmo gairdneri*, are not widespread in Maine, but several waters have well-established populations that offer quality fishing. Maine does not have an official rainbow trout stocking program, but during the last few years, private organizations have stocked rainbows in several Maine waters.

Rainbow trout are prized for their spirited runs and leaping abilities. Also, rainbows are capable of prospering in areas where water temperatures are too high for Maine's native brook trout.

Rainbow trout are the only Maine salmonids to spawn in spring, not fall. A stream-bred rainbow trout in its spawning colors is a thing of beauty. Instead of the faint trace of red seen in typical anaemic-looking hatchery-reared fish, wild rainbows show their colors in shades of deep rose.

Rainbow trout are active in the early season. Opening day anglers have every chance of taking a rainbow, although low water temperatures can cause the fish to put up a less than exemplary battle. Rainbow trout, like brown trout, feed on bait fish as well as insects, making them popular with a wide range of anglers.

Some Maine waters contain stream-bred rainbow trout. These populations exist because fish from previous stockings have managed to become self-sustaining and because rainbows, a popular game fish in neighboring New Hampshire, have traveled to Maine via streams connecting the two states.

Techniques

Fly casting - Rainbow trout are the fly fisher's delight. They are taken on streamers, bucktails, nymphs, and dry flies. The same tactics that work on brown trout are effective on rainbows, except that rainbows are more easily taken on colorful attractor patterns such as the Wright's royal, a variation of the royal coachman with a single hairwing.

In big waters such as the Kennebec River, fly fishers do well with bucktails such as black-nosed dace, and various shades of the Thunder Creek series.

In spring, spawning rainbow trout are fair prey to dry-fly anglers. Rainbows will not forgive a sluggish response, so be prepared to lift your rod the second a fish takes your fly. Spawning rainbow trout can be a real problem when they take to the tributaries. A 16-inch rainbow can make a fast, powerful run. If the stream is small and lined with brush, all the angler can do is hang on and hope for the best.

Fly fishers can take advantage of windy conditions. Look for rainbow trout feeding on the windward side of a lake or pond. The trout are attracted to the myriad insects that float in windrows along the shore. It is almost impossible to fish from shore during these conditions, since casting against the wind is so difficult and frustrating. It is better to use a boat and anchor near the shoreline. Using wet or dry flies, cast with the wind toward the shore. Few anglers like to fish during times of high winds and it can be dangerous when the wind is driving flying spray from the tips of whitecaps, but this is when rainbow trout take to the shoreline. Be sure your boat is big enough to handle the conditions; otherwise, wait for calmer weather.

Use a light- or medium-weight fly rod for rainbows. An 8- or 9-foot rod in 5 or 6 weight is perfect. Do have plenty of backing on your reel in case you hook a big fish; rainbows of 3 pounds and up can make long, line-sizzling runs.

Spin fishing - Rainbow trout are commonly taken on small, gold-colored spoons as well as Rapalas and similar bait fish imitations. Mepps spinners are also effective. This may be the best way to take trophy rainbows in Maine, since the bigger trout prefer fish to insects.

You will need light- or medium-weight spinning tackle; the size of the water being fished will dictate the size of the tackle. If you fish the smaller tributaries, ultralight tackle is the ticket.

Lines need not be more than 6-pound test, and 4-pound test allows for longer and more delicate casts. Do pay close attention to your drag setting, since the initial run of a rainbow trout can be enough to break almost any line if the drag setting is too tight.

Keep your lures small when casting and use the larger sizes only when trolling. Even then, you will have your best luck with the smallest Rapalas and other minnow imitations.

Trout in rivers are likely candidates for the spin fisher using small spinners. Spinners are effective even when rainbow trout are taking aquatic insects from the surface. Cast close to the rise, but not directly on it. Rainbow trout are rarely able to resist the whirring spinner blade as it passes near their feeding station.

Trolling - Rainbow trout will take a night crawler or minnow pulled behind a set of chrome-colored lake trolls. This is a productive way to fish in early summer, when the fish are in deeper water. Go slowly, as you would for lake trout. Fish in

40 to 50 feet of water. You can also use downriggers for rainbows. A good setup is a dodger a few feet in front of a live minnow, Rapala, or streamer fly.

In years past, anglers had success with a June-bug spinner and a night crawler or minnow on the trailer hook. You can duplicate the action of these antique lures by using a snelled hook with a single spinner blade, or even the all-in-one sets consisting of a snap for your hook on the end, a loop for the line on the other, and two spinner blades attached to the wire shaft with clevises. When using this rig, be sure to troll slowly, since the action will be impaired by too much speed.

Bait fishing - Live minnows, garden worms, and night crawlers are all effective on Maine's rainbow trout. Cast your offering upstream and let it tumble down with the current, just as you would a wet fly.

Best bets for Maine rainbow trout: Wild River, especially near its confluence with the Androscoggin River, Site 13; Kennebec River below Wyman Dam, Site 15; Megunticook Lake, Site 26; and Kennebec River below Shawmut Dam, Site 38.

Landlocked Salmon

Landlocked salmon, *Salmo salar sebago*, are Maine's glamour fish. These silvery battlers are known for their leaping ability, savage strikes, and swift, powerful runs. In Maine, landlocked salmon are found in both rivers and lakes.

Because of the fish's popularity, the Maine Department of Inland Fisheries & Wildlife regularly stocks landlocked Salmon in Maine lakes and rivers. In 1995, the agency stocked 190,458 landlocked salmon in Maine.

Landlocked salmon need cold, pure water in order to thrive. Fortunately, Maine is well endowed with waters suitable for salmon. In fact, Maine has more landlocked salmon waters than any other state in the nation.

An abundance of smelt, a slim, toothy bait fish, is another reason for the state's renowned landlocked salmon fishing. Smelt are a major forage species for landlocked salmon. In the early spring, just after ice-out, schools of smelt cruise shorelines as they prepare to ascend small streams and brooks to spawn.

At this time, anglers using smelt imitations can take salmon just beneath the surface. Dozens of artificial lures and flies have been designed for the sole purpose of imitating smelt. Commercial bait dealers trap live smelt and sell them as bait. Maine's smelt are the basis for a productive industry.

Landlocked salmon taken immediately after ice-out often have a yellowish hue, the result of a winter spent under the ice, away from sunlight. After a few days in the open water and exposure to direct sunlight, the fish soon regain their normal silvery appearance.

The flesh of landlocked salmon is more delicately flavored than that of sea-going salmon. Even anglers who are dedicated to catch-and-release often save at least one landlocked salmon to cook on the grill with a little pepper and a squirt of lemon juice.

Most of the landlocked salmon you catch will weigh 2 pounds or less, but 4-pound specimens are not uncommon, and fish weighing 8 to 10 pounds are always possible. The Maine record landlocked salmon weighed 22.5 pounds and was taken from Sebago Lake in 1907. You are not likely to hook a fish of that size, but even a 5-pound landlocked salmon can provide the freshwater angling thrill of a lifetime.

Techniques

Trolling with streamer flies - A 9-foot fly rod is best for this specialized form of fishing, but 8-footers will suffice. You will have the best results with a fairly soft rod-action, since landlocked salmon strike fast and a too-stiff rod is liable to tear the hook out on a strike. Modern graphite rods are sensitive and forgiving, but some of the older glass models are too stiff.

You don't need to worry about tapered leaders and fine tippets. Length of leader is the biggest concern. Level monofilament will do just fine. Use at least 15 feet of 6-pound test leader. If the fish are more than a few feet down, you may need up to 30 feet.

Most anglers use a sinking fly line, but a floating line will do if you add weight. Do make sure your line-to-leader connection is smooth and neat. If it isn't, it may catch on your top guide and allow the fish to escape.

Make sure your fly reel is loaded with plenty of backing and has a smooth drag. One of Maine's trophy landlocked salmon can tear a fly line off a reel faster than it takes to talk about it.

Trolling for landlocked salmon with streamer flies is best done during breezy or even windy days. Mainers refer to small whitecaps as "salmon chop." Some of Maine's lakes can be dangerous during high winds, so listen to the weather forecast. If a lake's boating advisory is in effect, don't go on the water.

Up to three persons can troll for landlocked salmon at the same time and not be in each other's way. A rod on either side plus one straight off the stern is a common setup.

When you begin trolling, start with most of your fly line out. If you don't get any strikes, try using a shorter line. In fact, salmon are often attracted to the bubbles of the prop wash and can be taken within 10 feet of your boat.

Landlocked salmon are capable of swimming at high speeds, as are smelt, so troll at a good clip. Work the shorelines and coves and especially the mouths of streams and brooks. If you find where the smelt are schooling, you will have also found landlocks. Look for dead smelt floating on the surface.

Landlocks tend to slash at bait fish, crippling them first and eating them at their leisure. Use a hook sharpener to keep your hooks needle-sharp and you will get more hookups.

When the fishing is slow, anglers sometimes tire of holding their rods and place them in a rod holder. The value of these devices is debatable, since they require a fish to hook itself. You will hook more fish if you are holding the rod when the fish strikes. Still, when cold sleet makes holding a rod a chore, you may need to resort to a rod holder.

Streamer patterns for trolling - Selecting the proper streamer fly pattern for landlocked salmon is a guessing game. What makes fly selection even more interesting is the fact that what the landlocks are crazy for today may be ignored tomorrow.

Streamers come tied on either a single, long-shanked hook, or on a tandem setup, with two single hooks fastened together by plastic-coated wire. Both types of fly are useful and both are suited to a specific task.

Single-hook streamers are, by virtue of their design, smaller than tandem streamers. In a lake where the forage fish run small, a single-hook streamer will take more fish. This is in keeping with the notion that you will take more fish if you match your lure size to the size of the natural bait. The drawback to using these is that the single, long-shanked hook allows the fish to apply leverage and possibly tear the hook out.

Tandem-hook streamers are preferred by the majority of anglers. When you go to a lake for the first time, begin with tandems; if you don't get a strike, switch to the smaller variety.

Streamers come in a wide variety of patterns, and new ones appear each year. Some anglers design their own patterns for specific waters. Still, you will not go wrong by sticking to tried-and-true patterns. Any of the following will take fish anywhere in Maine: gray ghost, black ghost, supervisor, Barnes special, pink lady, nine-three, Jerry's smelt, queen bee, and red-and-white.

Like milk, butter, and eggs, streamer flies are a common item in most general stores in Maine. Additionally, any sporting-goods store will have a selection of streamers. When you buy streamers, stay away from bushy, over-dressed flies.

If any group of Maine landlocked salmon anglers were asked what they considered the best all-around streamer fly, they would surely choose the gray ghost. Whatever other patterns you decide to collect, make sure you have a few gray ghosts.

Fly casting - Landlocked salmon do not feed exclusively on smelt, to the delight of fly fishers. Often, a hatch of mayflies will bring landlocks to the surface. The author keeps a 9-foot fly rod strung up and ready to fish at all times, just in case landlocked salmon decide to go on a surface feed. Hooking a 3- or 4-pound landlocked salmon on a dry fly is an exciting, nerve-shattering experience, and one not soon forgotten.

Fly casters sometimes take landlocked salmon in lakes, but Maine's rivers offer more opportunities. Early-season anglers use single-hook streamers and weighted nymphs. As the season progresses and aquatic insects begin to hatch, dry-fly fishers experience the thrill of taking landlocked salmon with surface offerings.

Never use a fly rod lighter than 6-weight. A 9-foot rod is ideal, and 8-footers are acceptable. Some anglers, especially on the larger rivers, use an 8- or 9-weight, 10-foot rod.

When a hatch is on, you can get by with a 4-pound test tippet, but when the water is low, you may have to switch to 2-pound test. Leader length is not as critical as with brown trout, but in low, clear water, you will be better off using a 12-foot tapered leader.

Fly selections for fly casting - Many landlocked salmon rivers in the central and southern sections of the state are quite fertile and contain the usual assortment of mayflies. Northern freestone rivers are usually less fertile and contain a higher percentage of caddis flies than mayflies.

Generally speaking, landlocked salmon rivers tend to be big, with heavy flows. For that reason, you should carry an assortment of Wulff patterns, as well as a few irresistibles, in sizes 10 and 12. These bushy flies float well and are visible even in fast water.

The author has had across-the-board good luck on Maine's landlocked salmon rivers with a single dry-fly pattern, the dun variant. This fly floats well when tied with the traditional quill body; in addition to imitating a specific mayfly, the dun variant is one of the best general patterns going. Carry a selection of dun variants in sizes 12 through 14.

Spin fishing - Spinning tackle is not popular for landlocked salmon fishing, but anglers who use it do well. A light spinning rod and reel, filled with 4- or 6-pound test line is suitable. Spinning tackle is not very effective in lakes, but works well in rivers and streams.

Most anglers use small casting spoons for landlocked salmon. It is important to impart action as you reel, in order to make your lure resemble a frantic bait fish.

Deep trolling - During the summer months, landlocked salmon are usually found in the deeper parts of Maine's ponds and lakes, often in as much as 60 feet of water. Anglers using specialized deep-trolling techniques can experience fast action at this time.

What Maine anglers call "trolling spoons" are also known as cowbells and lake trolls in other parts of the country. These consist of a set of spinner-type blades attached to a plastic-coated wire by means of a clevis. The number of blades varies, according to the size of the spoon set, but in every case the top blade is the largest, with the size gradually diminishing with each succeeding blade.

Trolling spoons are pulled slowly, so the blades barely turn. The light reflected from the blades, combined with whatever vibrations they create, attract fish. A 3-foot length of 8- or 10-pound test monofilament is attached to a snap swivel at the end of the spoon set. Lures are sometimes used on the end of a trolling rig, the floating Rapala being a favorite. You'll get the best results by using a live minnow, hooked to a sliding hook rig. Landlocked salmon, attracted by the flashing spoons, see the minnow and nail it.

Because of the terrific pull exerted by these spoons, the angler must resort to heavy rods and reels. Old-timers used non-multiplying reels and wire lines, but modern anglers use Penn-style multiplying reels and multicolored lead-core lines. These lines are divided into 10 colors, each color being 10 yards long. Thus, by taking note of how many colors were out when a fish is taken, you can get back to the same depth by letting out a like amount of colors.

Traditional deep-trolling rods were short and thick. Modern anglers prefer longer, more slender rods. A 10- or 12-foot rod, with just enough backbone to handle the weight of the spoons, allows a landlocked salmon to make a reasonable account of itself.

Anglers wishing to use medium to light tackle must use a downrigger. These devices allow you to fish in the deepest parts of a lake without using additional weights. Most downrigger users use live minnows or minnow imitations.

Regardless of what tackle you are using, begin trolling in about 30 feet of water. If you don't get strikes, keep working to progressively deeper water. When you get a strike, mark the spot and depth, because other fish will likely be at the same depth, feeding on bait fish.

Landlocks will often follow a trolled bait, tapping but not taking it. Resist the urge to strike until you feel a solid take. A 4-pound landlocked salmon, leaping clear of the surface and pulling a string of trolling spoons with it, is a remarkable sight.

Dodgers - Anglers who prefer to use streamer flies can still take landlocks in deep water during the summer. A 9- or 10-foot, 8-weight fly rod, large freshwater or small saltwater fly reel, and a sinking fly line or colored lead-core line are all you need.

You can also pull a dodger behind a downrigger. Dodgers are oblong blades designed to wobble when towed. A fly or lure, attached to the dodger by no more than 10 inches of 6- or 8-pound test monofilament, will dance about in a wild fashion. The dodger's flash attracts the fish, much as trolling spoons do. When the fish sees the lure or bait, it usually hits it.

Since dodgers exert little pressure on the rod, anglers can enjoy the battle to the fullest. Whatever you do, don't attach your lure or fly with a leader that is longer than 10 inches, or the dodger will be unable to impart any action. The closer the lure or fly to the dodger, the faster it wobbles. Some anglers use only 6 inches of monofilament. You will need to experiment with differing lengths.

Dodgers, like trolling spoons, don't need to be pulled very fast in order to function properly. Begin fishing at a very slow speed and keep your eye on the rod tip. The tip should slowly bounce up and down. Too rapid a bounce means you must slow down.

Bait fishing - In the spring, bait fishers prefer to troll a live minnow for landlocked salmon. It is important to not go as fast as you would with a fly, since the minnow can easily twist, making it useless.

Use a sinking fly line, with a 20-foot, 6-pound test leader to troll with a smelt or other minnow. You can use a floating fly line if you lengthen your leader.

Some anglers use spinning rods to troll live minnows, but a plastic rudder must be attached a few feet above the bait. The rudder helps to prevent line twist.

In summer, when the lakes stratify, live minnows can be used effectively with spinning tackle. Drift over the deepest parts of the lake and allow your minnow to bounce the bottom. If you have a fish locator, you can first locate the schools of fish and then anchor. Let your bait down to the bottom and leave the bail open until the line begins going out. Close the bail and strike.

Ice fishing - Landlocked salmon are a favorite ice fishing quarry. Landlocks follow schools of smelt, usually staying only a few feet under the ice, although they are sometimes taken in deep water too.

Tip-ups, baited with a live smelt or other bait fish, are standard fare for the winter angler. Long leaders are more important in winter than during open water fishing, since the fish have a better chance to inspect the line. Use at least 15 feet of 6-pound test leader. It is better to tie a number 6 hook directly to the leader than to use snelled hooks, since the line used in snelled hooks is usually thick and stiff. Don't use heavy weights and swivels. Instead, use only enough split shot to keep the bait from swimming to the top.

Here is a simple trick that will help you when ice fishing a strange lake for the first time. (This procedure works for other salmonids too.) After drilling your holes, lie face down over one hole and shade your face with your hands to help your eyes acclimate to the dark. Attach a sounder to your baited hook and let it down until it goes out of sight. Then, slowly bring it up until you can just see your bait. Set your tip-up for this depth. You will be fishing in that layer of water where objects are barely discernible. As it turns out, landlocked salmon and other gamefish often feed at this layer. The depth of this zone varies from lake to lake, since it is influenced by thickness of ice, amount of sunlight, and depth of snow cover.

Salmon do hit artificials in winter, although most anglers prefer bait. Use a short jig rod and an open-faced spinning reel. Open-faced reels don't freeze up as quickly as other styles. Begin jigging just beneath the ice and if you don't get a hit, continue fishing in progressively deeper water until you are near the bottom. Even if you are standing over very deep water, the majority of hits will occur close to the surface.

If you don't get a hit, keep trying new areas. However, you should return to unproductive holes later in the day. Salmon are likely to move in late afternoon. A hole that didn't produce in the morning may provide the best fishing in the afternoon.

Best bets for Maine landlocked salmon: West Grand Lake, Site 58; East Grand Lake, Site 79; Sebec Lake, Site 78; Sebago Lake, Site 6; and St. George Lake, Site 24.

This small splake was taken early in the ice-fishing season and was soon released to grow larger. A hybrid, splake retain characteristics of both parent species: brook trout and lake trout.

Splake

Splake are hatchery-reared coldwater game fish, the result of combining brook or speckled trout milt with lake trout eggs. While splake are physically capable of reproducing, in Maine they have not been known to successfully cross with either parent species in the wild. This ensures that existing populations of brook trout and lake trout will not suffer genetic degradation from the introduction of splake.

Splake grow faster than either parent species and can live as long as seven years. They can resemble either parent, causing potential identification problems for anglers. Regulations are usually the same for all three species when they occur in the same water. Generally speaking, splake have spots similar to lake trout, larger heads than brook trout, and a square tail. The vermiculations found on the back of brook trout are present but indistinct. In spite of these differences, only a trained biologist can identify a splake with 100 percent certainty. The only logical answer to this quandary is for the state to begin fin-clipping splake in an easily identifiable manner. This is already being done in some waters, mostly for the benefit of those Maine anglers who keep voluntary fishing record books for the Maine Department of Inland Fisheries & Wildlife.

Generally, splake are stocked in ponds, rather than in brooks and streams. Sometimes splake escape over dams and are taken by trout anglers. This has happened in the Sheepscot River, where splake entered from Sheepscot Lake.

It is still unclear how large a Maine splake can grow. The average 4-year-old splake measures about 22 inches. Larger fish have been documented in other states.

Techniques

Spin fishing - Splake are more easily taken on bait or flies, but anglers using small gold spoons can take the occasional splake. Spinning lures are not commonly used by splake anglers.

Splake are relatively small, so using ultralight tackle will let you enjoy the fight to the fullest. A one-piece graphite rod and a reel loaded with 4-pound test line is ideal.

Fly casting - Splake will hit small bucktails such as muddler minnow, Edson tiger light, Mickey Finn, and black-nosed dace. Nymph fishers can take splake with sinking lines and large nymphs, such as stone fly nymphs. Even so, splake are not a noted fly rod quarry.

Any fly outfit will do, but a 4- or 5-weight rod of 8 feet will provide the most sport.

Bait fishing - Splake will take live or dead minnows, worms, and night crawlers. Use small minnows (no longer than 2 inches). Common earthworms are just as good. Use a size 8 hook and no more weight than is needed to cast. Let your worm sit on the bottom for a few minutes, then slowly retrieve it in increments. Fish minnows the same as you would worms. As when fishing for brook trout, anglers fishing from shore should seek the south side of ponds in early spring and along rocky drop-offs. If you use a boat, fish in 10 to 20 feet of water. Ultralight and light spinning gear is the ticket for splake fishing, since splake are not found in weedy areas. Your hook is not likely to get stuck on the bottom in Maine's cold, relatively deep splake waters.

Ice fishing - More splake are taken by ice fishing than by any other method. Splake feed actively under the ice, and minnows or worms placed on or near the bottom in 10 to 40 feet of water are effective. Since splake are so active in winter, a large portion of the fish in a pond can be taken during the first few weeks of ice fishing season, after which the action slows. For that reason, some splake waters are closed to ice fishing.

Begin fishing near a point of land, if any can be found. Splake are fond of structure and often hang near rocky bottoms looking for bait fish. Use size 6 or 8 hooks, with no added weight other than a small split shot. Make sure your tip-ups are in good working order, because splake will drop a bait at the first sign of unnatural pressure. For this reason, splake can be difficult to hook.

Splake usually make a long run as soon as they take the bait. Wait for the fish to stop and turn the bait prior to swallowing it before you strike.

You can also take splake with small ice fishing jigs. Work the jig slowly and be ready to strike at the first hint of a take.

Best bets for Maine splake: Sheepscot Pond, Site 23; and Piper Pond, Site 45.

Largemouth Bass

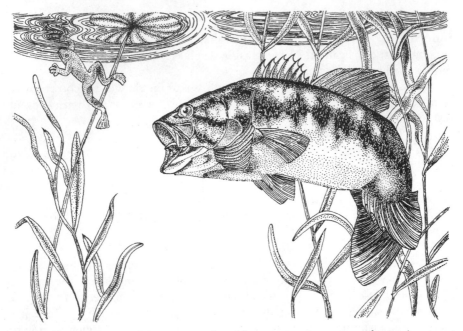

Largemouth bass, *Micropterus salmoides*, represent a new and growing sport fishery in Maine. Until recently, Maine anglers considered largemouths to be "trash fish." Now, many anglers are aware that largemouths can provide fast-paced, exciting sport. Maine's record largemouth bass weighed 11.63 pounds.

Maine largemouths do not grow as large as those found in the extreme southern states, simply because they have a shorter season in which to grow. As far as providing sport, the sheer numbers of largemouth bass in Maine make up for the slightly smaller average size. And nobody scoffs at the 4- to 6-pound fish so common in Maine.

Largemouth bass are voracious feeders, especially in the spring and early summer. Even when ice covers Maine lakes and ponds, largemouths cannot take a hiatus from feeding; they need the calories provided by bait fish in order to survive. Maine largemouth bass are lethargic during periods of extreme hot weather, but in the Pine Tree State such uncomfortable conditions soon pass. Even during heat spells, the diligent angler can entice Maine's largemouth bass to respond. Early morning and evening hours are best during the dog days.

Many lakes and ponds in southern and central Maine either lack sufficient dissolved oxygen or are not cold enough to host viable populations of coldwater game fish, so largemouth bass have been introduced in order to supplement the trout and salmon fisheries. Small ponds in particular have been targeted for largemouth bass. An angler could spend many years and not cover all of Maine's largemouth bass waters.

Maine largemouths begin to bite immediately after ice-out, but few anglers try for them then. You can have a prime southern Maine bass lake all to yourself if you go in late April. The fish will be in rather shallow water at this time. Concentrate on the mouths of small streams and brooks; the water there will be warmer, which is attractive to largemouth bass.

Generally, Maine bass are on their spawning beds in June. By July, the fish take to deep water during the day, returning to the shallows in the evening to feed.

Many Maine bass ponds and lakes are bounded by wetlands and boggy areas. These shorelines provide perfect largemouth bass habitat. Often, wave action will undercut the banks, providing cover for largemouths. All the bass has to do is wait for a bait fish or other prey to swim by, then dash out and grab it. A good number of Maine's slow-moving rivers provide similar habitat, although these areas are usually overlooked by the largemouth fraternity.

In these boggy areas, fish will continue to filter into the feeding spots on the edges of bogs and wetlands. If you take a fish in a certain spot today, you can bet that another one will soon station itself in the same spot.

Techniques

Spin fishing - Probably more Maine anglers use spinning tackle than fly tackle when fishing for largemouth bass. A medium-weight outfit with at least 8-pound test line is all you need. If you are hunting for a trophy, or are fishing waters that contain pike as well as bass, you might want a medium to heavy outfit with 12-pound test.

Maine bass are no different from bass in any other state. All the standard bass lures are productive but plastic worms seem to be the most popular. These and similar plastic baits such as salamanders are extremely effective on Maine largemouths. Although some anglers use a number of worm-hooking methods, the author has found that leaving the hook exposed results in more fish hooked and a longer life for plastic bait. Maine largemouths are not hook-shy and will not drop the bait if they detect the hook.

The boggy shorelines mentioned earlier are perfect spots for casting a plastic worm. The only way to fish these places is from a boat or canoe. Some anglers like to anchor within casting distance from shore and cast toward the bogs. On calm days, it is possible to dispense with the anchor. You must drop your bait as close to the shore as possible in order to draw the fish out. If a fish takes it and runs out toward deep water, you can allow the fish to take the bait as long as you wish. If, on the other hand, it heads back under its boggy hiding place, you must strike as soon as possible.

Be aware that if you make a bad cast and your bait hangs up in the brush, you will put the fish down in that area if you decide to physically retrieve the lure. If that does happen, especially before you have covered the area fully, go to another spot and return to the area you disturbed in an hour or so. Largemouth bass have short memories and your previous intrusion will be long forgotten.

Boggy shorelines are also great spots for topwater action, especially before the lily pads have reached the surface. As with plastic baits, try to drop your lure as close to the shore as possible.

Fall fishing is a hit-or-miss proposition, but some of the biggest bass of the year can be taken in September. By then, the water is uniformly cool and crystal-clear. Look for bass around points, where they will feed on bait fish. Try fishing dropoffs and around structure. The fish should be in 5 to 20 feet of water at this time of year.

Trolling - Trolling is not a suggested method of fishing for largemouth bass. Largemouth bass are sometimes taken as an incidental catch by anglers using dodgers and streamer flies or metal lures while brown trout fishing.

Fly casting - Fly fishing is an exciting way to take Maine's largemouth bass. Anglers using cork-bodied poppers or Henshall-style deer-hair flies can have top-notch sport. Mornings and evenings are the best for topwater action. You can fish from shore, by wading, or you can cast from a boat or canoe. Even in summer's heat, bass will rise to topwater offerings in mornings, evenings, and at night.

Leech patterns are preferred by daytime anglers. These flies are simple to tie. Note that leeches are prevalent in many of the boggy areas where large-mouth bass live, and the fish are used to feeding on them. The author's favorite leech pattern consists of a size 2 hook with a black floss body. Four long, black saddle hackles are tied in at the head and two bead-chain eyes are attached at the top of the head. When cast and allowed to sink a few feet before imparting action, these flies are deadly. You might consider them the fly fisher's version of the plastic worm.

Since most fly fishing is done near weed beds or structure, you need a rather stout leader. It needn't be long—6 to 8 feet is plenty—but it should test at least 8 pounds. A floating fly line for topwater and a sinking line for leech patterns round out the bill. Reels needn't be elaborate, since largemouths don't make long runs. You should use at least a 6-weight outfit; for windy days, or when topwater fishing, an 8-weight outfit with a weight-forward line is recommended. Fly rods should be from 8 to 9 feet long.

Bait casting - Baitcasting tackle is not too popular in Maine, but it should be, since it is ideally suited for fishing Maine's largemouth bass lakes. Modern bait casting reels allow the angler to make longer casts with lighter lures than did the reels of 25 years ago. Bait casters use the same lures as spin fishers and apply the same techniques. Bait casting tackle may be your best bet when fishing shallow, weedy ponds and lakes, since it is well suited for wrestling big fish in heavy cover. Standard bait casting tackle can easily coax a bass out and away from the rubbery stems of the lillies.

An angler working a boggy shoreline with bait casting tackle can cover the territory quicker than someone using spinning tackle. Bait casting tackle is also perfect for midsummer, when bass are found beneath floating lily pads.

Bait fishing - Maine anglers know live bait is deadly on lunker bass. Trophy hunters use the largest minnows available, up to 6 or 8 inches long. Heavy spinning or baitcasting tackle is preferred, and lines should be at least 12-pound test.

Bait fishermen rely on live minnows. The constant movement of the min-now draws bass from considerable distances. Use a bobber to keep the bait from getting wound around weeds and debris on the bottom.

Some anglers allow their boat or canoe to drift while dragging a lip-hooked minnow on the bottom. This is especially effective during Maine's short summer, when bass are in water between 20 and 40 feet deep.

Any minnow is effective on bass, but most anglers prefer golden shiners. Night crawlers, hooked once through the collar, are a close second to minnows. Use night crawlers as you would a plastic worm. That is, do not add unnecessary weight, and cast the bait close to the shore or structure. When a largemouth bass takes a night crawler, you must strike quickly.

Ice fishing - Only a handful of Maine anglers fish for largemouth bass through the ice, and those who do use live minnows and tip-ups. A better and more fast-paced method is to use a small metal jig. Largemouth bass respond well to jigs, and taking a 3 or 4 pound bass on a light jig rod is a real thrill.

Best bets for Maine largemouth bass: Cobbosseecontee Lake, Site 10; Great Pond, Site 11; Sebago Lake, Site 6; and North Pond, Site 12.

Smallmouth Bass

Smallmouth bass, *Micropterus dolomieui*, abound in Maine, especially in the eastern part of the state. Unbelievably, some ponds contain so many smallmouth bass that there is no size or bag limit, although other species in the same body of water are regulated. Smallmouths are also found in many of Maine's rivers and streams, where they provide action throughout the open water season. Maine's record smallmouth bass weighed 8 pounds.

Smallmouth bass are tireless fighters, given to lightning-fast runs and spectacular aerial displays. Such is the tenacity of these dogged battlers that anglers often overestimate their size, at least until the fish is safely in the net. Landlocked salmon anglers sometimes think they have hooked the trophy of a lifetime, only to find a 4-pound smallmouth bass on the end of their line. A day spent catching 1- to 3-pound smallmouth bass may mean sore arms that night.

Smallmouth bass become active in early spring, as soon as the water temperature nears 60 degrees; they stay active through September. Spawning takes place in June. The fish are extremely susceptible during this period, and will strike anything that comes near the bed. Anglers should always release any bass in the same area it was taken from, or the fish may become disoriented and be unable to return to the bed.

Bass living in ponds become difficult to catch when the water temperature is over 75 degrees. Fish in rivers remain active all season, however, because rivers provide cool, well-oxygenated water.

Smallmouth bass feed on other fish, crayfish, hellgrammites, and, to a lesser extent, insects. Maine's rocky lakes are such good smallmouth bass producers partly because of the large numbers of crayfish found in these lakes.

Techniques

Spin fishing - In spite of the smallmouth's fearsome reputation, heavy tackle is not required to catch them, since they are primarily a fish of open water. Smallmouth bass prefer rocky bottoms, not weed-infested coves. Unlike largemouth bass, smallmouths can be leader-shy. Lines should be no heavier than 6-pound test, and 4-pound test will bring more strikes. Open-faced reels are more commonly used, but closed-faced reels will suffice. A smooth, positive drag is probably more important than reel style. Smallmouth bass are masters at shaking off lures, so your hooks must be needle-sharp. Keep a hook hone in your tackle box.

When casting, have your drag on a medium setting to facilitate setting the hook. Be ready to loosen the drag when the fish makes a run. Improper drag adjustment probably accounts for more lost fish than any other factor. You must be able to sense when to use muscle and when to simply keep a tight line. Perhaps the most critical moment occurs when the fish is about to be netted. An unexpected burst of energy at the last moment can cause a broken line if the drag is set too tightly.

At one time, Daredevle spoons were used by more Maine smallmouth bass anglers than any other lure. The Daredevle is still a good choice, and you should have several in your tackle box, especially the red-and-white variety. Daredevles and similar spoons are highly effective for fishing from a lakeshore, since they have little wind resistance and can be cast a great distance. A lip-hooked bass can easily throw a spoon, so always keep your rod high in order to maintain tension.

Plastic grubs attached to a jig head are a highly effective combination. The plastic bodies come in an amazing variety of sizes, scents and colors, but they all have one thing in common: the fish are reluctant to spit them out. This allows for some degree of angler error in detecting a strike.

If you are fishing a river, cast the grub/jig combination toward whatever cover you can find, especially behind large boulders. Allow the jig to settle and gently twitch it back to shore. Fish will often take the jig as it sinks toward bottom, so be ready to strike if you notice slack line.

When fishing lakes and ponds, concentrate on rocky shorelines, especially around points of land. Cast your jig toward shore and fish it as described above. In summer, when the fish are in deeper water, you can drift in 20 to 40 feet of water. Drag the jig combination on bottom, and impart action by lifting it about a foot from bottom, then allowing it to settle back.

Spinners such as the Mepps are effective on smallmouths, especially in rivers. Fish the spinner as if it were a wet fly. That is, cast quartering upstream and slowly retrieve the spinner as it is carried downstream. To find out how deep the fish are holding, begin counting after the spinner hits the water. Start by counting to five, and then retrieving. If you get no action, increase the count until you find fish.

Minnow imitations such as Rebels and Rapalas are topnotch smallmouth lures, effective when casting or trolling. If you choose to troll, use the diving variety, the kind with the lip in front. Adjust your speed so the lure is riding within a foot of bottom. The faster you go, the deeper the lure will ride. Troll just off the shorelines, near points, and around rocky islands. This is a highly effective method for smallmouth bass in slow-moving rivers. Carry some lures in fluorescent orange, as these can take fish when nothing else works.

Fly casting - Smallmouth bass provide great surface sport, especially during the early morning and evening hours. Fly pattern isn't as critical as in trout fishing, but you should try to duplicate the shade and size of any natural insects that might be on the water.

You do not need a heavy fly rod, unless you are fishing one of the larger lakes where wind may be a factor. On calm days, you can get by with a 5- or 6-weight rod and line. Reels should have an effective drag.

If you wish to surface fish during the daylight hours, try small fly-rod poppers, as well as deer-hair bugs. You might want to use a weight-forward floating line, since poppers and bugs are difficult to cast due to increased wind resistance.

Anglers armed with a high-density sinking fly line and a few leech patterns can have a heyday with smallmouth bass. Woolly buggers, muddlers, and Matukas are also good choices. Cast the fly toward shore if fishing a lake and toward quiet sections of pools if fishing rivers. Allow it to sink and retrieve either by raising the rod and then dropping it, or by the hand-twist method. Sometimes the fish will nearly tear the rod from your hand, but other times they simply inhale the fly and hold it until you detect their weight.

Bait casting - Lightweight, modern bait casting reels and rods are suitable for smallmouth bass fishing, although few Maine anglers use them. An especially good technique is to use one of the so-called stick lures, the simple floating lures that require the angler to supply the action. When twitched, these lures dart about like a wounded minnow. They drive smallmouth bass wild.

If you use the old-style braided casting line, use a short section of monofilament leader on the end. Otherwise, standard monofilament is fine.

Because bait casting tackle allows the angler to cast and recast so rapidly, it is perfect for when you are floating down a river, where you do not get the opportunity to cast more than once to any particular spot.

Use the same lures mentioned in the section on spin fishing and fish in the same spots.

Bait fishing - Hellgrammites and crayfish are both top smallmouth baits. Note that it is illegal to import hellgrammites into Maine. They are also hard to find in stores, so you might want to learn how to harvest them yourself. A good way to do that is to take a section of fine screen and have someone hold it at a 45-degree angle in a stream. Go above the person holding the screen and turn over rocks. The hellgrammites will float downstream and be trapped on the screen. Hook hellgrammites through the collar and hook crayfish through the tail. Use little or no added weight and allow your bait to move about on bottom in a natural manner. When using crayfish, you may need to remove the large claw to keep the bait from grabbing hold of underwater debris. Live minnows and night crawlers are also effective when fished in this way.

Ice fishing - Smallmouth bass bite well in winter, but few Maine anglers fish for them. Set your baited tip-ups in from 10 to 20 feet of water, preferably around rocky points.

Smallmouth bass usually run a considerable distance when they first hit a bait. Allow the fish to take line before picking up your tip-up. When the fish stops running, wait until it takes off again before setting the hook.

Smallmouth bass also respond to ice jigs. A lightweight jig rod and ultralight reel are perfect for jigging for smallmouths.

Best bets for Maine smallmouth bass: Indian Pond, Site 67; Junior Lake, Site 59; Penobscot River, Site 46; Kennebec River, Sites 35 and 37; and West Grand Lake, Site 58.

Pickerel

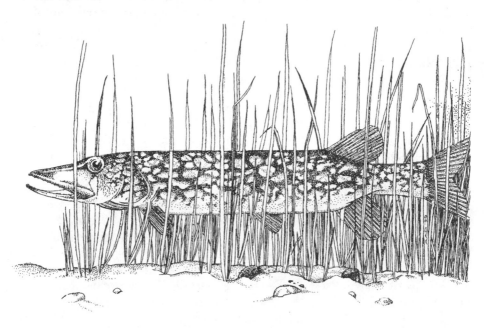

Pickerel, *Esox niger,* are widespread in Maine's warmwater ponds, lakes, and streams. These members of the pike family are splashy fighters and are easily taken on artificial lures, bait, and flies. Despite the fact that pickerel can provide almost year-round sport, Maine anglers do not spend much time fishing for them during the open water season, and only a small number bother fishing for them through the ice.

Because pickerel are so numerous in Maine waters, bag limits are extremely liberal. If you like fast-paced fishing with constant action, you will enjoy pickerel fishing. Pickerel are also great fun for children and are recommended as a good first fish for beginners.

Pickerel feed mainly on other fish, but are not reluctant to pick off a swimming frog or even a careless dragonfly. They are denizens of the weed beds, where they will sit motionless for hours, waiting for a bait fish to swim past. Pickerel are seldom taken in deep water.

Most Maine anglers head for the trout streams or lakes in early spring, the pre-spawn period for pickerel, ignoring the fact that the biggest pickerel can be taken when the water is cool. During the hot spells of Maine's brief summer, pickerel become somewhat lethargic. However, you can still catch pickerel then; even if they are not particularly hungry, they are so savage that they will strike anything that comes near their resting place. Even so, the best time to fish for them in hot weather is early and late in the day.

The largest pickerel taken in Maine weighed 11.61 pounds. Specimens weighing 4 and 5 pounds are taken each year.

Techniques

Spin fishing - Weed beds, sunken logs, and any other shallow-water structure are prime areas to cast for pickerel. Weedy sections of slow-moving rivers are also prime spots.

Since most pickerel you will catch will weigh under 3 pounds, light spinning tackle is ideal. Use a short wire leader or a shock tippet of 15-pound test monofilament line, since pickerel have sharp, dagger-like teeth, capable of severing light lines.

It would be difficult to name an artificial lure that pickerel would not strike. Favorites include Daredevles, Rapalas, and red plastic worms. If you like fishing from a boat, a canoe is your best bet. With it, you can glide noiselessly close to prime pickerel cover. If fishing from shore, concentrate on open areas near weeds. If you see a swirl just behind your lure, stop reeling for a moment and then continue. This will often elicit an explosive strike. Pickerel are not hook-shy, so if you hook and lose one, you can probably coax it into biting again.

If you find a likely looking spot that you are certain must hold a few pickerel, give it a thorough working over. Sometimes pickerel will ignore a lure the first few times they see it, only to smash it after repeated casts.

Pickerel are easily taken on topwater lures. Lightweight poppers are best, with green a favorite color. Cast near weed beds and let the popper rest before imparting action. Pickerel will often clear the water as they lunge after a surface lure.

Be extremely careful when handling pickerel, since their teeth can inflict a nasty bite. Never put your hand in a pickerel's mouth. Use forceps instead.

Fly casting - Pickerel are great fun on a fly rod. They strike streamers and bucktails and respond well to surface offerings. No special pattern is needed, but yellow, white, red, and orange are all good colors. If pickerel fail to respond to a slowly fished bucktail, try reeling your line in as fast as possible. This technique sometimes brings savage strikes.

Long leaders are not needed. Use a level or tapered leader of at least 8-pound test. An 8- or 9-foot fly rod of at least 6-weight is suggested. Although pickerel can make powerful runs, they seldom go for more than 10 feet, so fly reels need not be elaborate. You should still have backing behind your fly line, in case you hook a trophy. You will have no need of a sinking fly line, since pickerel are rarely taken in deep water.

Bait fishing - Most bait fishers use live minnows. Large minnows are preferred, up to 4 and 5 inches long. Pickerel are not reluctant to attack a fish only slightly smaller than themselves. The author was once reeling in a pickerel of about 15 inches, when the fish suddenly gained weight. A 6-pound pickerel had grabbed the hooked fish by the tail and wouldn't let go.

Minnows are best fished in conjunction with a small bobber, since without it, the bait would soon become entangled in the weeds. Be careful about striking too soon, as pickerel seldom swallow a bait fish without killing it first.

Lacking live bait, some anglers keep frozen strips of belly meat from white suckers. These are cut into thin, 6-inch, lancelot-shaped pieces, leaving the skin intact. The hook is pushed all the way through one end of the sucker strip.

Do not use any additional weight. A 9- or 10-foot fly rod is perfect for this method. While standing on shore or sitting in a canoe, extend the tip of the fly rod over the edge of a weedbed. Allow the sucker strip to sink and gently raise it, all the while manipulating the rod to cover all the territory possible without taking up a new position. In years past, this was done with a cane pole or telescoping metal rod.

Suckers live in most Maine lakes, and if you want to catch some for future use, look for them to run up small brooks and streams sometime in April, or as soon as blackflies begin to hatch. If you cannot find any suckers, you can get good results with old-fashioned pork rind strips. Use the largest strips you can find.

Ice fishing - Pickerel are eagerly sought by early-season ice fishers, since many pickerel ponds can be legally fished before the ice fishing season on coldwater gamefish begins. Fish the same places you would hit during open water season: the mouths of coves, along weedbeds. Use tip-ups, baited with live minnows.

Pickerel respond well to metal jigs. Lower a jig down to the bottom, and raise it only a few inches. Hold the jig motionless as long as possible, then gently give it a twitch. An open-face spinning reel and a short jigging rod are the perfect combination.

Best bets for Maine pickerel: Goose River, Site 29; Crawford Lake, Site 55; and Bog Lake, Site 49. Additionally, most shallow ponds in southern, central, and Downeast Maine offer good pickerel fishing.

Northern Pike

Northern pike, *Esox lucius*, exist in Maine through unsanctioned introduction. When pike began showing up in the Belgrade Lakes region, anglers worried that these efficient predators would raise havoc with existing fish populations. This has not happened. Instead, pike have made a place for themselves without threatening the trout, bass, and landlocked salmon.

Pike are voracious feeders, able to eat almost anything that is not more than half their size. The catholic appetite of pike is responsible for the demise of large numbers of ducklings each year, as well as muskrats and frogs. Other victims can include bragging-size bass, trout, pickerel, yellow perch, and other pike.

Pike are happiest when the water temperature is between 45 and 60 degrees. In Maine, water temperatures on the surface do not get above 60 degrees until sometime in May, but underwater temperatures can remain cooler for a longer period. Pike fishing is slow in summer. The warmer temperatures slow down the pike's biological processes, making them eat less.

Although you might pick up a pike anywhere in the lake, weed beds seem to be their favorite hangouts. Schools of bait fish, which pike feed on, use weed beds as protective cover. Pike will sit motionless near a prime spot, then attack when a hapless bait fish (or anything else) swims by.

Pike are not nocturnal, as are bass and trout, nor do they bite well in the middle of a bright, sunny day. Peak feeding times are mid-morning and mid-afternoon.

Pike grow large in Maine, as witnessed by the 26.74-pound state record. Given a pike's potential for growth, this record is destined to be broken someday. Maybe you will be the angler to do just that.

Techniques

Spin fishing - Use medium to heavy spinning rods and reels. Light tackle has no place in pike fishing, since you need plenty of power to wrestle large pike out from weeds and other snags.

Large spinners, spinner baits, buzz baits, Rapalas, and large spoons are all good pike producers. Use at least a 10- or 12-pound test line and a short wire leader. The leader is needed to keep the pike's needle-like teeth from severing your line.

If you can locate an underwater weed bed, here is a good way to fish it. Using large spinners, cast over the weed bed and begin counting as you allow your lure to sink. When it hits the weeds, stop counting. If you had a count of 15, for instance, all you need to do is cast again, count to 12 or 13, and begin reeling. This allows you to pull your lure just over the tops of the weeds, which is where pike will be waiting. Aquatic weeds, like all other weeds, grow higher as the season progresses, so late spring and early summer will be the best times to employ this method.

When the weeds have grown above the water's surface, you need to cast as close to them as you can. You can anchor off the weed beds and cast toward them in a "wagon wheel" pattern, or you might actually tie off on the weeds and cast parallel to them. If you hook a big fish by the latter method, have a partner take the boat or canoe out to open water as soon as possible. Large spoons such as Johnson's Silver Minnow and Daredevles are favorites for this type of fishing. Allow the spoon to flutter toward the bottom, then reel for a few feet and let the spoon flutter again.

Pike will also hit topwater offerings. Use the largest bass poppers you can find. To give you an idea of how large a topwater lure you can use, a special pike lure was once manufactured that was identical in size and shape to a duckling. You needed a powerful outfit to fish it, but it worked.

Fly casting - Fly fishers often abandon spring landlocked salmon fishing in order to tangle with a trophy pike. Make sure your reel has a smooth drag and load it with 100 yards of 18-pound test backing. Rods should be at least 8-weight, and weight-forward fly lines are best. You need a shock tippet of 50-pound test to take the place of a wire leader.

Aim your casts toward weed beds and on the shady side of any obvious structure. Use the largest, bushiest streamers you can find. Hook sizes of 2 and 3 are best. You can have success by using standard saltwater patterns, especially flies designed for striped bass such as Lefty's deceiver and McNalley smelt.

Throwing a deer-hair bass bug to a waiting pike may be one of fly fishing's greatest thrills. Mid-morning, mid-afternoon, and early evening are the best times for topwater action. If your shock tippet causes your bass bug to sink, you will have to dispense with it and hope your pike will be hooked in such a way that it cannot bite your line.

Bait fishing - Pike like large bait. Use a stout rod and reel, wire leader, a size 2 hook, and the largest golden shiner or sucker you can find. Any other large minnow will work, but suckers and golden shiners are best. You might want to use a bobber to keep your bait from getting wound up in the weeds. Adjust the bobber so the bait is at least 3 feet beneath the surface. Cast the baited hook and bobber near a likely looking weed bed and let it sit. Allow your line to play out freely as the bait carries the bobber around. When a pike hits, the bobber will plummet as the fish dashes off with the bait.

You must make sure your line is perfectly tight before you strike. Holding your rod high, follow the fish with the rod. When you are ready to strike, lower the rod and point it at the fish. Then, when you feel pressure, strike as hard as you can.

Of course, if the pike heads for the weeds after it takes your bait, you have no choice but to strike fast and hope for the best.

Bait fishers can also take pike by slowly drifting a live minnow near bottom during the warmer months. A three-way swivel is helpful for this type of fishing. Attach one end of the swivel to your line. Attach a 2-foot section of the same pound test line to the second end of the swivel and tie a wire leader to it. Affix your hook to the leader. Now attach a 1-foot section of lighter line to the third end of the swivel. Attach a few split shot to the end of the weaker line. If the split shot get hooked on bottom, the lighter line will break, saving your hook.

As you drift, be ready to pay out line when a pike hits. For this reason, it is good to hold the rod in your hand rather than placing it in a rod holder.

Ice fishing - Northern pike have a huge following of hard water anglers. Use tip-ups, baited with large minnows. Fish near weed beds in from 10 to 20 feet of water. If you don't take fish, you might change tactics by going into a shallow cove and fishing with small minnows in 5 to 10 feet of water. Pike sometimes take advantage of the shallows and their tiny resident bait fish.

Pike will hit ice jigs, but you need a stout rod. Use a medium-weight spinning reel with 15-pound test line and a short wire leader. Regulations on pike vary with different waters, so be sure to consult the rule book.

Best bets for Maine's northern pike: Pike fishing is pretty much limited to the Belgrade Region's chain of ponds. Try these for both open water and ice fishing: Great Pond and Long Pond, Site 11; and North Pond, Site 12.

White Perch

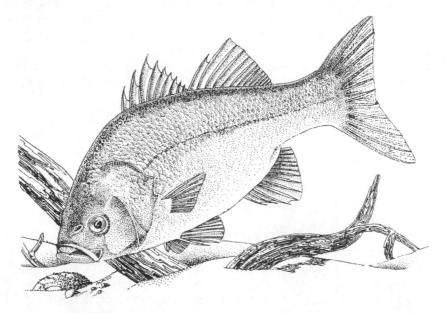

White perch, *Morone americana*, are everybody's fish. These scrappy panfish are closely related to striped bass and bear no relation to the perch family except in name. White perch are natives of brackish water, and their presence in Maine's freshwater lakes, ponds, and streams can be attributed to a combination of of natural causes and private stocking efforts. The largest recorded white perch from Maine, a world record, was a 4.75 pound specimen measuring 19 inches.

White perch are a schooling species, with the schools segregated according to age groups. If you are catching small fish, all you need to do is search for a school of older, larger individuals.

White perch are aggressive feeders and are taken on flies, artificial lures, and bait. When taken on light tackle, white perch put up a fight that would do justice to any of the more famed species. Anglers used to taking these fish can tell immediately when they have hooked a white perch. Short but powerful runs, during which the fish bores toward the bottom, characterize the actions of white perch on the end of a line. In tenacity, white perch are equaled only by landlocked salmon and smallmouth bass.

White perch are present in such numbers that you can pretty much take as many fish as you can use without harming the fishery. Only a handful of waters have bag limits on white perch, and that is due to the insistence of local residents rather than any biological need for protection. In fact, the author has seen the average size of white perch increase after a pond was subjected to higher than average fishing pressure. Do take good care of your catch. Keep an ice-filled cooler on board and place your fish on ice as soon as possible. The result will be worth the effort. Maine law requires that all fish taken must be immediately released unharmed, or killed at once.

Maine people are fond of fish chowder, and the ultimate chowder uses white perch as the primary ingredient. The meat is flaky but firm, and sweet and delicate. When skinned and filleted, rolled in flour or cornmeal, and fried, white perch become an epicurean delight. It is no wonder, then, that these easily caught fish are so prized by their followers.

Anybody can catch white perch, but not everybody can consistently catch the largest specimens. The following techniques will help you in that department.

Techniques

Spin fishing - Most anglers use light spinning gear when white perch fishing. Since these panfish rarely weigh more than 2 pounds, light tackle is needed to fully appreciate their exceptional performance. A 1-piece rod, tiny reel, and no more than 4-pound test line is the perfect white perch outfit. White perch are aggressive feeders and will strike any artificial lure that approximates the size of a natural forage fish.

Although white perch will hit small spinners and spoons, this is not the best way to take the most fish or the largest specimens. Vertical jigging, however, is a very effective method. Lures for this type of fishing include the metal jigs used in ice fishing and the many varieties of jig combinations consisting of weighted heads and plastic bodies. Use lightweight jigs for the best results. Although Maine does not have any walleyes, an angler from another state could use the same techniques used for walleyes to take white perch.

Serious white perch fishers rely on electronic fish finders to locate schools of perch. Once a school is located, all you need to do is drift over it and work the jig. It sometimes helps to add a bit of minnow or worm to the jig, but it is not necessary.

Fly casting - White perch tend to feed on the surface in the evening. Unfortunately, it is mostly the smaller perch that exhibit this behavior. Still, if you are fishing a body of water that has average specimens nearing 1 pound, this can be great sport.

In order to extract the uttermost enjoyment from catching white perch on flies, use the lightest rod you own. White perch are not leader shy and a 4-pound or even 6-pound test tippet will not put them off. Any fly reel will suffice, because even the largest white perch don't make long runs.

Dry flies should approximate the size of any naturals on the water, but more clever deception is not needed, for these fish will readily take any pattern. If you have never taken white perch on dry flies, you may miss the first few strikes. White perch do not reject artificials as quickly as trout, plus they have rather small mouths. Count to one before you raise your rod to strike.

Some anglers enjoy trolling with streamers and bucktails so much that they insist on trolling for white perch. This is not the most effective method, but it is a good way to locate schools. Use a few size B.B. split shot ahead of your fly to ensure that it is down at least 10 feet. You will get more hits if you occasionally impart action to your fly. Twitch your rod; grab the line and give a sharp tug. This will stimulate interest in your offering.

In late summer and early fall, white perch give evidence of their saltwater genesis by congregating in immense schools and frantically thrashing the surface. This is not always indicative of a feeding frenzy, but they do feed when exhibiting this behavior. If you see herring gulls swarming in some distant cove, make for it as quickly as you can. The birds are attracted to the swarming fish and you can get in on the action too. Be careful about approaching too close, as this may cause the fish to sound.

Bait fishing - Anglers using bait usually take more and larger fish than those using artificials. Any type of light-action rod and reel will do, but ultralight spinning gear is preferred. Most anglers use earthworms or night crawlers. These old standbys are certainly effective. But to catch the largest perch possible, use live minnows.

The type of minnow doesn't seem to matter, except that dace, small suckers, and banded killifish are more durable than gold or silver shiners. As you might expect, the larger the bait, the better chances of taking a large perch. Bait fish of about 2 inches in length are best. Be sure to change the water in your bait pail frequently, or your bait may die from lack of oxygen.

Using a size 6 hook, hook the bait through the membrane just behind the lips. This does not severely injure the bait and it also makes hooking a fish easier, because white perch tend to swallow bait fish head first. If you have a fish locator, you are ahead of the game, if not, try fishing in from 20 to 40 feet of water. White perch do not seem to care about cover, and prefer a flat, muddy bottom. Don't use any terminal gear except your hook and a small split shot to keep the bait down near bottom.

Don't cast your bait, since that will shorten its life. Just let it down alongside the boat. Once the bait is near bottom, gently raise and lower your rod tip. If you feel a bite, count to five and strike. Some anglers like to anchor as soon as they catch a few fish. It is possible to keep a school of perch around for some time, because other fish are attracted to the struggles of a hooked fish. Two anglers can work a school to good effect. Sometimes you will see several fish following the one on your line, a sure sign that you are fishing to a school.

You can use the wind to your advantage by drifting over a school. When the fish stop biting, go back to where you began and repeat the process.

Ice fishing - In winter, white perch can be found in 50 to 60 feet of water. If the lake or pond you are fishing is not that deep, just head for the deepest spot.

Most anglers use tip-ups, baited with live minnows, while others prefer to use a light jig rod. You might want to set out a few tip-ups and jig at the same time. Generally the tip-ups will produce the largest perch.

If you are certain that you are in a good area, do not despair if the fish do not bite immediately. White perch have definite feeding schedules and it is possible to go without a bite for several hours, only to have all your flags flying at once as if somebody turned on a switch.

White perch behavior is directly influenced by lunar phases. Again, this may be due to their brackish-water beginnings. During his 40-some years of white perch fishing, the author has become convinced that it is a waste of time to go fishing during a full moon. The closer the moon is to its new phase, the better the white perch fishing.

Best bets for Maine white perch: Millinocket Lake, Site 76; Cobbosseecontee Lake, Site 10; and Megunticook Lake, Site 26. These lakes are noted for large white perch, but they represent only a small percentage of the Maine lakes that can provide great white perch fishing.

Other Species

Maine waters contain various species of game fish and panfish that are either limited in distribution, or are not popular with large numbers of anglers. Nevertheless, these less-popular species have their fans, anglers who enjoy having the sport all to themselves.

Bullheads

Bullheads, known as "hornpout" in Maine, are found in vast numbers throughout the state. A small variety of catfish, bullheads are easily taken on worms or dead minnows. When evening falls, bullheads come to the shallows to feed. One evening's still fishing can result in dozens of tasty bullheads. These fish average less than one pound, but the occasional specimen may approach 3 pounds. Any tackle that can toss out a baited hook and small sinker is adequate, but ultralight spinning gear provides the most sport.

Yellow perch

Although yellow perch are the basis of a huge sport fishery in the midwest, most Maine anglers ignore these tasty panfish. Many lakes in southern and central Maine have yellow perch. Yellow perch are school fish, with year-classes staying together. Perch are easily taken on worms and small minnows. Ultralight spinning gear is preferred for open water fishing, and small metal jigs are used during the winter. Yellow perch bite well through the ice. Cooked, their flesh is white, flaky, and sweet.

Yellow perch spawn in late April, depositing their eggs on brush or blowdowns along the edges of ponds and lakes.

Redbreasted sunfish

Redbreasted sunfish are Maine's answer to the bluegill. These spunky panfish are found in many Maine lakes, most notably those in the Rangeley region. Redbreasted sunfish attain weights up to 1 pound, true heavyweights of the sunfish family. The author once took a 12-inch redbreasted sunfish, which is about as long as any sunfish ever gets.

Redbreasted sunfish are almost totally ignored by Maine anglers. These fish provide great sport on light tackle and are easily taken on the fly rod with small poppers. Redbreasted sunfish take to the spawning beds in June, where they will strike anything that comes near them in defense of their beds. Small spinners, worms, and flies are all good sunfish lures.

Cusk

Cusk, a type of landlocked codfish, inhabit most northern Maine lakes as well as some lakes in the central region. These fish are bottom feeders and are primarily nocturnal. Most cusk are taken through the ice at night. Many waters have special regulations which allow nighttime cusk fishing.

While not shining fighters, cusk are perhaps the most delicious fish in Maine. Fresh cusk fillets, slowly cooked in butter with a dash of lemon, are an epicurean delight. Cusk are the basis for some ambrosial fish chowders, a staple of Maine's north country.

Use any tackle for cusk fishing. Simply leave a dead minnow on the bottom and the cusk will do the rest. Cusk can also be taken after ice-out on jigs, near the mouths of rivers. Some anglers apply fluorescent paint in order to attract the fish in the sunless depths. A bit of minnow will sweeten up the jig, resulting in more hits.

Whitefish

Whitefish are denizens of northern Maine lakes. These fish are usually taken by anglers fishing for other species. Whitefish will hit small spoons, bite on a tiny, baited hook, and take dry flies. If you see a school of fast-moving fish taking insects from the surface of a northern Maine lake, it may be whitefish. Rather than casting to a whitefish, determine where the fish is heading and land your fly in its path. Whitefish put up a tremendous fight and are delicious table fare. Maine has two types of whitefish, lake whitefish and round whitefish. Lake whitefish attain the largest size and provide the best sport.

Black crappie

Black crappies exist in Maine due to accidental or illegal introduction. These fish first showed up in Sebago and Sebasticook lakes and are steadily extending their range. Maine's largest black crappie weighed 3.25 pounds. Anglers use small bucktails, live minnows, and small spinners to take Maine crappies.

MAINE'S RECORD GAME FISH ───────────

Fresh water

Brook trout	8 pounds, 8 ounces
Brown trout	23 pounds, 8 ounces
Lake trout	31 pounds, 8 ounces
Rainbow trout	No official record is available, but to qualify for the One That Didn't Get Away Club, a rainbow trout must weigh at least 5 pounds.
Landlocked salmon	22 pounds, 8 ounces
Northern pike	26 pounds, 12 ounces
Pickerel	6 pounds, 12.8 ounces
Largemouth bass	11 pounds, 10 ounces
Smallmouth bass	8 pounds

Salt water

Striped bass	67 pounds
Bluefish	19 pounds
Mackerel	No official record is available, but to qualify for the One That Didn't Get Away Club, a mackerel must weigh at least 2 pounds.

MAP LEGEND

Interstate	(00)	Campground	▲
US Highway	(00)	Cabins/Buildings	▪
State or Other Principal Road	(00) (000)	Peak	5,281 ft.
National Park Route	(00)	Hill	
		Elevation	5,281 ft. ✕
Interstate Highway	⟹	Gate	•—•
Paved Road	⟹	Mine Site	✕
Gravel Road	⟹	Overlook/Point of Interest	▣
Unimproved Road	======⟹		
Trailhead	◯	Bridge	
Town	◉	Boat Landing	◣
Main Trail(s) /Route(s)	— — —	Marsh or Wetland	
Alternate/Secondary Trail(s)/Route(s)	– – –	National Forest/Park Boundary	
Parking Area	(P)	Map Orientation	N
River/Creek			
Spring	⟨	Scale	0 0.5 1 Miles
One Way Road	One Way		
Fishing Site	2		

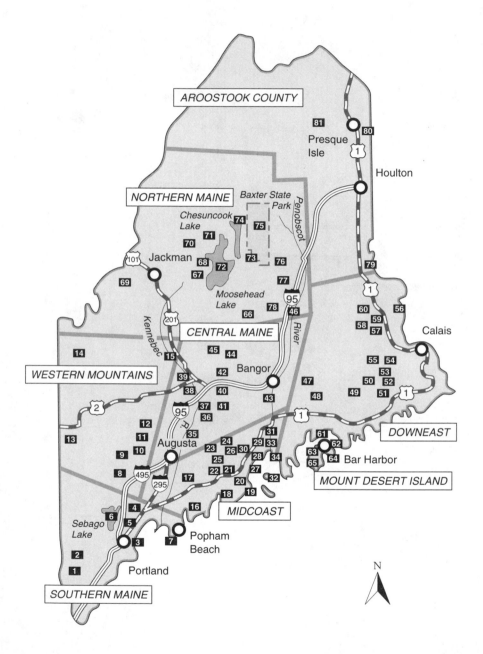

AROOSTOOK COUNTY

81 Presque Isle 80

Houlton

NORTHERN MAINE

Baxter State Park

Penobscot

Chesuncook Lake 74 75

71 70

68 72

Jackman 101 67

73 76

79

69 Kennebec 201

Moosehead Lake 66 78 77 46 95 River

1

60 56
58 59 57

Calais

CENTRAL MAINE

14

45 44

WESTERN MOUNTAINS 15 42 Bangor

55 54
50 53 52
49 51

39 38
2 40
37 41 95 R 36 43

47 48

1

1

12 35
13 11 10
9 24
23 26 30
25 29 33
22 21 28 34
17 20 27 32

31 61 62
63 64 Bar Harbor
65

DOWNEAST

MOUNT DESERT ISLAND

Augusta 495 295

18 19 16

MIDCOAST

4 6 5
Sebago Lake
3 7 Popham Beach

2
1 Portland

N

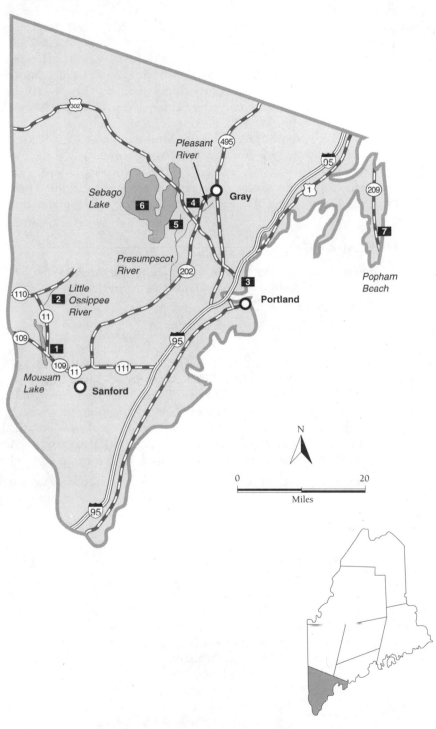

71

SOUTHERN MAINE

Southern Maine is the most populated section of the state, yet it has dozens of lakes, ponds, rivers, and streams. Many of southern Maine's rivers offer fast trout fishing amidst pastoral surroundings. Some of the heaviest fish stocking takes place in this region.

Saltwater anglers in southern Maine get the first crack at early-arriving striped bass and bluefish. Wading, fishing from shore, and fishing from boats are all popular. Charter boats and party boats abound. These boats usually provide bait and tackle, making saltwater fishing accessible to anglers without the proper equipment.

Sebago Lake is the second largest lake in Maine and is an early hot spot for lake trout and landlocked salmon. Later, Sebago becomes a favorite spot for warmwater species.

Most anglers driving north on U.S. Route 1 never suspect that just a few miles inland from the coastal congestion lies some of the finest fishing in the state.

1. MOUSAM LAKE

Key Species: *brook trout, brown trout, lake trout, largemouth bass, smallmouth bass, white perch, black crappie, pickerel*

Best Way to Fish: *canoe, boat*

Best Time to Fish: *May through September*

MAG: *2, B-2*

Description: This narrow, 900-acre lake is heavily stocked with brook, brown, and lake trout. From 1993 to 1995, 2,200 brown trout, 2,059 lake trout, and 5,839 brook trout were stocked in Mousam Lake. Numerous coves and inlets make this a perfect lake to fish from a canoe. Not much opportunity exists to fish from shore. The wide variety of species and easy access make Mousam Lake a good choice for families with children. Campgrounds are located in nearby Acton, Lebanon, and Alfred. Motels are available in Sanford, Biddeford, and Kennebunk.

Fishing index: In the summer months, lake trout will be found in a deep trench that runs up the middle of the main body of the lake. Depths here range from 66 to 88 feet. Troll with large minnows and lead-core line or use downriggers. A fish locator will reduce the time needed to locate groups of fish.

Look for brown and brook trout near the mouths of the various brooks. If flies are on the water, try to match the hatch. Be sure to have some red quills as well as some caddis patterns. If no insects are present on the surface, you can troll with Jerry's smelt, Mooselook Wobblers, or Flash Kings in orange and gold. Bait fishers will do well to drift, using a small minnow suspended near the bottom. May and June are best for brook and brown trout. Use medium-weight spinning tackle. Fly fishers should use a 9-foot rod in 5 or 6 weight.

Warmwater species can be taken throughout the open water season. This is one of the better lakes in Maine for black crappie. Use lightweight spinning or fly tackle. Fly fishers can take crappie by casting small streamers and bucktails. Gray ghost and any of the Thunder Creek series are good choices. Anglers using spinning tackle should use small jigs and Mepps spinners. Small minnows are best for anglers using bait. In May, look for crappies to be schooling in the lower portion of the lake. Concentrate on the cove near the dam, as well as the large island in the middle of the lower section. In warm weather, crappies will be in relatively deep water. A fish locator is handy for finding the schools. Once you catch one crappie, drop your anchor and fish hard.

The lower section of the lake is best for largemouth bass. You can take largemouth bass here throughout the open-water season. Look for smallmouth bass around the many points of land in the upper section of the lake.

In summer, try for white perch in the main section of the lake, in about 20 feet of water. Pickerel lurk in the shallow coves throughout the lake.

Directions: From Sanford, head north on Maine Route 109. The lower section of Mousam Lake and the boat ramp are on the left.

For more information: Call the Maine Department of Inland Fisheries & Wildlife in Gray.

2. LITTLE OSSIPEE RIVER

Key Species: *brown trout, brook trout, landlocked salmon*
Best Way to Fish: *wading*
Best Time to Fish: *May and June*
MAG: *2, A-2*

Description: This freestone river has occasional deep, slow runs and long pools. The river receives annual stockings of brook trout and brown trout and in 1993 and 1994, 792 landlocked salmon were stocked. Special regulations apply here. The fishing season runs from April 1 through October 31. Artificial lures only are allowed and all trout caught must be released alive at once. Be sure to read the open-water fishing regulations before fishing.

A large portion of the Little Ossipee River is contained within the Vern Walker Wildlife Management Area, public land managed by the Maine Department of Inland Fisheries & Wildlife.

Fishing index: This heavily stocked river is a fly fisher's paradise, with its wide variety of conditions, ranging from beaver ponds to fast riffles. An 8- or 9-foot, 5- or 6-weight rod will serve well here. Be sure to use a leader of at least 12 feet and carry some fine tippet material, stuff down to 2-pound test. May is the absolute best month and June still offers good fishing. Bring plenty of mayfly patterns, especially red quills and Hendricksons, as well as an assortment of caddis patterns. After the mayfly hatches, slow down and switch to terrestrial patterns.

Spin fishers should use ultralight spinning rods and line no heavier than 4-pound test. Try small Mepps spinners, small Flash Kings in gold and orange, and small Dardevles.

Directions: From Sanford, take Maine Route 11 north to North Shapleigh. In North Shapleigh, take the Mann Road on the right. Park in the lot at the end of the Mann Road. You can fish upstream and downstream from this point.

For more information: Call the Maine Department of Inland Fisheries & Wildlife Regional Office in Gray.

3. PORTLAND SHORELINE

Key Species: *bluefish, striped bass*
Best Way to Fish: *bridge*
Best Time to Fish: *July through September*
MAG: 5, E-4

Description: Several bridges, as well as the shoreline at Mackworth Island, provide shore-based anglers with the opportunity to catch bluefish and striped bass. Mackworth Island is home to the Baxter School for the Deaf. Private campgrounds are available in Portland and Scarborough, and motels are plentiful in the Portland area.

Fishing index: The Martin Point Bridge, the highway bridge on U.S. Route 1, and the shores of nearby Mackworth Island can be crowded when fishing is hot. Most anglers come here for bluefish. These battlers are not daunted by the urban setting and provide fast fishing. You can tell when the blues are in because the bridges and shoreline will be lined with anglers. If you can snag some menhaden, these make good bait, as do whole mackerel. Some anglers use heavy-duty spinning tackle to cast Rapalas or large poppers. One especially good lure is cigar-shaped and has a concave head with a single treble hook on the back. This lure is semi-buoyant, so you can let it sink and then give it a twitch to bring it back to the surface. Bluefish love it. Use a 3-foot steel leader and medium or heavy spinning gear.

Large runs of bluefish are not necessarily an annual event. It is impossible to predict the intensity of the runs from one year to the next.

Look for school-size stripers to arrive in early or mid-May. Medium-weight spinning rods are perfect for schoolies. Use the same plastic lures you would use for freshwater bass; try lead-head rubber-bodied jigs, Shadows, and, if you can find them, small plastic eels. Larger stripers come into the area in late June and July. At this time, it is best to use heavier gear. Use medium-heavy spinning rods and 12- or 15-pound test line. The same lures you use for schoolies will work on the bigger fish.

Fly fishers should use at least an 8-weight outfit. Use a 15-inch section of 40-pound mono as a shock tippet. Weight forward lines will make casting easier, especially when facing a headwind. Use poppers when either bluefish or stripers are visible, and try large streamer flies at other times.

Directions: From Portland, take U.S. Route 1 north to the Martin Point Bridge. Look for the road leading to Mackworth Island on the right. You will see a sign for the Baxter School for the Deaf. Fish from the shore at Martin Point Bridge or from the shoreline at Mackworth Island.

For more information: If the bluefish are in, you will see many other anglers, most of whom will be willing to give advice. Fly fishers may call the L.L. Bean fly fishing hot line for tackle tips.

Low water on the Pleasant River. This still pool is typical of the many tranquil spots on this heavily stocked southern Maine trout stream.

4. PLEASANT RIVER

Key Species: *brown trout, brook trout*
Best Way to Fish: *wading*
Best Time to Fish: *April through June*
MAG: *5, D-2*

Description: This high-quality trout stream is not far from Portland, Maine's largest city. The idyllic setting is the kind you see on calendars: glassy runs, tumbling riffles, ferns growing along the bank, and ancient maple trees spreading their limbs over quiet pools. For the most part, the Pleasant River is easily waded. In spite of streamside brush and obstructions, some bank fishing is possible, especially in the summer when lower water levels let you jump from rock to rock as you fish. Special fishing regulations are in effect, in the form of no-kill and artificial lures only from the U.S. Route 302 bridge downstream to the River Road bridge. Motels are available in North Windham and camping is available at nearby Sebago Lake State Park.

Fishing index: The Pleasant River is a good place for early season fly fishing. The catch-and-release section, from the U.S. Route 302 bridge downstream to the River Road bridge, was the beneficiary of a recent stream improvement project. The river has good mayfly and caddis fly hatches in May. If you come in April, bring a sinking fly line and plenty of brightly colored bucktails and streamer flies, such as Mickey Finn and Edson tiger light. Spin fishers should

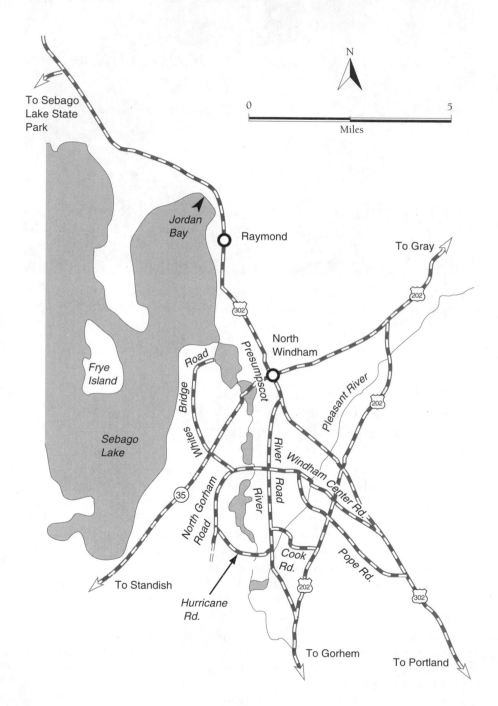

Angler survey boxes, such as this one on the Presumpscot River, are present on many Maine waters. Maine's fishery managers rely upon this information in designing their management plans for each water. Be sure to do your part and fill out a card.

bring an assortment of ultralight spoons and spinners. The Pleasant River receives heavy annual stockings of brown trout and brook trout.

Directions: In North Windham, drive south on U.S. Route 302 to the U.S. Route 302 bridge over the Pleasant River, just out of town. Other access points include the Cook Road Bridge, the bridge at Pope Road, and the bridge at Windham Center Road.

For more information: Call Maine Department of Inland Fisheries & Wildlife Regional Office in Gray.

5. PRESUMPSCOT RIVER ————————————

> **Key Species:** *brown trout, brook trout, landlocked salmon*
> **Best Way to Fish:** *wading*
> **Best Time to Fish:** *April through September*
> **MAG:** *5, D-2*

Description: Clear and cold, this river is an outlet of Sebago Lake (Site 6). Even in dry weather, a good head of water can be expected, making for good angling when other streams and rivers are too low. Special fishing regulations on various sections of the river include fly-fishing-only, no-kill on landlocked

The cool, clear Presumpscot River. This angler is about to work a run with a small dry fly.

salmon, a one-fish bag limit on trout, and closed sections of river; check the open water fishing regulations carefully before fishing. Water levels can rise quickly here, so be on the alert when wading. It is possible to fish without wading, but you will be somewhat limited. Windham has plenty of motels and nearby Sebago Lake State Park offers camping.

Fishing index: This is a good place to take landlocked salmon in the early spring. Use size 8 or 10 bucktails and streamers. In late April and May, trout can be taken on the surface during the mayfly hatches. Be sure to carry some red quills and Hendricksons. You should also carry some dun variants in size 14. Variants are more durable than traditional winged flies and are proven fish takers during the red quill hatch. Even when no flies are showing, skipping a heavily dressed dun variant across the surface will elicit a strike. This river is heavily stocked. In 1995, 2,000 brook trout, 1,060 landlocked salmon, and 3,500 brown trout were planted here. Good-sized carry-over fish are present here as well, offering the possibility of hooking into a real trophy.

Directions: From North Windham, drive south on Maine Route 35. The bridge over the Presumpscot River is 0.4 mile from town. Look for a gravel road by the bridge, leading to a good-sized parking area. Begin fishing downstream. Look for an obvious path on the left side of the river. You can also gain access to the river from the Windham Center Road and the Hurricane Road, both downstream from Maine Route 35.

For more information: Call Maine Department of Inland Fisheries & Wildlife Regional Office in Gray.

6. SEBAGO LAKE

Key Species: *lake trout, brook trout, landlocked salmon, brown trout possible, smallmouth bass, largemouth bass, white perch, black crappie, pickerel, cusk*
Best Way to Fish: *boat, canoe*
Best Time to Fish: *late April through September*
MAG: *5, C-1*

Description: Second in size only to Moosehead Lake, 28,771-acre Sebago Lake is an amazing 316 feet deep. This lake is one of the original homes of the landlocked salmon, *Salmo sebago*.

Fishing is a popular industry in the Sebago region. Motels, marinas, and tackle shops abound. Although small boats and canoes are useful in sheltered areas and near the shore, you really need a boat of 16 feet or more if you plan to visit any of the offshore areas. Sebago Lake is nearly round, and this open aspect is conducive to potentially dangerous high winds, which can whip the lake to a froth.

Sebago Lake is situated in a built-up part of Maine, but its large size ensures plenty of room for all. Some limited fishing can be done from shore at Sebago Lake State Park, but you really need a boat or canoe in order to take full advantage of the lake's resources. The park offers campsites as well as two boat ramps. Another public boat ramp is located off U.S. Route 302 in the town of Raymond, at the north end of Jordan Bay. Motels can be found along U.S. Route 302 between North Windham and Portland.

Fishing index: As soon as the ice melts, usually in mid or late April, hundreds of boats descend upon Sebago. Landlocked salmon are the main target for these early-season anglers. Sebago Lake has a large number of lake trout, and liberal bag limits have been imposed. Lake trout are especially active in the early season. The near-surface action continues through May and June and can even last into July during years with a late spring. Later on in the summer, anglers turn to deep-trolling methods for salmon and lake trout. Dodgers, fished with downriggers, are the usual fare for summertime trolling. Popular spots for landlocked salmon include: the mouth of the Songo River, the mouth of Northwest River and north to the mouth of Muddy River, and the mouth of Jordan Bay. Lake trout will be found here too, but in deeper water. You can get results by drift fishing large minnows on the bottom in the deep holes on the east side of Spider Island. Brook trout are found near the river mouths and close to the shore and can be taken by slowly trolling a night crawler behind a small spinner.

Sebago Lake has immense potential for warmwater species, a fact most trout and salmon anglers tend to dismiss. Try the Dingley Islands, the north end of Spider Island, and the shoreline around Raymond Neck for smallmouth bass. Try fly-rod poppers on calm days. Use a 6-weight rod and weight forward line. Muddler minnows are effective underwater imitations. Use a sinking fly line and slowly twitch the fly while you retrieve it. Effective spinning lures for smallmouths include Mepps spinners, 6-inch plastic worms in black and purple, and plastic-bodied lead-head jigs. Jig bodies with glitter tails are especially good. Ultralight spinning rods loaded with 4-pound test line are

A pair of ducks swims near the sandy shoreline at Sebago Lake State Park. The lake is slightly choppy in this photo, perfect for trolling for landlocked salmon.

perfect for feisty smallmouths. For largemouth bass, crappies, yellow perch, and pickerel, try the north end of Jordan Bay, the shallows between Dingley Islands and Kettle Cove, and the Sticky River basin. Largemouth anglers do well in the early morning and evening with poppers, and daytime anglers prefer plastic worms of 6 inches and larger. Use a medium-weight spinning rod or bait-casting rod for largemouths. Use at least 6-pound test line. Eight-pound test is better because Sebago can produce some huge largemouths. Bait fishers should use nightcrawlers or large golden shiners. Pickerel anglers should stick to the shallows. Try small Daredevle spoons and spinners with yellow hackle on the treble hooks. Yellow streamer flies and bucktails are also good pickerel lures, since pickerel feed voraciously on yellow perch. Anglers seeking yellow perch and crappies should fish in about 20 feet of water, using worms, small shiners, and small twister-tail jigs. A fish locator is a great help in locating schools of crappie and yellow perch.

Directions: From North Windham, head northwest on U.S. Route 302 to Casco. In Casco, look for a sign on the left for Sebago Lake State Park.

For more information: Contact Sebago Lake Marina.

7. POPHAM BEACH

> **Key Species:** *striped bass, bluefish*
> **Best Way to Fish:** *surf casting*
> **Best Time to Fish:** *July through September*
> **MAG:** *6, E-5*

Description: This sand beach is located at the mouth of the Kennebec River on the Gulf of Maine. Historic Forts Baldwin and Popham are located on the point of land just north of the beach. Popham Beach State Park offers parking, swimming, surfing, and picnicking.

Fishing index: Striped bass fishing is good from late June through September. Surf casters line Popham Beach when the fish are in. Although most anglers use bait, such as sandworms and live eels, Popham Beach is an excellent spot for fly fishers. Striped bass are often found near shore, just outside the breakers. The water is so clear that you can often see stripers as they chase your fly or lure. Use a 9- or 10-foot, 9- or 10-weight rod. Large streamer flies such as Lefty's deceiver are effective, as are various squid imitations such as Page's Simple Squid. Whitlock's Sand Eels and Tabory's Sand Eels are good choices as well. Cast your fly and retrieve by quickly hand-stripping the line. A wading line basket can be a great help. The author has found that a heavy-duty plastic storage container can easily be converted into a line basket by simply cutting two holes on either side and attaching a belt or rope. You can often take bluefish as well as stripers, especially during July and August. Because of the presence of bluefish, you should use a shock tippet of 40-pound test mono. Bluefish will hit the same flies and lures used for stripers. Because this beach is popular with swimmers, it is best to time your visits at dawn and dusk during July or August.

Directions: From Bath, head south on Maine Route 209, which ends at Popham Beach.

For more information: Contact the Maine Bureau of Parks and Recreation, Department of Conservation. Fly fishers might want to call the L.L. Bean fly fishing hot line.

Popham Beach as seen from a boat in the mouth of the Kennebec River. Striped bass and bluefish come close to this sandy beach, offering great sport for surf casters. Boaters take fish here by trolling with large diving plugs.

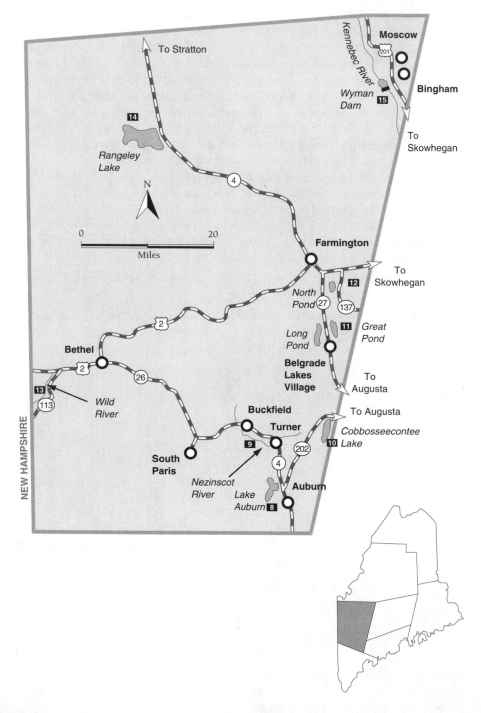

To Stratton

Kennebec River

Moscow

201

Wyman Dam

15

Bingham

To Skowhegan

14

Rangeley Lake

N

0   20
Miles

4

Farmington

To Skowhegan

12

North Pond   27

137

11   Great Pond

Long Pond

Belgrade Lakes Village

To Augusta

Bethel

2

26

13

113

Wild River

Buckfield

Turner

To Augusta

Cobbosseecontee Lake

10

9

202

4

South Paris

Nezinscot River

Lake Auburn   **8**

Auburn

NEW HAMPSHIRE

WESTERN MOUNTAINS

Maine's western mountain region is a place of breathtaking beauty. Mountains, lakes, and fast-moving rivers offer something for everyone. The freestone rivers of Maine's western mountains are a trout fisher's paradise. Brook trout are the most common species found in this part of the state. Rainbow trout can also be taken in a few spots.

This region is famous for its gemstones, including the famous Maine tourmaline. Feldspar was once mined here in great quantities, and rock hounds can search for gems at the abandoned pits.

Maine's western mountains are also famous for their grand old resorts. Visitors can stay in Victorian splendor at many inns and hotels. Most of these businesses are open year-round because of the great downhill skiing in this region.

8. LAKE AUBURN

Key Species: *brook trout, brown trout, lake trout, landlocked salmon, smallmouth bass, pickerel, white perch*

Best Way to Fish: *boat, canoe, shore*

Best Time to Fish: *April through June*

MAG: *11, E-4*

Description: This cold, deep 2,260-acre reservoir lies on the outskirts of the city of Auburn. Rocky shorelines and water up to 118 feet deep make for good fishing for a variety of species. Even though this lake is found in an urban setting, the shoreline has little development, giving a sense of wildness. A portion of the southern end of the lake is closed to all water-related activities, but the rest of the lake is open to fishing and recreational boating. Swimming is not allowed, so competition from water-skiers is not a problem. This lake is a noted early-season producer. While the northern lakes are still icebound, anglers are catching fish in Lake Auburn. The greater Lewiston-Auburn area offers plenty of motels, and there are campgrounds at Hebron and Monmouth.

Fishing index: In April, anglers seeking white perch of up to two pounds congregate along the shore by the Maine Department of Transportation turnoff along Maine Route 4 in Auburn. Earthworms are the most popular bait. At the same time, other anglers try for lake trout, landlocked salmon, and the occasional brown trout near the turnoff on Lake Shore Drive. Thompson Brook enters the lake here via a culvert, and even if most of the lake still has ice, this section will have open water. Live smelt fished on bottom are the most popular bait at this time.

Once the lake is free of ice, anglers take salmon by trolling with streamer flies such as Jerry's smelt or gray ghosts. Live smelt, Flash Kings, and Mooselook Wobblers are also effective. Go at a good clip and work the shorelines carefully. Landlocked salmon will be relatively close to shore. You may need to use a sinking fly line if the fish are holding deeper than 10 feet. Good spots to begin are the shorelines along Lake Shore Drive, around Salmon Point, and the western shore along Spring Road.

Smallmouth bass fishing picks up after the landlocked salmon have taken to deeper water, usually sometime in June. The rocky shoreline offers good bass fishing almost anywhere you can legally fish. The bottom of this lake contains great structure—drop-offs, submerged boulders, and lots of declivities—making Lake Auburn a perfect place to drift with small plastic-bodied lead-head jigs. Use ultralight spinning tackle and 4-pound test line. Let the jigs hit bottom, then raise and lower your rod tip. Most bites will occur when you raise the rod, but sometimes a smallmouth bass will hit the jig on the way down, so strike if you see the line stop before you think it should. Fly fishers can take smallmouths by fishing leech patterns with a sinking line. Either cast, drift, or troll, and be sure to give the fly plenty of action by constantly working the rod. Smallmouths will hit poppers and deer-hair bugs in the mornings and evenings, and all day on still, drizzly days.

Directions: In Auburn, head north on Maine Route 4. Look for the Maine Department of Transportation scenic turnoff and boat ramp on the left.

For more information: Contact Dag's Bait Shop.

9. NEZINSCOT RIVER

Key Species: *brook trout, brown trout, smallmouth bass*
Best Way to Fish: *bank, canoe*
Best Time to Fish: *late April through early June*
MAG: *11, C-4*

Description: This heavily stocked trout stream in Maine's western mountains is scenic even by Maine standards. In 1995, 2,500 brown trout were stocked here. You can fish by wading, from the bank, and by canoeing. Special fishing regulations include catch-and-release, artificial-lures-only, and an open fishing season from January 1 to December 31 from the Turner Mill dam downstream to Meadow Brook. From Meadow Brook to the Androscoggin River, the Nezinscot River is open to fishing from January 1 to December 31 with a daily limit of two trout. Check the open water regulations before fishing.

The east and west branches of the Nezinscot River join each other in Buckfield, the starting point for the Nezinscot River canoe trip. Except for a few mild rapids, this mostly calm section of river is easily negotiated from Buckfield to Turner Center, a distance of 12 miles. You are required to make one easy portage at Turner. This would be a good day trip for anglers looking for smallmouth bass and the occasional brown trout.

A campground is located along Maine Route 117 in Turner, and there are plenty of motels in the Auburn-Lewiston area.

Fishing index: There is excellent brown trout fishing in that section of the river between Turner Center and the Nezinscot River's confluence with the Androscoggin River in Turner. Begin fishing downstream from the dam in Turner Center. The river here offers varied habitat, from deep pools to fast riffles. Fly fishers should use small bucktails with a sinking fly line. Carry some red quills, Hendricksons, dun variants, and Adams dry flies in sizes 12, 14, and 16 in case mayflies are hatching.

Spin fishers should use ultralight rods and 4-pound test line. Try small spinners and Super-Dupers. Do not neglect the edges of deep pools. Trout will be hiding near the banks and under overhanging limbs. Spinning tackle does well on dark days, especially later in June when mayfly hatches have slowed down.

Directions: From Auburn, take Maine Route 4 north to Turner and turn right on Maine Route 117, also called Turner Center Road. Park near the dam in Turner Center. To reach the Buckfield site, take Maine Route 4 north to Turner and turn left at the intersection of Maine Routes 4 and 117. Follow Maine Route 117 for 7 miles to where Maine Route 117 crosses the Nezinscot River.

For more information: Call the Maine Department of Inland Fisheries & Wildlife Regional Fish and Wildlife Headquarters in Gray.

10. COBBOSSEECONTEE LAKE

Key Species: *Largemouth bass, smallmouth bass, brown trout, brook trout, splake, white perch, pickerel, redbreasted sunfish*
Best Way to Fish: *boat, canoe*
Best Time to Fish: *May through September, January and February*
MAG: *12, C-4*

Description: This is a 5,543-acre lake with a maximum depth of 100 feet, and extensive shallow, weedy areas. Cobbosseecontee Stream offers an 8-mile canoe trip, beginning at the outlet. You will need a boat of some sort to fish this lake. Special regulations include a slot limit on bass. Cobbosseecontee Lake receives annual stockings of brown trout. In 1995, 3,900 12- to 14-inch browns were stocked here. Motels are plentiful in the Augusta area, including along U.S. Route 202 between Manchester and Augusta. There is a campground in Winthrop.

Fishing index: This site is noted for trophy largemouth bass. Both largemouth and smallmouth bass fishing remain good through the open water season. Bass anglers use large plastic worms in a variety of colors; you never know which will work best. Black and purple are tried and true shades, but it pays to carry a good assortment of worms in every color. Topwater action is good early and late in the day, and any surface lure will work. In summer, bass will congregate around bottom structure and vertical jigging with lead-head jigs will pay off. A fish locator will help you locate the structure and its resident bass.

In winter, bass are taken on large gold shiners fished with tip-ups. Begin fishing in relatively shallow water, from 10 to 20 feet, but do not neglect the deeper areas of 50 feet or so because bass often spend at least part of their day in deep water. You will also take bass by jigging with medium-sized Swedish Pimples, lead-head jigs, and Rapala jigs. As when using bait, begin in fairly shallow water and continue fishing deeper until you find where the fish are holding.

For bass as well as brown trout, try off Horseshoe Island, in the center of the lake, and Hersey Island, at the north end of the lake by the boat ramp.

Brown trout can be taken in May and June by trolling with streamer flies. Gray ghost, black ghost, queen bee, Jerry's smelt, and supervisors will all take fish. Try trolling with a floating line and just enough weight to keep the fly from rolling on the surface. If you do not get action in an hour or so, either add a longer leader and more weight, or go to a fast-sinking fly line. You will also take browns by trolling with Flash Kings and Mooselook Wobblers.

Look for pickerel in the weed beds along U.S. Route 202 in Winthrop. Medium-sized minnows, Dardevles, red plastic worms, and yellow bucktails will all take pickerel here. Pay particular attention to the edges of the weed beds, as well as the area within 10 to 15 feet in front of the weeds.

This is also an excellent lake for white perch. Local anglers take them during the open water season and through the ice. White perch of one pound or more are common. Most wintertime anglers bait the hooks on their tip-ups with small silver or gold shiners or banded killifish when fishing for white perch. You can also take white perch by jigging with a small Swedish Pimple. You may need to add a bit of cut-up minnow to the treble hook of your jig if perch are reluctant to bite. Open water anglers use worms and night crawlers for perch, drifting with the wind and letting the bait flutter just above the bottom. A few anglers have found that larger perch are more frequently caught on small minnows. Plastic-bodied lead-head jigs are effective for open water white perch. Fish these by drifting, allowing the jig to play the bottom. Be sure to work your rod tip up and down to impart action.

In July and August, early morning and evening are the best times to fish, since this popular lake sees considerable boat traffic during the day.

Directions: Heading north on Interstate 95, take Exit 30 in Augusta. From there, take U.S. 202 for 4.5 miles to Winthrop. A state-maintained gravel boat ramp is on the left, just off U.S. 202. Another ramp is located off Maine Route 135 in East Monmouth.

For more information: Contact Harpo's Emporium or Elma's Tackle Shop.

11. GREAT POND AND LONG POND

Key Species: *landlocked salmon, pike, smallmouth and largemouth bass, white perch, pickerel, brown trout and brook trout possible*
Best Way to Fish: *boat, canoe*
Best Time to Fish: *May through September*
MAG: 20, E-5

Description: Great Pond is a highly productive 8,239-acre lake in the Belgrade Lakes chain. Neighboring Long Pond is a long, narrow lake of 2,714 acres. Belgrade Lakes Village separates the two lakes. Both contain the same species of fish, and both are easily accessible. Both lakes also see a considerable amount of fishing pressure. Some bank fishing is possible. On Great Pond, there is a 2-fish bag limit and a 24-inch minimum length on pike; on Long Pond, there is a 16-inch minimum length on landlocked salmon. Campsites are available in Belgrade Lakes Village, Norridgewock, and Skowhegan. Nearby Waterville offers plenty of motels.

Fishing index: During the first few weeks of the fishing season and through May, anglers seeking landlocked salmon, pike, and white perch vie for space around the inlet of Long Pond in Belgrade Lakes Village. This is usually the first spot to be free of ice, a magnet to winter-weary anglers. Worms, fished on bottom, are the most popular bait for white perch; live smelt and night crawlers are used for landlocked salmon. This area is also a good (but crowded) place to troll for landlocked salmon after ice-out. Use any streamer fly that imitates a smelt; gray ghost and Jerry's smelt are two favorites, with Jerry's smelt taking the edge. Some anglers troll with chrome or copper-colored Mooselook Wobblers. When using lures or streamer flies, troll at a fast clip and use an erratic trolling pattern. You may want to use a short wire leader in case you hook a pike. Note that Long Pond is thought to hold the largest pike in Maine; fish weighing more than 20 pounds are a distinct possibility.

In June, largemouth and smallmouth bass, pike, and pickerel will be at the peak of activity. Most shoreline areas in either lake will produce bass, but the southern end of Long Pond has the greatest amount of shallow, weedy water. Use plastic worms, crankbaits, and spinnerbaits for largemouths here. Stickbaits are effective if you impart plenty of action. Be sure to let the bait sit motionless every so often. This will spur a reluctant bass into activity. You can have good surface action during the early morning and evening hours if you use poppers. This is also the best time to fish for pike in either lake, so even if you are primarily interested in bass, be sure to use fairly stout tackle in case you hook a huge pike. For pike, cast near the weeds, using large Mepps spinners, large spinnerbaits (orange is a good color), and large Dardevles.

In summer, anglers using downriggers and live minnows, or lead-core line with minnows behind a set of lake trolls, troll for landlocked salmon in the north end of Long Pond and in the deep water off Hoyt Island in Great Pond. Anglers using worms or small minnows fish to schools of white perch throughout the season.

Directions: From Augusta, head north on Maine Route 27 and stay on 27 until you enter Belgrade Lakes Village. In the village, look for signs for the state boat ramp on Great Pond on the right and for another state-sponsored ramp on Long Pond, on the left.

For more information: Contact Harpo's Emporium.

12. NORTH POND

> **Key Species:** *largemouth bass, pike, pickerel, white perch, brown trout and smallmouth bass possible*
> **Best Way to Fish:** *boat, canoe, shore*
> **Best Time to Fish:** *May through September*
> **MAG:** *20, D-4*

Description: North Pond is a shallow, weedy 2,115-acre lake featuring easy access. Some fishing from shore is possible, but a canoe or boat is best. The daily limit on pike is one fish, with a 24-inch minimum length. From October

Northern Pike grow big in North Pond. This beauty fell to a small minnow fished through the ice.

1 through November 30, all landlocked salmon, lake trout, and bass must be released alive at once. Campgrounds are located in Belgrade Lakes Village and Norridgewock, and motels are available in Waterville.

Fishing index: Beginning in late April or early May, anglers using worms, night crawlers, or minnows take schooling white perch from shore near the inlet, just off Maine Route 8 in Smithfield. After the perch runs fade, largemouth bass fishing and pike fishing come to the front. North Pond produces some of the largest bass in the state. Plastic worms are a favorite lure. Use 8-inch worms rather than the standard 6-inch variety. The larger worms appeal to the lunker bass found here. Also effective for largemouth bass are plastic salamanders and twist-tail plastic grubs in the larger sizes. Use at least 8-pound test line; you may need it to wrestle large bass out from the numerous obstructions. Topwater lures are effective here, but the weedless variety are better than those with exposed hooks. The lake is weedy, with a maximum depth of only 20 feet, so largemouth bass and pike can be found almost anywhere.

Until recent years, North Pond was mainly known as a premiere largemouth bass water, but the introduction of pike has added a new and exciting dimension to the angling possibilities. Anglers using large gold shiners fish for pike near the weed beds. A bobber will help keep your shiner out of the weeds. Large, splashy spinnerbaits with orange, yellow, or green bodies are good pike lures here, especially in spring. Try to work your spinnerbait so it moves as much water as possible, which will infuriate the mean-tempered pike.

Little Pond, a shallow extension of the southwest end of North Pond, is a good place to look for pickerel, as is the shoreline at the north end of North Pond. Try casting brightly colored bucktails near the weed beds for pickerel. Use Mickey Finns, Edson tiger lights, and yellow perch bucktails. Small or medium Dardevles are good for pickerel here. A strip of pork rind on the treble hook of a Daredevle will bring more strikes, but if the fish strike short, remove the pork rind.

Directions: From Farmington, drive east on U.S. Route 2 for 17 miles, until the intersection with Maine Route 137 on the right. Turn right on Maine Route 137 and drive 3.5 miles to the intersection with North Shore Drive on the right. Drive 0.9 mile on North Shore Drive and look for the boat ramp on the left.

For more information: Call the Maine Department of Inland Fisheries & Wildlife Regional Office in Sydney.

13. WILD RIVER

Key Species: *brook trout, brown trout, rainbow trout possible*
Best Way to Fish: *wading*
Best Time to Fish: *May through June*
MAG: *10, B-1*

Description: This freestone mountain stream runs through the White Mountain National Forest. Wading can be difficult during periods of high water, but the large number of streamside boulders enables the angler to hop about and reach prime spots. Maine Route 113 bounds the eastern side of the river, providing unlimited access. The Wild River flows between Maine and New Hampshire and enters the Androscoggin River in Gilead. The daily bag limit on trout is two fish. In 1995, Wild River was stocked with 1,600 brook trout and 2,000 brown trout. The White Mountain National Forest has five campgrounds in Maine. Motels and inns are available in Bethel.

Fishing index: Fishing is good from where the Wild River joins the Androscoggin all the way to the New Hampshire border. The river is stocked with brook trout and brown trout, but rainbow trout, originating in New Hampshire, provide unexpected bonuses. Huge boulders in the stream create numerous pockets as well as medium-sized pools. Trout seem to hang on the edges of these pockets near the swift sections, and will dart out into the pockets to intercept a lure or fly. Try Slaymaker's Thunder Creek series streamer flies. These sparsely tied flies are ideal in clear water and the painted eye is helpful in drawing strikes. Variants and size 14 royal coachman dry flies are good choices for dry flies. Angleworms are the most popular bait. Anglers using spinning gear should try small spinners fished with ultralight spinning gear. Cast your streamer fly, worm, or spinner to the head of a pool and slowly work it back. Fish dry flies with a dead drift.

The following tips should help you get the most out of this site. Water levels are low from July through September, so early morning and evening are the best times then. On bright days, concentrate your efforts on shaded sec-

Wild River is studded with boulders. The calm pocket water on the downstream side of each boulder provides a perfect spot for trout to lie in wait for food.

tions of the deeper pools. Since some of the large boulders here create considerable shade, finding good locations should not be a problem. Use special care while wading. The intense clarity of the water can be deceiving. It is usually deeper than it appears. Use the lightest tackle you have, since the river has no snags for a trout to get wrapped up in. As in other crystal-clear streams, you will have the best luck using the lightest possible line.

Directions: From Bethel, take U.S. Route 2 west to a bridge over the Wild River in Gilead. You can park on the left, just before the bridge, on Maine Route 113. From there, you can also follow Maine Route 113 south, and find numerous places to park and fish along the way.

For more information: Contact the Forest Service, Northeast Forest Experimental Station.

14. RANGELEY LAKE

Key Species: *landlocked salmon, brook trout*
Best Way to Fish: *boat, bank*
Best Time to Fish: *May through September*
MAG: *28, E-4*

Description: Rangeley Lake was a popular fishing destination even during the Victorian era. Nineteenth-century anglers reached the lake's hotels and sporting camps after a lengthy stage ride from Portland and a short steamboat trip. Brook trout weighing up to 10 pounds were the ultimate goal. Today, this 6,000-acre lake set amidst magnificent mountain scenery is still a popular destination for anglers. Camping is available at Rangeley Lake State Park.

Rangeley Lake is heavily stocked. In 1995 alone, 3,132 landlocked salmon and 9,216 brook trout were stocked here. Boats and canoes are useful, and some bank fishing is available. The lake is subject to special fishing regulations, including a ban on live fish as bait (the use of dead fish, salmon eggs, and worms is permitted), a ban on taking smelt except by hook and line, a slot limit on brook trout, and a daily bag limit on landlocked salmon of one fish. Read the open water fishing regulations carefully before fishing.

Fishing index: The average ice-out date is May 9. For the next four weeks, anglers descend on Rangeley Lake to take landlocked salmon by early-season trolling methods (see the section on landlocked salmon in this book).

If you launch your boat at Rangeley Lake State Park, you can begin trolling immediately. Use streamer flies such as gray ghost, black ghost, nine-three, and Jerry's smelt. Mooselook Wobblers in copper or chrome finish and orange and gold Flash Kings are also effective. A 9-foot, 6-weight fly rod with a fast-sinking fly line is ideal for trolling here. If you elect to troll with spinning gear, be sure to use a rudder ahead of your lure to prevent line twist. The section of lake bordering the park, as well as the area to the west near South Bog Islands, is a prime place for landlocked salmon. To the east of the state park, try trolling between Doctors Island and Haines Point.

If you lack a boat, try taking brook trout from the town ramp in Rangeley Village. Earthworms are the most widely used bait. Later in the summer, you can take brook trout by trolling with a streamer fly and a dodger. Use a sinking fly line or lead-core line. A small gray ghost is as good a choice as any for a fly.

Directions: To reach Rangeley Lake State Park and its campsites and boat ramp, head south from Rangeley Village on Maine Route 4. At the end of Rangeley Lake, about 3.5 miles from the village, look for South Shore Drive on the right. Follow signs on South Shore Drive to Rangeley Lake State Park. You can also launch your boat at the town ramp in Rangeley Village.

For more information: Contact the Rangeley Region Chamber of Commerce, or for more information about Rangeley Lake State Park, contact the Maine Bureau of Parks and Recreation.

15. WYMAN DAM ON KENNEBEC RIVER

Key Species: *landlocked salmon, brown trout, brook trout, rainbow trout*
Best Way to Fish: *wading, bank*
Best Time to Fish: *April through October*
MAG: *30, D-3*

Description: This tailwater fishery of the Kennebec River is a popular early-season spot for anglers seeking coldwater species. Fishing from the bank is the safest method, since the water is fast and deep, making wading difficult. Spe-

The pool below Wyman Dam on the Kennebec River is a popular opening-day destination for eager anglers. This brawling section of river is home to a self-sustaining population of rainbow trout.

cial fishing regulations include an artificials-only fall season and restricted bag and length limits on landlocked salmon, trout, and lake trout. Private campgrounds are available in Madison and Skowhegan, and motels are located near Skowhegan on U.S. Route 201.

Fishing index: Although brook trout, brown trout, and lunker landlocked salmon are present, rainbow trout attract the majority of anglers. A self-sustaining population of rainbow trout exists here, something of a rarity in Maine. These Maine-born fish represent a great hope for rainbow trout aficionados, because they are thought to be genetically suited to Maine's environment.

The opening week of fishing season is hectic, as anglers from far and wide arrive in hopes of landing a lunker rainbow trout or landlocked salmon. Most early-season anglers rely on spinning tackle and Rapalas and Rebels, but fly fishers use streamers and bucktails fished with a fast-sinking fly line.

Brown trout fishing is good and fly fishers using caddis patterns take good fish in the evening throughout the season. Action will be good throughout the summer. Solitude is another plus; you can fish here in August or September and not encounter another angler.

Directions: From Bingham, head north on U.S. Route 201 toward Moscow, just across Austin Stream. In Moscow, look for a sign on the left indicating Wyman Dam.

For more information: Call the Maine Department of Inland Fisheries & Wildlife in Strong or Augusta.

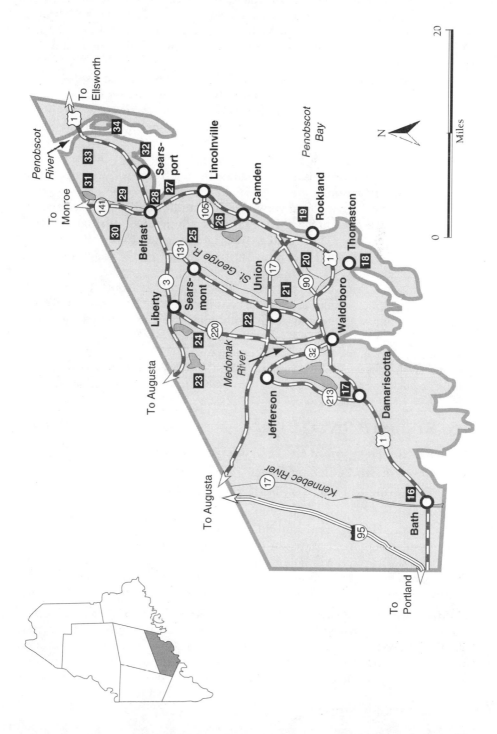

MIDCOAST MAINE

The Midcoast region displays the splendid irregularities of the Maine coastline. Coves, rocky points, peninsulas, and river mouths add to the stark beauty of this rugged shore. In Midcoast Maine, the mountains nearly touch the sea. You can go boating on the ocean in the morning and climb a mountain that same afternoon.

Midcoast Maine is known for some of the best white perch fishing in the state, but largemouth and smallmouth bass fishing can be red-hot too. Anglers usually pass through this region on their way to the more storied waters of the north, not realizing that they are passing up some of the state's better angling opportunities.

Brown trout are a Midcoast success story. Several rivers and numerous lakes and ponds hold browns, providing fast fishing from ice-out until the end of the open water season.

The Midcoast region contains two trophy landlocked salmon waters, St. George Lake (Site 24) and Swan Lake (Site 31). Both lakes also contain large numbers of brook trout. The rapid growth rate of fish in these lakes is mind-boggling. A 9-inch trout stocked in April of one year may weigh over two pounds the following April.

As with southern Maine, the areas adjacent to U.S. Route 1 are tourist havens, but in the Midcoast region, the commercial edge has worn off. This is an area of rolling hills, winding roads, and typical New England villages, each with a white-painted church and pointed steeple. Instead of factory outlet stores and garish neon signs, you will see homemade signs touting handicrafts and used lobster traps. Roadside flea markets and vendors selling shrimp and clams from the backs of pickup trucks take the place of fast-food restaurants.

16. KENNEBEC RIVER, BATH

Key Species: *striped bass, bluefish*
Best Way to Fish: *boat, bank*
Best Time to Fish: *late May through September*
MAG: 6, C-5

Description: This is a powerful tidal river with many rips and backwaters. Boats smaller than 14 feet are not recommended, since the river can become dangerous during high winds and when the tide is running. You can fish from shore near the state boat ramp in Phippsburg. This site is also a great place for wildlife viewing. Seals, a variety of shorebirds, and bald eagles are common.

Fishing index: This section of the Kennebec River is a world-class site, offering by far the best striped bass and bluefish angling in Maine. Striped bass and bluefish can be found from the boat ramp in Bath all the way down to the open ocean at Popham Beach. Striped bass anglers should begin by searching for flocks of gulls, an indication that stripers are on a feeding spree. Sometimes you can see frantic bait fish being driven out of the water as they are herded and slaughtered by stripers.

16 KENNEBEC RIVER, BATH

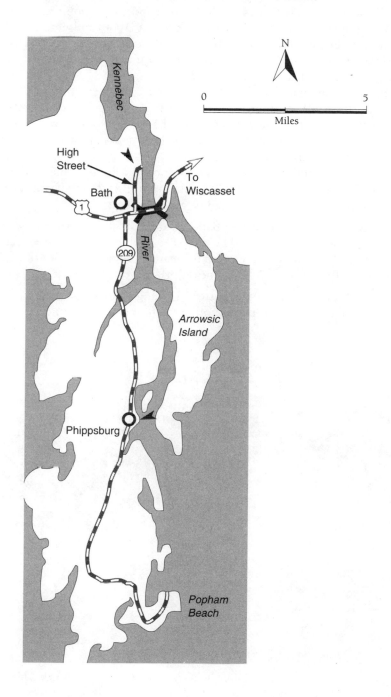

If you manage to get within casting distance of a school of feeding stripers, you can take fish with either spinning or fly tackle. Any spinning lures that you would use for largemouth bass will also take stripers, but soft plastic minnow-shaped lures are best. Fly fishers can have great sport with poppers. Be sure to give your popper plenty of action. Do not worry about presentation at this point; your main concern should be to get the lure in front of the fish as soon as possible, because a feeding spree can end as quickly as it begins. If no surface activity is evident, try trolling with Rapalas or Rebels. Anglers using live eels as bait can fish on bottom by anchoring in deep water in the middle of the river. An electronic depth finder is helpful for this type of fishing. Most school stripers will weigh between 3 and 8 pounds. Larger fish often top the 36-inch minimum length requirement. The smaller fish enter the river in late May, the larger fish about a month later.

Bluefish are attracted to the river by migrating schools of menhaden. The most common method of fishing for bluefish is to troll with Rapalas and Rebels. Bait fishers often use menhaden, dead or alive, for bait.

Directions: From U.S. Route 1 in Bath, take High Street north to a sign for the state boat ramp on the right. The ramp area will be crowded on weekends in July and August. An alternate ramp is located about 7 miles south of Bath, just off Maine Route 209 in Phippsburg. Both ramps offer plenty of parking.

For more information: Contact Kittery Trading Post. These people have all the answers, so be sure to stop in if you are entering Maine from the south.

An angler casts for striped bass on the Kennebec River near Bath. Many boaters cruise the river, watching for telltale signs of surface activity. Feeding frenzies can be wild and furious while they last.

17. DAMARISCOTTA LAKE

Key Species: *brown trout, lake trout, landlocked salmon, smallmouth bass, white perch, pickerel*
Best Way to Fish: *boat, canoe, bank*
Best Time to Fish: *May through September*
MAG: *13, D-4*

Description: Damariscotta Lake has three distinctly different sections: the north, middle, and south basins. The north basin is the deepest, at 114 feet; the middle basin is next at 46 feet; and the south basin is 34 feet deep. Damariscotta Lake State Park is set on the northeastern shore of the north basin. A boat or canoe is recommended, but there is limited fishing from shore in Jefferson, near the mouth of Davis Stream. Campgrounds are located in Jefferson and Warren, and there are motels on U.S. Route 1 between Newcastle and Warren.

Fishing index: North Basin: Early-season trolling near the stream mouth in Jefferson is a good way to take landlocked salmon and brown trout. Use streamer flies, smelt, Flash Kings, or Mooselook Wobblers. Lake trout will be holding in the same area, but in deeper water, further out in the lake. A deep hole just south of the state park produces lake trout in summer. This site produces lake trout weighing 10 pounds and more.

Middle basin: The islands in the center of the middle basin are great spots to cast for smallmouth bass from June through September. Use lead-head jigs with plastic bodies. The sparkle-tail variety, especially yellow ones, are killers on smallmouth. Curly-tail jigs are also highly effective. Muscongus Bay, the lower leg of the middle basin, is also a good smallmouth spot. Smallmouth bass of up to 5 pounds are taken here.

South basin: This shallow, narrow section is known for pickerel and white perch, but it is possible to take brown trout around the several islands. White perch here can weigh more than two pounds. Local white perch addicts use worms, minnows, and night crawlers, slowly drifted on the bottom. This method also takes the occasional brown trout. You can also take white perch here by jigging with small Swedish Pimples or plastic-bodied lead-head jigs. Anglers using bait take pickerel with large shiners suspended by a bobber. Fish any weedy areas along the shoreline for pickerel. Fly fishers also take pickerel by casting colorful streamers and bucktails; Mickey Finn is a choice pattern. Anglers using spinning tackle should use Dardevles, casting toward weedy areas and slowly retrieving the lure. Sometimes pickerel will make furtive slashes at your lure; if you change to a fast retrieve you will often elicit a strike.

Directions: From Waldoboro, drive north on Maine Route 32 toward Jefferson. Watch for a sign for the public boat ramp and Damariscotta Lake State Park on the left. Another boat ramp is located on Maine Route 213. This boat ramp is private and a fee is charged.

For more information: Contact the Maine Department of Inland Fisheries & Wildlife office in Augusta.

18. St. George River, Thomaston

Key Species: *striped bass, bluefish, mackerel possible*
Best Way to Fish: *boat*
Best Time to Fish: *late May through September*
MAG: *8, A-2*

Description: Upstream from the town landing in Thomaston, this river is swift and narrow. Downstream from the town landing, the river widens out and becomes more like a sheltered part of the ocean than a river. Opportunities for fishing from shore are limited except at the town landing. Camping is available at Camden Hills State Park in Camden and at private campgrounds in Thomaston and South Thomaston. Motels line U.S. Route 1 between Thomaston and Camden.

Fishing index: A medium-sized motorboat is all you need to fish upriver from the town landing. In late May, school stripers enter the river and fishing is good all the way upstream to the bridge over Maine Route 90. Most anglers troll with Rapalas or Rebels. Larger fish, some reaching or surpassing the legal length limit of 36 inches, enter the river in July. When menhaden are running, local anglers take bluefish from the town landing by using sections of menhaden as bait.

Downstream from the town landing is a good spot for boaters to take striped bass, bluefish, and mackerel. You must navigate well to avoid getting tangled in the many lobster traps and buoys. This is a working waterfront as well as a prime recreation area, so expect company. Fishing remains good through September. The author has taken bluefish downstream from the town landing in late September, and lunker striped bass are still in the upper stretches of river at that time of year.

Directions: Headed north on U.S. Route 1, look for a sign for the public boat ramp in Thomaston.

For more information: Contact The Outdoor Sportsman.

19. Rockland Breakwater

Key Species: *mackerel, striped bass, bluefish, cunner*
Best Way to Fish: *shore*
Best Time to Fish: *June through September*
MAG: *14, E-4*

Description: The Rockland Breakwater is a mile-long jetty built of massive blocks of granite. The breakwater itself is a scenic destination for hikers, but local anglers value it as a prime spot to fish from shore for saltwater species. This is a highly recommended site for families with children because of the endless variety of marine life, the magnificent scenery, and the lighthouse at the very end of the breakwater. Motels and inns are plentiful in Rockland.

Fishing index: Most anglers come for mackerel, bluefish, and striped bass. One other desirable species also live here. Cunners—a member of the wrasses,

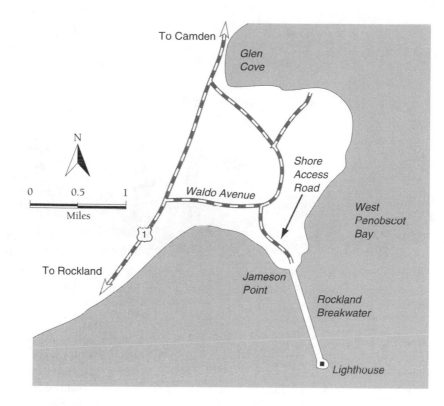

To Camden

Glen
Cove

N

Shore
Access
Road

0   0.5   1

Miles

Waldo Avenue

West
Penobscot
Bay

1

To Rockland

Jameson
Point

Rockland
Breakwater

Lighthouse

a mostly tropical group of fishes—live in the crevasses between the boulders. Cunners are easy to catch and good eating. All you have to do is lower a baited hook into one of the deep holes between the boulders that make up the breakwater and wait for a bite. You can use anything for bait, including bits of clam, strips of mackerel, or even a piece of baloney. Cunners weigh up to three pounds, and when skinned and filleted they are the makings of a gourmet meal.

Mackerel are usually taken by anglers with spinning tackle, using small spoons or small diamond jigs. When a school of mackerel passes by, you can fill a bucket in just a short time.

Striped bass and bluefish are taken by local anglers using mackerel and live eels as bait. Anglers using spin tackle take fish on a variety of lures, including large spinners, Swedish Pimple jigs, diving plugs (mackerel-colored Rebels are choice), and poppers. Fly fishers can take fish on top with fly-rod poppers. If surface activity is not present, use large, bushy streamer flies. Any heavily dressed, colorful pattern will do. Expect most striper activity early in the morning, on a coming or going tide. Walk the breakwater, looking for signs of activity.

The 1-mile-long Rockland Breakwater is a prime spot to cast for mackerel, stripers, and bluefish. A variety of marine life and the lighthouse on the end make this a favorite spot for the whole family.

Directions: From U.S. Route 1 in Rockland, head north and look for Waldo Avenue on the right. Go 0.5 mile down Waldo Avenue and look for the sign for Shore Access Road on the right. Go 1.4 miles down Shore Access Road. Near the end of the road, look for the Samoset Resort golf course on the left. There is ample parking at the end of the road. Follow the obvious path to the break-water, which is visible from the parking area.

For more information: Contact The Outdoor Sportsman.

20. OYSTER RIVER

Key Species: *brook trout, brown trout possible*
Best Way to Fish: *wading*
Best Time to Fish: *April through June*
MAG: *14, E-2*

Description: Oyster River is really a good-sized stream. Dense streamside brush makes fishing here difficult, but also keeps fishing pressure to a minimum. The route described here is easy to follow and should present no problems. However, the upper reaches of Oyster River flow through the Rockland Bog, a vast, almost trackless wetland. Anglers and hunters have gotten lost in this wild area, ironic when you consider how close the bog is to the city of Rockland. Rockland offers plenty of motels, and campgrounds are located in South Thomaston, Warren, Camden, and West Rockport.

20 Oyster River

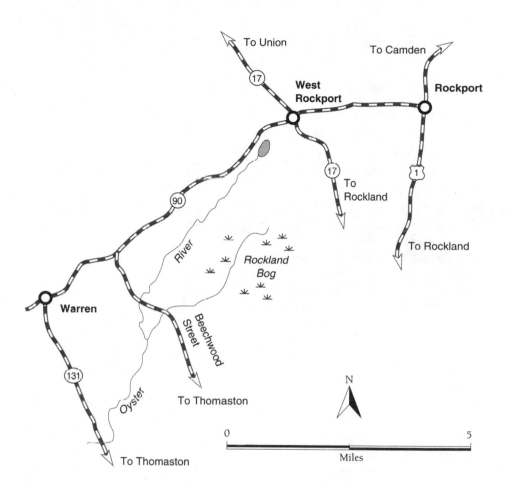

Fishing index: Some fly fishing is possible here, but casting is often difficult. You will do best by fishing downstream with small bucktails or streamers such as the gray ghost. So-called "long lining" is effective here. Stand above a productive-looking pool and strip out line until all your fly line is in the water. Let the fly hang in the current, giving it an occasional twitch, then reel in quickly.

Bait fishing accounts for most of the trout taken here. A worm, slowly fished on the bottom or allowed to drift through the deepest pools, is sure to bring a strike.

Native brook trout and some carry-over brown trout from past stockings will be active from mid-April until late June.

Directions: From Rockport, drive west on Maine Route 90, following the signs for Warren. At the four-way intersection of Maine Route 90 and Maine Route 17, go straight. About 5 miles past the intersection, look for Beechwood

Street on the left. Look for a stream crossing about a mile down Beechwood Street. You can fish from the bridge on Beechwood Street all the way downstream to where Oyster River crosses Maine Route 131.

For more information: Contact the Maine Department of Inland Fisheries & Wildlife Regional Fish and Wildlife Headquarters in Bangor.

21. SEVEN TREE POND

Key Species: *brown trout, white perch, largemouth bass, smallmouth bass, pickerel*
Best Way to Fish: *bank, canoe, boat*
Best Time to Fish: *April through September*
MAG: *14, D-1*

Description: Seven Tree Pond is a 490-acre flow-through pond for the St. George River. The pond is set in the hilly farm country typical of this part of Maine. It receives annual stockings of brown trout, usually 400 to 500 fish from 10 to 14 inches long. Within two years of stocking, these fish can gain several pounds and reach lengths of 17 to 20 inches. The upper half of the pond is the shallow end, with depths from 5 to 20 feet; the north end is from 20 to 45 feet deep. The pond is mentioned in *Come Spring*, a historic novel about colonial life in Maine by Ben Ames Williams. Ayer Park provides parking, picnicking, and a boat ramp.

Special regulations include a fall fishing season from October 1 to November 30; all trout, landlocked salmon, lake trout, and bass are to be released alive at once. Seven Tree Pond is a good example of the Open Water Fishing Regulations booklet sometimes mentioning fish that do not exist in the body of water cited. Landlocked salmon and lake trout are not even found in Seven Tree Pond. For this reason, you should not rely on the regulations booklet as a guide to fish species in a given body of water.

Fishing index: As soon as the ice leaves, usually in late April, white perch perform their annual spawning ritual near shore at Ayer Park, on the north end of Seven Tree Pond. Most anglers fish from shore using earthworms, but you can take spawning perch on small Mepps spinners and small lead-head jigs. Ultralight spinning tackle and 4-pound test line is best for perch fishing. Evening is the best time of day, but the fish remain until early morning. Since few anglers fish for spawning perch in the morning, you can have the shore to yourself as you catch a mess of tasty white perch. This is also the time to do some trolling for brown trout. Use a 9-foot fly rod of at least 6 weight and a sinking fly line. Troll with live minnows, tandem-hook streamer flies (gray ghost, black ghost, yellow perch, and Jerry's smelt), or lures such as Mooselook Wobblers and Flash Kings. Bass fishing is good all along the shoreline in May and June. Use poppers or deer-hair bass bugs in the early morning and evening; at other times, try black plastic worms. Both largemouth and smallmouth bass will respond to these lures. Later on in the summer and into September, try drifting with lead-head jigs for smallmouths in the south end of the pond.

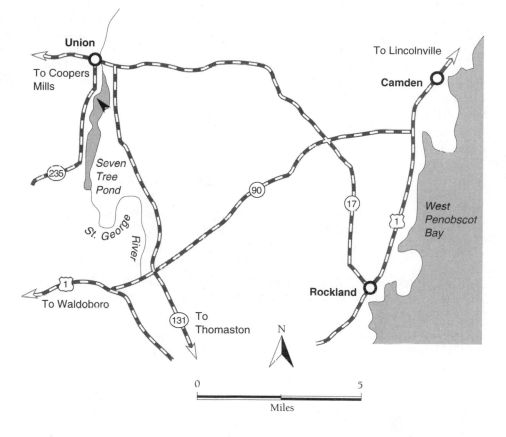

Directions: From Rockland, take Maine Route 17 north to Union. In Union, take Maine Route 235 south for about one mile. The park and boat ramp are on the left where the St. George River enters the pond.

For more information: Contact The Outdoor Sportsman.

22. MEDOMAK RIVER

Key Species: *brown trout, smallmouth bass, pickerel*
Best Way to Fish: *canoe, bank*
Best Time to Fish: *May through September*
MAG: *13, D-5*

Description: This small, quiet river flows through rolling farm country. The Medomak sees little fishing pressure except in early spring. From June through September, you may well have the river to yourself. The river is easily fished at several bridges, from shore, or from a canoe. Special fishing regulations include an artificials-only rule from August 16 to October 31 in the section from Winslow's Mills in Waldoboro to tidewater.

Fishing index: Medomak River is stocked annually with brown trout, but sees little pressure from trout anglers. Local anglers take browns in late April and May by fishing from the bank with night crawlers (wading is not recommended because of a silty bottom and sharp drop-offs in the larger pools). Fly fishers can take browns by using small bucktails (black-nosed dace, Edson tiger light, or any of the Thunder Creek series) on a sinking fly line. If you come in spring, bring some red quills and a few Adams in size 12, 14, and 16. Use medium or light tackle here because the river, for the most part, is really just a large stream. While May and early June are the best times for brown trout, smallmouth bass can be taken throughout the season. Smallmouth bass fishing is fantastic in September, when it is possible to take 30 or more fish in a day. Use ultralight spinning tackle and small plastic-bodied jigs.

If you do not have a canoe, stop at the various bridge crossings and fish the deep holes. Medomak Pond, a flow-through for the river, is a small but choice spot for brown trout and white perch.

Directions: From U.S. Route 1 in Waldoboro, take Maine Route 220 north for 7 miles. Look for a turnoff by a small bridge. Other sites include the U.S. Route 1 bridge in Waldoboro and the Wagner Bridge Road bridge, reached by driving north for 4 miles on Upper Depot Street from its intersection with U.S. Route 1 in Waldoboro.

For more information: Contact the Maine Department of Inland Fisheries & Wildlife Regional Fish and Wildlife Headquarters in Gray or the department office in Augusta.

23. SHEEPSCOT POND

Key Species: *splake, brown trout, lake trout, smallmouth bass, pickerel, white perch*

Best Way to Fish: *boat, canoe*

Best Time to Fish: *April through September, January and February*

MAG: *13, B-4*

Description: This productive, easily accessible 1,215-acre lake has a maximum depth of 150 feet. Sheepscot Pond is about halfway between Augusta and Belfast. You will need a boat or canoe to fish here because the shoreline is private, except for the area near the boat ramp. Prevailing winds can make the lake choppy on windy days, so pick a calm day to use a canoe.

Special fishing regulations include a minimum length of 14 inches on brook trout, splake, and lake trout. Nearby Lake St. George State Park in Liberty offers camping, and motels can be found on Maine Route 3 between Palermo and Augusta.

Fishing index: The depth of this lake makes it good habitat for lake trout. Try the deep hole off Iron Ore Point. In winter, use a large, dead shiner fished on the bottom; in summer, troll a large minnow behind lead-core line and trolling spoons.

Sheepscot Pond also receives annual stockings of splake. In 1995, 2,750 splake were planted here. In spring, or through the ice, try for splake around Bald Head and Leemans Arm. Fish with small minnows in about 20 feet of water (see splake in the species section for more details). As in most splake waters, the first few weeks of ice fishing season produce the most fish. Early and late in the day are the best times for splake; however, you should get slow but steady action throughout the day.

White perch grow large here, and the shallower water close to shore is best for them. When fishing for white perch in winter, use small minnows, Swedish Pimple jigs, or lead-head jigs in chartreuse with sparkle tails. In summer, use worms, small minnows, and lead-head jigs. For smallmouth bass, try Oak Point, off the west shore. Use Dardevles, Mepps spinners, or lead-head jigs. Early morning, mid-morning, late afternoon, and evenings are best for smallmouths.

Directions: From Augusta, take Maine Route 3 and head east for 20 miles. The state boat ramp is on the right, along the highway.

For more information: Contact Elma's Tackle Shop.

24. St. George Lake

> **Key Species:** *landlocked salmon, brook trout, smallmouth bass, white perch*
> **Best Way to Fish:** *boat, bank, canoe*
> **Best Time to Fish:** *April through September*
> **MAG:** *Map 14, B-1*

Description: This is a spring-fed lake with incredibly clear, cold water. In spite of some shoreline development, the lake retains a wild feeling because its rocky shoreline is lined with large pines and spruce trees. Lake St. George State Park is located on its shores, and lakeside camping is available. This is a good site for families with children.

St. George Lake is heavily stocked. In 1995 alone, 7,945 brook trout and 1,000 landlocked salmon were stocked here. Special fishing regulations on landlocked salmon include a one-fish bag limit and a 16-inch minimum length. The special open water fishing season runs from October 1 through October 31, with artificials only. All fish caught during that time must be released alive immediately.

Fishing index: Brook trout and salmon are the popular species here, but good smallmouth bass fishing can also be had all around the lake's rocky shoreline. In spring, anglers using worms as bait fish from shore by the boat ramp for stocked brook trout. Just after ice out, landlocked salmon are on top, ready for trollers. Streamer flies that imitate smelt are popular here, as are live smelt. Late afternoon through dusk is the best time of day to fish. From June through September, anglers take landlocked salmon in deep water using live minnows fished behind Dave Davis lake trolls with lead-core line. (See the species section for specifics on this technique.) Some of the largest landlocked salmon

A Midcoast angler displays an average-sized smallmouth bass from St. George Lake. Smallmouths are great acrobats and when hooked will spend as much time in the air as they do in the water!

have been taken in September, when fishing is fairly slow. St. George Lake is noted for trophy landlocked salmon, fish of 8 pounds and more. The author believes that fish weighing twice that much may be present here.

A companion body of water, Little Pond, is connected to St. George Lake by a narrow channel. This pond is shallow and weedy, great for largemouth bass, pickerel, and white perch. Most anglers use worms for white perch. Pickerel are sometimes taken by bass fishers using plastic worms, but live minnows are preferable. Largemouth bass anglers rely on plastic worms; black is a favorite color. In May, anglers using worms fish from shore for spawning white perch by the dam on Maine Route 173 in Liberty Village. Parking is limited, so you may wish to come by boat.

Directions: From Belfast, take Maine Route 3 west to Liberty Village. It is 17 miles from Belfast to the state boat ramp, located on the left of the highway.

For more information: Contact Elma's Tackle Shop.

25 ST. GEORGE RIVER HEADWATERS ———

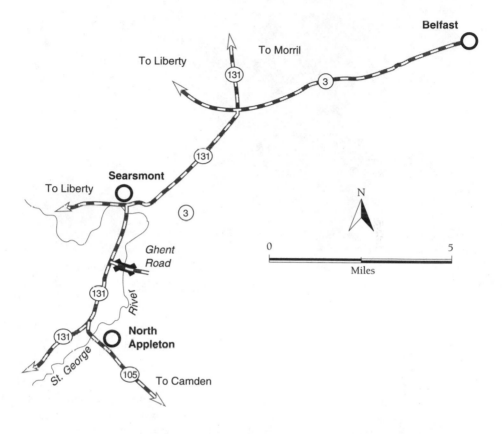

25. ST. GEORGE RIVER HEADWATERS ———

Key Species: *brown trout, brook trout and smallmouth bass possible*
Best Way to Fish: *wading*
Best Time to Fish: *April through November*
MAG: *Map 14, B-2*

Description: The St. George River, a 42-mile-long scenic trout stream, is specially managed for brown trout. It is one of a handful of Maine trout rivers where year-round angling is permitted. Wading is the best way to fish the river, but you can also fish from the bank in many areas. A whitewater canoe race takes place here each April, but fishing from a canoe is not practical. Special regulations include a 12-inch, 2-fish daily limit on trout, an open season from January 1 through December 31, and a 2.5-mile-long no-kill section from the Ghent Road in Searsmont to the upstream side of the Maine Route 105 Bridge in Appleton. Camping is available at Camden Hills State Park on U.S. Route 1 in Camden. There are motels in Camden, Northport, and Belfast.

Savoring the red quill hatch on the St. George River. Here, an angler keeps tension on a hefty brown trout. Long rods and fine leaders are the key to success here.

Fishing index: The river is heavily stocked with brown trout (in 1995, 3,000 8- to 10-inch trout were stocked in Appleton). There is a good carry-over rate, and fish up to 15 inches long are relatively common. Some native brook trout and smallmouth bass are present. This site is a haven for fly fishers, since most of the river is easily waded. In May and early June, fly hatches can be profuse, with a good variety of mayflies, as well as caddis flies. In early spring, stick to bucktails and nymphs. Fall fishing is sometimes a hit-or-miss proposition, but this is when some of the largest fish in the stream are taken. Dry-fly patterns to use in the fall include creme variants, hairwing royal coachmen, and any midge pattern in sizes 20 through 26. Bucktails, muddler minnows, black-nosed dace, and Jerry's smelt are all effective as well. In midsummer, water levels can drop, making the fish sluggish, except during morning and evening. Terrestrial patterns work well here when aquatic insects are not showing. One of the author's favorite terrestrials is a red, cork-bodied beetle in size 14.

Night fishing during periods of low water can be very productive. Sometimes you can hear the huge brown trout as they splash about and slurp in anything that happens to be on the water. Pay attention to the shallows, since the trout tend to be in unlikely places at night. Use big, bushy wet flies; black is the best color. Leech patterns are effective at night, too.

Directions: To get to the no-kill section of the river in Searsmont, take Maine Route 3 from Belfast and drive west for 7 miles to the intersection of Maine Route 131. Take Maine Route 131 south through Searsmont Village and continue south for 2 miles to the Ghent Road, on the left. You will see a bridge at the bottom of the hill. Park on the right side of the road, just past the bridge. The no-kill section starts below the bridge and continues on to the next bridge in North Appleton. The section above the bridge is not as heavily fished.

For more information: Contact the Maine Department of Inland Fisheries & Wildlife Regional Fish and Wildlife Headquarters in Bangor.

26. MEGUNTICOOK LAKE

Key Species: *brown trout, rainbow trout, smallmouth bass, large-mouth bass, white perch*
Best Way to Fish: *boat, canoe, bank, shore*
Best Time to Fish: *April through September*
MAG: *14, C-3 and D-3*

Description: This scenic 1,220-acre lake is studded with islands. The water is cold and crystal-clear, and the lake has a maximum depth of 64 feet. Fernald's Neck, a Nature Conservancy preserve, extends into the center of the lake. Another local landmark is Maiden Cliff, a rugged promontory on Mount Megunticook that is visible from most parts of the lake. Camden Hills State Park, in Camden, offers camping. Motels dot U.S. Route 1 between Camden and Lincolnville.

Fishing index: In spring, anglers fishing from shore near the boat ramp on Maine Route 52 take brown trout by fishing with worms and night crawlers on the bottom. Those in boats successfully troll around the islands with tandem streamers and single-hooked streamers such as Jerry's smelt, Mooselook Wobblers, and Flash Kings. White perch are taken in all parts of the lake. Most anglers prefer to drift in 10 to 40 feet of water, using worms and night crawlers as bait. You can do equally well with artificials. Use small lead-head jigs with plastic bodies, either the sparkle-tail kind or curlytails. Smallmouth bass are found near the islands and on the edges of rocky ledges; action can be good in spring, summer, and fall. Use the same jigs you would use for perch when fishing for smallmouth bass here. Smallmouths at Megunticook Lake seem to prefer yellow bodies above all other shades. Anglers also catch smallmouths by fishing a live minnow on bottom while slowly drifting. Purposely fishing for largemouth bass is almost a waste of time here because largemouths, while present, are vastly outnumbered by smallmouths.

Rainbow trout are a new addition to this site. In November 1994, the Megunticook Fish and Game Association stocked 3,600 10- to 12-inch rainbows at the lake. The association was working in cooperation with state biologists as part of an experimental 3-year project. Following that initial stocking, in May 1995, the author caught and released a 12-inch rainbow while trolling with a Jerry's smelt. Though small, the fish put up a good account of itself, a harbinger of things to come when the rainbows grow larger. These rainbows should provide exciting dry-fly action for fly fishers in May and June. Try size 14 hairwing royal coachmen. Early morning and evening should

An angler smiles as a feisty white perch strains her ultralight spinning rod at Megunitcook Lake. Notice the landing net at the bottom of the photo. When perch get over 12 inches, it is good practice to net them.

be the best times of day to take rainbows on dry flies, because then the water is calmest. You are encouraged to release any rainbow trout you catch here so that the species can have a better chance to prosper. Navigational buoys are set out to mark hidden ledges. You can profit by fishing near these buoys; the ledges harbor bait fish, which in turn attract trout and bass.

Directions: From U.S. Route 1 in Camden, take Maine Route 52 north for 3 miles. The state boat ramp is on the left. An alternate boat ramp is located on Maine Route 105 in Camden. There is a public swimming beach at the south end of the lake, just past the boat ramp.

For more information: Contact The Outdoor Sportsman.

27. BELFAST SHORELINE

  Key Species: *striped bass*
  Best Way to Fish: *boat, bank*
  Best Time to Fish: *late May through September*
  MAG: *14, A-4*

Description: The Belfast shoreline borders Belfast Bay, which is part of Upper Penobscot Bay. Weed beds just offshore harbor bait fish, which in turn attract striped bass. Boaters have difficulty reaching these weed beds at low tide because of rocks and shallow water, but shore-based anglers can fish here during any stage of the tide. Access is available at Belfast City Park, a scenic

27-28 Belfast Shoreline/Belfast Footbridge

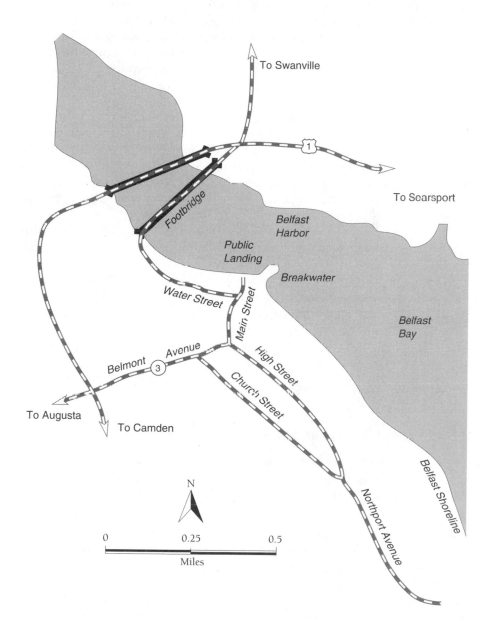

To Swanville

1

To Searsport

Footbridge

Belfast
Harbor

Public
Landing

Breakwater

Water Street

Main Street

Belfast
Bay

Belmont Avenue

3

High Street

Church Street

To Augusta

To Camden

N

Northport Avenue

Belfast Shoreline

0   0.25   0.5
Miles

day-use picnic area on the shores of Belfast Bay.

Fishing index: Striped bass enter the upper regions of Penobscot Bay in late May and remain all summer. Anglers using bait take school stripers as well as legal-sized fish by fishing on bottom. Favorite baits include whole mackerel, menhaden, live eels, and marine worms. You can dig your own marine worms on the local mudflats at low tide, and you can catch mackerel from the Belfast footbridge.

The author once made the mistake of trolling here using two rods at once. A 3-pound striper hit on the port rod at the same time as a considerably larger fish hit the Flash King on the starboard rod. In the ensuing battle, the smaller fish was landed and the larger fish escaped. Later that week, a friend of the author's fished here with lead-head jigs and took over 50 school-sized stripers in a few hours' time.

Most local anglers stand on dry land as they cast their bait out toward the kelp beds, but an angler willing to wade may have good sport using spinning or fly tackle. Fly fishers should use a weight-forward, sinking fly line with large, bushy streamer flies. If the stripers are visible on the surface, use poppers fished on a floating line. Anglers using spinning lures should try plastic eels and plastic minnow imitations such as shadow lures. Lead-head jigs with either white, green, or yellow bucktail or plastic curlytail bodies are effective as well.

A moving tide is best, either coming in or going out, because stripers disperse during extreme high and low tides. When the tide is moving, however, the fish always pass by this section of shoreline.

This is a popular spot for night fishing. Whole mackerel are the preferred bait then. Stripers of 20 pounds and more can be taken here during the nighttime hours.

Directions: From Camden, head north and east on U.S. Route 1 toward Belfast. At Belfast, take the first right turn just past an Irving service station on the left. Continue driving for about 0.5 mile and look for the sign at the entrance to Belfast City Park, on the right.

For more information: Contact The Outdoor Sportsman.

28. BELFAST FOOTBRIDGE

Key Species: *mackerel, striped bass, smelt, bluefish*
Best Way to Fish: *bridge*
Best Time to Fish: *June through September*
MAG: *14, A-4*

Description: This old highway bridge at the head of Belfast Harbor is now a public right-of-way for pedestrians and anglers, and a popular spot for shore-based anglers. You can fish from the bridge and watch lobster fishermen hauling traps at the same time. One of the East Coast's few remaining fish canneries is located near the bridge. U.S. Route 1 is lined with motels between Belfast and Searsport, and there are two campgrounds on the same stretch of highway.

Fishing index: From late June through September and sometimes into October, mackerel run under the footbridge with each tide. Anglers using bait catch mackerel on frozen shrimp, bloodworms, and cut-up mackerel. Swedish Pimple jigs and small Diamond Jigs are the most popular artificial lures for mackerel.

Striped bass, bluefish, and smelt are incidental catches. Local anglers employ the unusual but productive method of casting a diving plug and letting it wobble with the tide, without reeling in. Bluefish strike the plugs, seemingly out of spite. Be sure to fasten your rod securely if you try this. You should also bring an ice-filled cooler to preserve your catch.

In 1995, the mackerel run was small because unusually heavy rains had decreased the salinity of the seawater in Upper Penobscot Bay. This was an atypical occurrence. Striped bass were not daunted by the influx of fresh water, and anglers using herring or mackerel for bait had the best striped bass season in 25 years.

Depending on the stage of the tide, you may have to reel your fish up for a considerable distance after you get it out of the water. Make sure your line is strong enough to lift at least a 2-pound dead weight. If you hook a truly large fish, it is better to work your way to either end of the bridge and land the fish from the shore.

Directions: From Camden, take U.S. Route 1 to the intersection with Maine Route 3 in Belfast. Take the Belfast exit, and follow Main Street to its end at the Belfast waterfront. Turn left on Water Street and park off the road by the footbridge, next to Stinson Canning Company.

For more information: Contact The Outdoor Sportsman. You can also get a firsthand report from any angler you meet on the bridge.

Anglers flock to the Belfast Footbridge for mackerel, stripers, and bluefish. This old highway bridge is now a public right-of-way, offering easy access to great salt-water fishing.

29-30 GOOSE RIVER/PASSAGASSAWAUKEAG RIVER

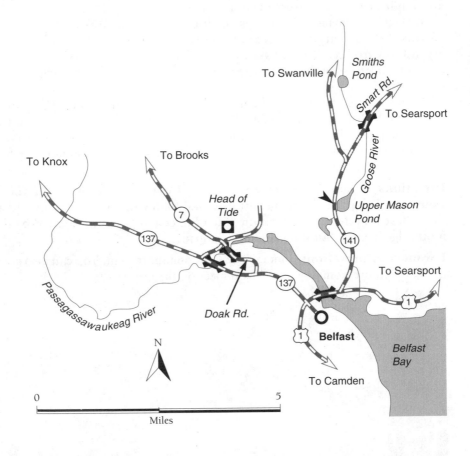

29. GOOSE RIVER

Key Species: *pickerel, white and yellow perch, brook trout*
Best Way to Fish: *canoe, bank*
Best Time to Fish: *May through September*
MAG: *14, A-4*

Description: Goose River, from the Belfast canoe launch on Maine Route 141 upstream to Smith's Pond, is about four miles long as the crow flies and at least twice that given all the twists, turns, and oxbows. A canoe is the best way to fish this river, but some fishing is possible from shore, especially by the Smart Road bridge. Wading is not possible; most of the river is too deep, and the bottom is covered in deep mud.

Goose River is a great spot for a leisurely day or half-day trip. Although the river is hardly a mile from the road on either side, it retains a truly wild aspect. In spring, waterfowl nest along the shore. Migrating warblers, red-winged blackbirds, and untold numbers of frogs unite in song, providing the angler with a relaxing natural concert. Families with children will also appreciate this river's unspoiled, soothing atmosphere. U.S. Route 1 in Belfast and Searsport is lined with motels, and there is a campground on U.S. Route 1 in Searsport.

Fishing index: Pickerel abound along the edges of the river's channel. Above Upper Mason Pond, the river has one riffly section, a good place to seek brook trout in late April and May. The section of river near the bridge on the Smart Road is also a good bet for brook trout. The rest of the river, all the way to Smith's Pond, is slow and fairly deep, with schools of yellow and white perch, plus lots of pickerel. Cast upstream as you paddle upstream, and troll on the way back. At night, local anglers fishing from shore catch large bullheads from the deep holes near the Smart Road bridge.

Directions: From Belfast, head north on U.S. Route 1 and turn left on Maine Route 141 immediately after crossing the bridge over the Passagassawaukeag River. Head north on Maine Route 141. After about 1.2 miles you will see a small parking area by the river and a sign for the Belfast canoe launching area. This launch offers the easiest river access and plenty of parking space. The Smart Road bridge is an alternative launch site but has little space for parking.

For more information: Both bait and advice are available from The Outdoor Sportsman and Ed's Bait Shop. Ed is a storehouse of knowledge, so do pick his brain!

30. PASSAGASSAWAUKEAG RIVER

Key Species: *brook trout, brown trout*
Best Way to Fish: *shore, wading*
Best Time to Fish: *April through June*
MAG: *14, A-4*

Description: This easily accessible river is often too high to fish in early April, because of whitewater resulting from snowmelt. As soon as water levels drop, anglers have plenty of room to fish from shore. Wading is possible, but the rocky bottom is very slippery, so you will need felts or other safety devices. The area below the falls at Head of Tide is tidewater. Most anglers call this river the Passy, rather than attempting to pronounce the full Native American name. Motels and campgrounds are located on U.S. Route 1 between Belfast and Searsport.

Fishing index: Sea-run brook trout enter the river in early spring. These sporty fish can be taken on bait as well as flies. Most anglers use worms, but small bucktails such as Edson tiger light and red-and-white are effective as well. In May, the section above Head of Tide holds stream-run brook trout that respond well to attractor patterns such as the royal coachman. Note that the sea-run brook trout do not enter the river all at once. When the run begins, it can last for many weeks, with groups of fish ascending the river on a daily basis. Sometimes cold weather and high water will keep the fish out of the river for a day or two.

In 1994, 130,890 brown trout fry were introduced into the river. As of the 1996 season, the first in which the outcome of this stocking could be assessed, results look encouraging. Some of these fry may go to the sea and return as adults, as do the native brook trout. Use light or ultralight spinning tackle and light fly tackle here, since the river is really no more than a large stream.

Directions: In Belfast, take Maine Route 137 west for about 3 miles to a bridge over the Passagassawaukeag River. Park well off the road on either side of the bridge and begin fishing downstream. To reach Head of Tide, continue on Maine Route 137 and turn right at the intersection of Maine Route 7. In less than a mile, you will see another bridge over the river. Park on the right side of the road and walk down the bank to the area beneath the falls. Be careful; the bank is steep and often slippery.

For more information: Contact The Outdoor Sportsman.

31. Swan Lake

> **Key Species:** *brook trout, landlocked salmon, lake trout, small-mouth bass, white perch*
> **Best Way to Fish:** *boat, canoe, bank*
> **Best Time to Fish:** *late April through early September*
> **MAG:** *22, E-5*

Description: This easily accessible lake is managed for coldwater game fish. The hills and mountains that surround Swan Lake give it a wild appearance, despite the seasonal and year-round cottages that dot the shoreline. In November, after the fishing season is closed, local anglers like to stand near the dam at the south end of the lake and watch the landlocked salmon perform their annual spawning ritual. Swan Lake is a heavy producer of smelt, a major factor in the fast growth of the lake's game fish. Special regulations include a minimum length on lake trout of 23 inches and a one fish per day bag limit. U.S. Route 1 between Belfast and Searsport is lined with motels. Camping is available along U.S. Route 1 in Searsport, and Swan Lake State Park, on the north end of the lake, offers a day-use picnic area and swimming beach.

Fishing index: Swan Lake receives heavy annual stockings of brook trout. Due to the large smelt population, trout and salmon have a high growth rate and brook trout of 15 to 18 inches are common. Swan Lake is not currently being stocked with lake trout, but a small population exists as a result of previous stockings. A deep trench running down the center of the lake is home to this site's lake trout.

Landlocked salmon fishing can be spotty here, but there is always the chance of catching a trophy fish. Ice-out fishing is best. Troll close to the rocky shoreline, using sparsely dressed smelt imitation streamer flies, Mooselook Wobblers, Flash Kings, or live smelt. Some anglers take landlocked salmon here all season long on live smelt and minnows, using lead lines and downriggers.

In April and early May, anglers line the road near the boat ramp on Maine Route 141. White perch congregate here in the evening and are readily taken on earthworms. Sometimes trout and landlocked salmon show up with the perch, adding an extra touch of excitement. This is a good spot to introduce a child to the joys of angling.

One of the best places for brook trout, even during the summer, is the northeast end of the lake. Underwater boulders provide cover for schools of minnows, which in turn attract brook trout. Anglers using bait take trout on worms and small minnows. Fly fishers often find caddis flies or winged ants on the surface and take fish on caddis and ant imitations. Small leech patterns, fished slowly and with a sinking fly line, also take brookies here. The water is always cool in this spring-fed lake, so the trout remain active here when other lakes are not producing.

Directions: From Belfast, head north and east on U.S. Route 1, and turn left on Maine Route 141, also known as Swan Lake Avenue. Follow Maine Route 141 past the dam at Swan Lake. The state boat ramp, the only facility on the lake, is located to the east of the dam, along the road.

For more information: Stop at Ed's Bait Shop on the way to Swan Lake.

32. FORT POINT STATE PARK FISHING PIER

Key Species: *mackerel, striped bass, bluefish*
Best Way to Fish: *pier*
Best Time to Fish: *June through September*
MAG: *15, A-2*

Description: Fort Point State Park is located on a peninsula at the head of Penobscot Bay and the mouth of the Penobscot River. This beautiful little park is off the beaten path, and the 200-foot fishing pier is never crowded. Floats alongside the pier can accommodate visitors who arrive by boat. There is a boat landing on the east side of Cape Jellison, off the West Cape Road. At the park, you can see the remains of historic Fort Pownall; an entrance fee is charged during the summer months. Camping is available off U.S. Route 1 in Searsport and on Verona Island, 3.5 miles upriver from Fort Point.

Fishing index: In summer, schools of mackerel swim near the fishing pier. Most anglers fish for mackerel with Swedish Pimple jigs or Diamond Jigs. Cast the jig as far as you can, allow it to sink a bit, and reel in quickly, jerking the rod as you reel to impart action to the jig. It is almost impossible to reel too fast to catch mackerel. Striped bass and sometimes bluefish offer opportunities for bigger game.

The best way to take stripers or bluefish here is to catch a mackerel and use it for bait. Hook the mackerel through the back, being careful not to touch the spine, and let it swim freely. When a striper or bluefish hits, strike as hard as you can in order to set the hook properly. If the mackerel is too close to the surface, you may need to add some weight to keep it down. Dead mackerel work nearly as well and do not need to be weighted. Once you have caught your mackerel, you can cook it at one of the park's seaside cooking sites.

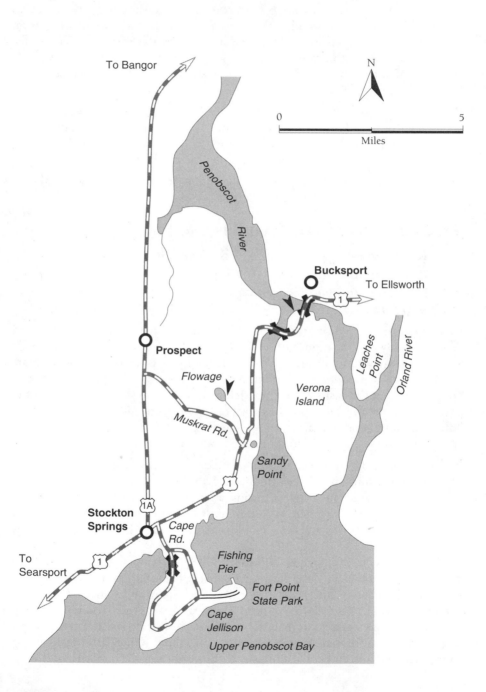

To Bangor

N

0   5

Miles

Penobscot River

Bucksport

To Ellsworth

(1)

Prospect

Flowage

Verona Island

Leaches Point

Orland River

Muskrat Rd.

(1)

Sandy Point

Stockton Springs

(1A)

Cape Rd.

To Searsport

(1)

Fishing Pier

Fort Point State Park

Cape Jellison

Upper Penobscot Bay

This bluefish put up a terrific fight on a fly rod. Note the small spoon still hooked to its jaw. Sometimes schools of hungry bluefish invade Upper Penobscot Bay, providing fast-paced action.

Directions: From Scarsport, head north on U.S. Route 1 to Stockton Springs. In Stockton, turn right off U.S. Route 1 just after the sign for Stockton Springs. In town, look for the Cape Road to the right, just past the post office, and a sign directing you to Fort Point State Park.

For more information: Call the Maine Department of Conservation Central Region Office.

33. SANDY POINT FLOWAGE

Key Species: *brook trout*
Best Way to Fish: *canoe, bank*
Best Time to Fish: *late April through June*
MAG: *23, E-1*

Description: This small pond and surrounding 543-acre parcel is managed by the Maine Department of Inland Fisheries & Wildlife. The pond is an impoundment, surrounded by wetlands and forest. Waterfowl nesting boxes have been built throughout the wetland, providing homes for the once-scarce wood duck. Wild rice has been introduced and serves as food for a wide variety of waterfowl. Easy access and the chance to get up close to nature make this a perfect spot for families with children. Some fishing can be done from the shore by the dam and boat ramp. Motels are available on U.S. Route 1 and U.S. 1A, and a campground is located on Verona Island.

Fishing index: Native brook trout are the main species here. Local anglers using worms begin fishing from shore in April, as soon as the ice leaves the pond. In May and June, when aquatic insects hatch, fly fishers canoe to the head of the pond where a small stream enters to take native brook trout on dry flies in the evening. Try small hairwing royal coachmen, Adams, dun variants, and caddis patterns. This pond gets little fishing pressure even though it is so close to busy U.S. Route 1.

Directions: Drive east on U.S. Route 1 in Stockton Springs. After going under a railroad bridge in Sandy Point, look for the Muskrat Road, on the left. The first right turn on the Muskrat Road, just a short distance from U.S. Route 1A, leads to the dam and boat landing on the Sandy Point Flowage.

For more information: Call the Maine Department of Inland Fisheries & Wildlife Regional Fish and Wildlife Headquarters in Bangor.

34. VERONA ISLAND

> **Key Species:** *striped bass*
> **Best Way to Fish:** *bank, boat*
> **Best Time to Fish:** *June through September*
> **MAG:** *23, E-2*

Description: Verona Island is set in the mouth of the Penobscot River, at the head of Penobscot Bay. The waters surrounding the island are an unheralded yet productive striped bass fishery. Fishing from shore is limited to the area around the boat ramp. You really need a boat to fish here effectively.

Historic Fort Knox, in Prospect, overlooks the river and Verona Island. The Waldo-Hancock suspension bridge connects the island to the mainland at Prospect, and a shorter, more modern bridge is its link to the mainland at Bucksport. There is a campground on Verona Island near the entrance to the Waldo-Hancock suspension bridge, and Bucksport offers plenty of motels.

Fishing index: Striped bass come to this section of the river in late May. Most of the early arrivals will be school fish weighing 3 to 6 pounds. Later in the summer, mature fish of 36 inches and more will enter the river. When the striped bass are running, you will see a handful of local anglers trolling around the island, but the crowds that haunt the more highly publicized striper rivers are not present here. Another plus is that the island's boat ramp is ideal, enabling you to launch even a large boat at any stage of the tide.

Most anglers troll with artificials. One popular lure is made from a length of black surgical tubing (any length from 8 to 10 inches will do) slid over a section of wire leader, with a single hook at the end. Other anglers have good luck using silver or blue Rebels. If you fish here in early summer, you can get by with medium-weight spinning tackle.

The deep water near the shore in front of Fort Knox is a good place to begin. You can troll completely around the island if you wish. If you head right after leaving the boat ramp, you can follow Leaches Point, on the left, to the mouth of the Orland River, another good spot. If you have plenty of fuel, you can fish the Penobscot River upstream all the way to Bangor, about 20 miles as the crow flies. A few anglers fish for school stripers in May and June by standing on shore by the boat landing. Lures for this include lead-head jigs with yellow or white bucktail tails, and small Rebels or Rapalas.

Directions: From Searsport, take U.S. Route 1 east and cross the Waldo-Hancock suspension bridge to Verona Island. A state boat ramp is on the left, just before you leave the island to enter Bucksport.

For more information: Contact The Outdoor Sportsman.

From late May through September, school-sized striped bass like this one offer continuous sport in the lower reaches of the Penobscot River.

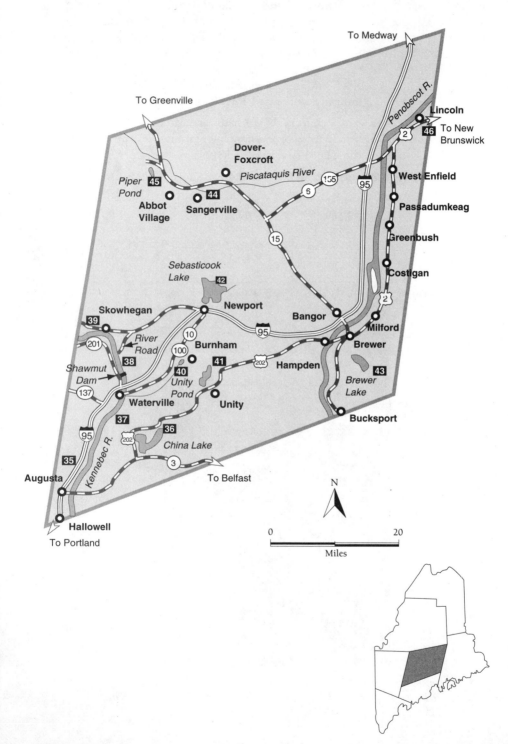

To Medway

To Greenville

Penobscot R.

Lincoln

To New
Brunswick

Dover-
Foxcroft

Piscataquis River

West Enfield

Piper
Pond

45

Passadumkeag

Abbot
Village

44

Sangerville

15

Greenbush

Costigan

Sebasticook
Lake

42

2

Skowhegan

Newport

Bangor

Milford

39

River
Road

10

Burnham

Brewer

201

100

202

Hampden

Brewer
Lake

43

38

Shawmut
Dam

40

Unity
Pond

137

Waterville

Unity

Bucksport

37

36

202

China Lake

35

3

Augusta

Kennebec R.

To Belfast

N

Hallowell

0   20

To Portland

Miles

CENTRAL MAINE

Central Maine holds two fantastic fishing areas, the Belgrade Lakes and the Kennebec River. Pike fishing in the Belgrades has become nationally famous, and the Kennebec River offers some of the best brown trout fishing in the nation.

This is Maine's heartland, a place where fishing and hunting are a way of life. Every general store has a fishing tackle selection, and you can still buy a dozen shotgun shells rather than a whole box.

Central Maine also offers some of the best largemouth bass fishing in the state. Bass fishing's newfound popularity has resulted in timely legislation designed to produce the heaviest fish possible. What is great fishing today will no doubt be even better in the future.

35. KENNEBEC RIVER, HALLOWELL TO AUGUSTA

Key Species: *brown trout, landlocked salmon, smallmouth bass, pickerel, white perch*

Best Way to Fish: *canoe, boat, shore*

Best Time to Fish: *May through July*

MAG: *12, C-5*

Description: This is a tidewater section of the Kennebec River; the Edwards Dam, in Augusta, is the head of tide. Much controversy exists over the continued use of this ancient dam, since the electricity produced here is not needed and the dam keeps the above-mentioned key species as well as shad, alewives, and Atlantic salmon from prime upriver spawning grounds.

If you do not have a boat or canoe, you can fish from shore by the boat ramps in Hallowell and Augusta and beneath the Edwards Dam in Augusta. There are plenty of motels in Augusta.

Fishing index: Even Maine residents are sometimes surprised to learn that the Kennebec River in Augusta and Hallowell provides some of the state's best brown trout, smallmouth bass, and striped bass fishing. Landlocked salmon fishing is good too, thanks to a recent stocking program and an impressive growth rate for game fish living in this fertile river.

Anglers fishing from shore in Hallowell use worms to take large white perch in spring and early summer. In early spring, boaters take brown trout, smallmouth bass, and landlocked salmon by trolling from the boat ramp in Hallowell to the dam in Augusta. Diving plugs such as Rapalas and Rebels are effective for all three species. Some fly-rod devotees take fish by casting or trolling with streamer flies.

The month of June is prime for school stripers. The fish congregate in the swift water below the Edwards Dam. Most of the fish you take will be school-sized, but sometimes a fish of 40 pounds or more will show up. It is best to have at least a medium-weight spinning rod and a reel with the largest line capacity you can find. Even so, in the spring of 1995, a friend of the author's who was fishing from a boat and armed with proper tackle hooked a fish that could not be stopped. Such experiences show that you should always be prepared to hook a monster when fishing in this amazing river. Fishing is best on an incoming or outgoing tide, and low tide is not usually productive.

Directions: The state boat ramp is on Route 201 in Hallowell, on the left. Parking is ample, and there is plenty of space to fish from shore. To get to the state boat ramp in Augusta, head north on U.S. Route 201 to the rotary in Augusta, and take the first right on the rotary. This takes you to a bridge over the Kennebec River. The boat ramp and small park are on the left.

For more information: Call the Department of Inland Fisheries & Wildlife in Augusta.

36. CHINA LAKE

Key Species: *brown trout, occasional salmon, occasional lake trout, occasional brook trout, largemouth bass, smallmouth bass, white perch, pickerel*
Best Way to Fish: *canoe, bank, boat*
Best Time to Fish: *May through September*
MAG: *13, B-3*

Description: This 3,922-acre lake is located just outside Augusta, Maine's capital city. The wide variety of species present makes China Lake a popular destination for Maine anglers. Hilly farmland and lakeside camps ring the shoreline, and the lake has a maximum depth of 85 feet. The shoreline may be crowded in springtime, during the white perch run, but boaters rarely experience crowded conditions. China Lake offers fishing from boats or canoes, or from the shore. Lodging is available at various motels on Maine Route 3 between Augusta and South China. You can also camp at Lake St. George State Park in Liberty.

Fishing index: Fishing is good throughout the season, but shore-based anglers flock here in May to take advantage of the huge white perch spawning runs near the breakwater at the north end of the lake in China Village. Most local anglers stick to worms fished beneath a bobber, but you can take your share of white perch with small spinners and lead-head jigs.

At the same time, anglers with boats troll for brown trout with streamer flies and live minnows at the north end of the lake in China and in that section of the lake just out from the boat ramp in East Vassalboro. In May and early June, you should troll fairly fast; as the season progresses, go slower and fish deeper. When brown trout were first introduced to this lake, fish weighing from 4 to 8 pounds were commonplace, but as with any new fishery, the average size has diminished somewhat. Still, fish of 4 and 5 pounds are taken each year, with the occasional larger specimen also appearing.

In summer, large brown trout are taken by deep trolling with live minnows as bait. Use the largest set of trolling spoons you can find. The preferred color is gold, but a gold and chrome combination is effective, too.

Bass fishers do well throughout the season, especially early and late in the day. Try fishing the shorelines with poppers or deer-hair bass bugs. During the day, try using plastic worms. You can do well with large minnows around the edges of weed beds.

Directions: From Augusta, take Maine Route 3 east toward China. Turn left at the intersection of U.S. Route 202 and head north to China Village, the breakwater, and a state boat ramp. Another state ramp is located in East Vassalboro, off Maine Route 32.

For more information: Contact Elma's Tackle Shop.

37. KENNEBEC RIVER, WATERVILLE

Key Species: *brown trout, smallmouth bass*
Best Way to Fish: *boat, canoe*
Best Time to Fish: *late April through June, and again in September*
MAG: *21, E-1*

Description: The river here is wide and powerful. You will need a boat or canoe to fish here effectively, since few opportunities exist to fish from shore. At the outset, this appears to be an urban setting, not a place where anyone would seriously consider fishing, but once you get out on the river the majestic oaks and willows that line the shore help create a feeling of solitude.

The area in front of the boat ramp is fairly deep and smooth, but a short distance downstream, the river becomes swift and relatively shallow. If you intend to go any distance downstream, be warned that you will probably hit some rocks with your propeller. You should use some kind of a prop guard. Anglers using a canoe may not be able to paddle back upstream if the river is in spate, so it may be wise to stick to the relatively quiet sections.

Special fishing regulations include a year-round open water season with a minimum length on salmon, trout, and lake trout of 12 inches and a daily bag limit of 2 fish in the aggregate. Motels are plentiful in Waterville.

Fishing index: This section of the Kennebec River may well contain more and bigger brown trout than any other body of water in the East. Fish weighing 4 pounds or more are not uncommon. Smallmouth bass weighing about 2 pounds are so numerous that you can take dozens of them in a day. Larger bass are always possible.

Early in the season, the best way to take both brown trout and smallmouth bass is to troll with diving Rapalas or similar minnow imitations. Your lure should ride just off the bottom for best results.

Later in the day, insect hatches bring thousands of brown trout to the surface. During the few but exciting hours between late afternoon and early evening, fly fishers can expect to see many hundreds of trout, especially during the red quill hatch. Consequently, red quills and small dun variants are excellent producers of fat brown trout. Terrestrials are productive in summer, even during daylight. Look for feeding lanes, places where the current carries surface matter to stationary trout. Most often, this will be along a steep bank or at the end of a ledge. Land-based insects are always falling from streamside

37-40 KENNEBEC RIVER WATERVILLE/SHAWMUT DAM/GREAT EDDY/SEBASTICOOK RIVER

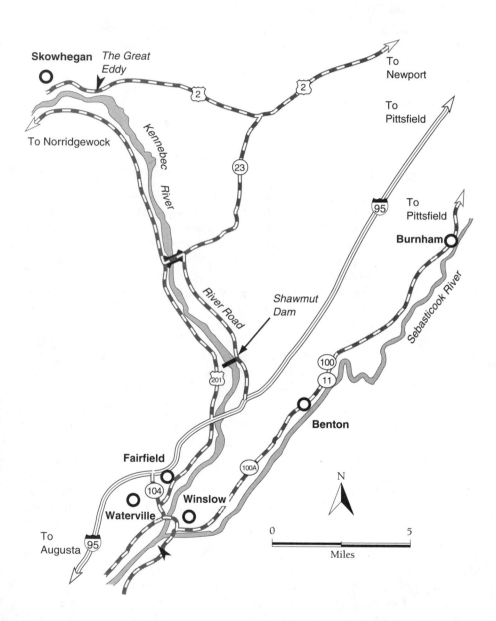

Skowhegan   The Great Eddy

To Newport

To Pittsfield

To Norridgewock

Kennebec River

2

2

23

95

To Pittsfield

Burnham

Sebasticook River

River Road

Shawmut Dam

201

100

11

Benton

Fairfield

100A

104

Winslow

Waterville

N

Benton

To Augusta   95

0   Miles   5

trees into the water. Try ants, grasshoppers (the Letort hopper is the author's favorite), beetles, and yellow jacket imitations.

Directions: From Augusta, take Interstate 95 north and get off at Exit 34. From Exit 34, take Maine Route 104, also called Main Street, to the intersection of Water Street at a rotary. On Water Street, look for signs for the boat ramp on the left, where you will find a modern ramp and ample parking.

For more information: Contact the Maine Department of Inland Fisheries & Wildlife Regional Fish and Wildlife Headquarters in Sydney.

38. KENNEBEC RIVER, SHAWMUT DAM ——————

Key Species: *rainbow trout, brown trout, smallmouth bass, landlocked salmon possible*
Best Way to Fish: *wading*
Best Time to Fish: *May and June*
MAG: *21, D-2*

Description: This section of river is a tailwater fishery, one of the few spots in Maine with an ongoing rainbow trout program. Wading is the best way to fish here, although it is possible to launch a canoe downstream from the dam. Special regulations on this section of river include artificial lures only, a minimum length limit on landlocked salmon, rainbow trout, and brown trout of 16 inches, and a daily bag limit on salmon, trout, and lake trout of one fish. Motels are located in the greater Waterville area, and Lake St. George State Park in Liberty offers lakeside camping.

Fishing index: Smallmouth bass were once about the only major sport fish in this formerly very polluted river, but this has changed. While smallmouth bass fishing remains good, brown trout and rainbow trout now provide excellent sport as well. This area is exceptionally good for fly fishers; the river here is easily waded and wide enough for you to get away from shoreline vegetation that might hinder your back cast. If you have a canoe, smallmouth bass be can taken by trolling with small orange Rapalas and by casting with lead-head jigs. Fly fishers take smallmouths by casting black leech patterns and muddler minnows.

Rainbow and brown trout are eagerly sought by fly fishers. In late April and early May, nymphs, Edson tiger light bucktails, single-hooked gray ghost streamers, Jerry's smelt, and, to an extent, wet flies such as soft-hackle flies take their share of trout. As water temperatures warm and quill Gordons, red quill, and Hendricksons begin to hatch, dry fly fishing reigns supreme. From late June and through the fall, trout contain their surface activity to the evening hours. Small dun variants, blue-winged olives, and various midges are all effective during the last half hour before dark. Daytime fly fishers might want to stick to a sinking fly line and nymphs, soft-hackle flies, or small leech patterns.

Few anglers, including the author, bother to fish here with anything but flies, but small Mepps spinners would also be effective for the trout, especially the rainbows.

The success of this rainbow trout fishery is attributable to the efforts of the Kennebec Valley Chapter of Trout Unlimited. Since 1992, this group has been releasing rainbow trout into the Shawmut tailwater. Fish over 22 inches long have been taken since then. Trout Unlimited strongly urges anglers to practice catch-and-release when fishing here.

Directions: From Fairfield, head north on U.S. Route 201 and drive about 5 miles, then look for the Shawmut Dam on the right. There is ample parking along the road. Walk down to the area below the dam and begin fishing. You can also get to the tailwater area by taking the River Road across the river from U.S. Route 201. You can see the dam easily from the road.

For more information: Contact the Maine Department of Inland Fisheries & Wildlife Regional Fish and Wildlife Headquarters in Sydney.

39. THE GREAT EDDY

> **Key Species:** *brown trout, smallmouth bass, white perch, landlocked salmon possible*
> **Best Way to Fish:** *canoe, boat, bank*
> **Best Time to Fish:** *May and June*
> **MAG:** *21, B1*

Description: The Great Eddy is a wide spot in the Kennebec River. The men of Benedict Arnold's ill-fated expedition came through the Great Eddy on their way to attack Quebec. You can easily fish from the bank along Route 2, but the Great Eddy is generally too deep for wading. However, the river can be waded upstream from the Great Eddy, where the water gets riffly and shallow. A boat or canoe will let you cover more water.

The river here is open to year-round fishing. Special regulations include a minimum length on landlocked salmon and trout of 12 inches and a daily bag limit of two fish in the aggregate.

You will find a picnic area and boat ramp at Kennebec Banks, on the Great Eddy. Skowhegan offers plenty of motels, and there is a campground on U.S. Route 2, just past the Great Eddy.

Fishing index: The brown trout fishing here is excellent. In early spring, local anglers fish from shore with night crawlers and take brown trout of up to 4 pounds. From shore, it is possible to take fish by spinning and fly casting, but the biggest trout always seem to show just out of casting range, a frustrating situation.

If you have a boat or canoe, troll upstream from the boat ramp to the head of the Great Eddy, where the water becomes too shallow for navigation. Drift back and cast toward shore. If you repeat this process, you will be able to mark spots where you get a strike and be prepared the next time you pass by. Work both shores in this manner.

In May, profuse hatches of red quills make the surface of the river come alive with brown trout. This spectacle resembles the feeding binges of striped bass in salt water. Try to get as close as possible to rising trout because the strong current will quickly make bellies in your line if you try a long cast. Use a red quill or small dun variant and drift it over feeding trout, being ever watchful of line drag. This is big water and the fish, especially during the red quill hatch, are not too leader-shy.

In most cases, you can easily get by with a 3-pound test tippet. Use at least a 9-foot, 6-weight fly rod and floating, weight-forward fly line.

Downstream from the Great Eddy, the river becomes tranquil. It is dotted with islands, where local residents pick fiddlehead ferns in the spring. These islands are good places to fish for smallmouth bass. Try trolling with small orange Rapalas. Fly fishers can do well by casting and slowly retrieving leech imitations, woolly buggers, and muddler minnows.

Directions: From Skowhegan, take U.S. Route 2 east. Two miles from town, you will see the boat ramp and picnic area at Kennebec Banks, on the shores of the Great Eddy.

For more information: Contact the Maine Department of Inland Fisheries & Wildlife Regional Fish and Wildlife Headquarters in Sydney.

40. SEBASTICOOK RIVER, BURNHAM

> **Key Species:** *smallmouth bass, pickerel, white perch, crappie, brook trout and brown trout possible*
> **Best Way to Fish:** *canoe, bank*
> **Best Time to Fish:** *May and June*
> **MAG:** *21, C-4*

Description: This is a slow-moving river, best for warmwater species. It is easily accessible and a good spot to fish with children because of the wide variety of species available. Bank fishing, wading, and canoeing are all popular fishing methods. Dams at Winslow and Benton are also popular spots, with wading and bank fishing available. A hand-carry boat ramp is located above the dam in Winslow, and the river is navigable all the way upstream to Benton. Special fishing regulations include an extended artificials-only fishing season with a 16-inch length limit and a reduced bag limit on salmonids. Check the Open Water Fishing Regulations booklet for details.

Fishing index: The pool below the dam in Burnham is a good place to start. Use ultralight spinning tackle for the above-mentioned warmwater species. Small Mepps spinners can be deadly here on white perch and crappie. Small lead-head plastic-bodied jigs in chartreuse and yellow are effective too. Use Dardevles and Mooselook Wobblers for pickerel, casting the lures, allowing them to sink, and slowly reeling them back. Be sure to impart plenty of teasing action in order to stimulate pickerel. Smallmouth bass are taken on spinnerbaits and curlytail jigs. Watch the line as your jig sinks, because smallmouths often pick up the lure as it falls to the bottom.

On weekdays, you may have this place to yourself. However, this site can be a popular place on weekends and evenings in May, when local anglers come to catch white perch. If you want to get in on the action, or simply enjoy the social aspect of fishing, use light spinning tackle and worms or night crawlers. Most local anglers use bobbers, but you will get more hits (and lose more hooks) by fishing your worm on the bottom. A small split shot may be needed to add extra weight for casting.

You can launch a canoe above the dam, although there is no formal ramp. Upstream, you will come to some islands, as well as riffly areas, coves, and weed beds. Good smallmouth bass and crappie fishing can be found in this part of the river.

Directions: From Winslow, which is across the Kennebec River from Waterville, take Maine Route 100A north to Benton, where the road becomes Maine Routes 100 and 11. Continue north on Maine Routes 100 and 11 to Burnham, where you will see a dam on the Sebasticook River, right along the road.

For more information: Contact the Maine Department of Inland Fisheries & Wildlife Regional Fish and Wildlife Headquarters in Sydney.

41. UNITY POND

> **Key Species:** *brown trout, largemouth bass, smallmouth bass, white perch, pickerel, cusk, crappie*
>
> **Best Way to Fish:** *canoe, boat*
>
> **Best Time to Fish:** *May through September, January through March*
>
> **MAG:** *21, D-5 and 22, D-1*

Description: This 2,528-acre lake is set in the midst of rolling farm country. Much of the lake is surrounded by marshes. Unity Pond is the largest lake in Waldo County, and though popular with local anglers, it is never crowded. Motels are available in Hampden and Bangor.

Fishing index: Although Unity Pond receives annual stockings of brown trout, this species is largely underfished. May is the best month to find brown trout near the surface. Troll for browns during the day, using Mooselook Wobblers, live minnows, gray ghost streamers, Jerry's smelt, and yellow perch streamers. Try dry flies in the evening. Use red quills, Hendricksons, caddis patterns, and dun variants. Look for brown trout near the shoreline at the southeast end of the pond and around the islands.

The most popular species here is largemouth bass. The area to the west of the boat ramp, near the railroad trestle, is a prime spot for bass early and late in the day. Use 6- or 8-inch black, red, and purple plastic worms. Cast toward the brushy shore and allow the worm to settle, and retrieve it by raising and lowering the rod, reeling in the slack, then repeating the process. Use at least an 8-pound test line because the bass will head for the cover of the shoreline brush. Poppers will produce early in the morning and toward evening. Two old favorites include Jitterbugs and Hula Poppers. June is the best month for bass.

Black crappie are also found here, but are rarely taken in large numbers. This may be because few Maine anglers are experienced in fishing for crappie. You should use small minnows, fished in about 20 feet of water. You can also use small lead-head jigs; the curlytail variety is a good choice. A fish locator will help you find schools of crappie. Crappie tend to run large here, up to 2.5 pounds.

Pickerel abound along the marshy shores of Unity Pond. Try using any heavily dressed yellow bucktail. Spinning lures include Daredevles and red

These white-perch anglers are staying close to shore, using the trees as a windbreak. Tip-ups, with live minnows as bait, are commonly used for perch.

plastic worms. Schools of white perch provide plenty of action throughout the summer months for anglers using bait. Use small minnows or worms, fished on bottom. Try drifting in 10 to 30 feet of water. If you get more than one bite in any location, go back to that point and drift over it again.

Ice fishers park near the boat ramp and walk out toward the center of the lake, where they fish in 20 feet of water for brown trout, crappie, and bass. Most anglers use tip-ups, baited with small minnows. Suspend the minnows at varying depths because while bass may be near the bottom, crappie may be at any level and brown trout can often be taken directly under the ice.

Directions: From Hampden, just south of Bangor on U.S. 1A, take U.S. 202 west to Unity. Upon entering town, look for a cemetery on the right and a gravel road just past the cemetery. Follow the gravel road to the boat ramp.

For more information: Contact the Maine Department of Inland Fisheries and Wildlife Regional Fish and Wildlife Headquarters in Bangor.

42. SEBASTICOOK LAKE

Key Species: *largemouth bass, smallmouth bass, white perch, pickerel, cusk, crappie*
Best Way to Fish: *boat, canoe, bank*
Best Time to Fish: *May through September*
MAG: *22, A-2*

Description: This 4,288-acre lake is managed for warmwater species. Once polluted, the lake has bounced back and now provides good fishing. A prehistoric fish weir, recently discovered at this site, is one of the oldest signs of human habitation in the country. Anglers fish from boats or canoes and from the shore. Special regulations include an extended open water season from October 1 through November 30, during which all trout, lake trout, landlocked salmon, and bass must be released alive at once. Newport offers motels, and there is a campground on U.S. Route 2, just west of town.

Fishing index: Numerous points and inlets provide good holding spots for largemouth bass. Anglers using large golden shiners take largemouths by hooking the shiner through both lips and slowly drifting it on the bottom at the mouths of inlets. Plastic worms are effective along the shorelines. Try brightly colored worms with sparkle added to the body; the water here is often murky, and brighter lures are more likely to attract bass.

The rocky eastern shoreline is perfect for smallmouth bass. Use night crawlers, drifted on the bottom. Be sure to hook the crawler near the head in order to present a more lifelike appearance. Lead-head jigs with white, yellow, or green plastic bodies are effective here, as are small spinnerbaits. In May and early June, anglers fishing from the bridge and roadside catch white perch and crappie on worms, night crawlers, and small minnows. At this site, the author's favorite bait is a small minnow, fished on bottom. If you do not get an immediate hit, slowly bring the minnow back by gently lifting the rod and reeling in the slack. When you feel a bite, give slack line and when the line tightens up, strike the fish.

This is a popular spot in the evening, so come early in order to find a good location. This is also a good opportunity to share fishing techniques with other anglers. The narrow section on the side of the bridge opposite the main body of the lake is surrounded by marshlands and is a perfect place to cast plastic worms for largemouth bass from a canoe. A gravel boat ramp is located just past Durham Bridge, on the left.

The middle and north end of the lake has the deepest water and is a good place to take white perch on the bottom in summer. Use worms and small lead-head jigs. A Swedish Pimple is effective here if you tip the hook with a bit of worm or minnow.

Directions: In Newport, look for a small park on Maine Route 7 and 11, next to the American Legion hall. The park offers benches and a concrete boat ramp.

For more information: Contact the Maine Department of Inland Fisheries & Wildlife Fish and Wildlife Headquarters in Sydney.

In May, this shoreline at Sebasticook Lake is lined with anglers fishing for spawning white perch. Note the rocky ledge extending into the lake in the center of the photo. This is a prime spot for bass and crappie.

43. BREWER LAKE

Key Species: *white perch, landlocked salmon, pickerel*
Best Way to Fish: *boat, canoe*
Best Time to Fish: *May through September*
MAG: *23, C-3*

Description: A boat ramp at the north end of the lake provides access to 881-acre, 49-foot-deep Brewer Lake. You will need a boat or canoe to fish here. Brewer Lake is dotted with cottages and is a popular spot for sailboats. Nearby Holden offers a campground, and motels are available in Bangor and Brewer.

Fishing index: Brewer Lake is a popular panfish lake, and few anglers take advantage of the landlocked salmon fishery. Nevertheless, salmon fishing is good here. The lake receives annual stockings of salmon and has a healthy population of fish weighing 4 pounds or more.

From June through September, white perch anglers can take fish away from the shorelines, anywhere the water is more than 20 feet deep. Bait fishing is most productive; the most popular baits are earthworms, night crawlers, and small minnows, in that order.

You can take salmon by trolling around the shorelines in early spring. Use tandem streamers such as gray ghost. The ever-faithful Jerry's smelt is another good choice. You can also take salmon by trolling with Mooselook Wobblers in chrome or copper, and with orange and gold Flash Kings. Be sure to use a rudder if you plan to troll with spinning tackle. Troll fast and follow an erratic pattern. When summer comes, a 48-foot-deep hole in the center of the lake holds many salmon, drawn by the cool water. Use deep-trolling techniques, such as lead-core line and a minnow behind a set of lake trolls, or a minnow or Jerry's smelt fished with a downrigger.

Pickerel can be found around the islands at the north and south ends of the lake. Use small Dardevles, Mepps spinners, or any bucktail containing yellow or orange.

Directions: From Bucksport, head north on Maine Route 15. In Orrington, just one mile from the Brewer line, turn right on the Snows Corner road. Continue on the Snows Corner Road, and go straight through a 4-way intersection, which will lead you to the lake. Turn right at the 2-way intersection and follow that road to the boat ramp.

For more information: Contact the Maine Department of Inland Fisheries & Wildlife Regional Fish and Wildlife Headquarters in Bangor.

44. PISCATAQUIS RIVER

Key Species: *brown trout, brook trout*
Best Way to Fish: *wading, bank*
Best Time to Fish: *June through September*
MAG: *31, between B-5 and C-5*

Description: This specially regulated river has good fly hatches and few fly fishers. Some sections are too deep to wade, but can be fished easily from the bank. Most Maine anglers pass right by this river on their way to the storied waters of the north woods. Expect lots of solitude. In Guilford, a mile-long public lane bounds the river. You can sit on a bench and watch for rises, as the British gentry did a century ago.

Fishing index: The Piscataquis River is a genuine success story for brown trout. In years past, the river was stocked with brook trout, but few fish survived the warm summer temperatures. Since their introduction, brown trout have managed to carry over, and annual stockings have kept the population at a maximum. Brown trout up to 15 inches are common. Be sure to fill out a card at the angler survey box by the Maine Route 23 bridge; your input is valuable.

In May, when the red quills are hatching, red quills, Hendricksons, or small dun variants will take fish. Try dry-fly fishing with small dun variants if no insect activity is present. In May and early June, a few variants should be all you need for dry flies. Later, caddis flies begin to hatch and any caddis imitation will be effective. The author once hooked and lost a mighty brown trout here when the current pulled his line at the end of a cast and submerged his caddis imitation. The fish had struck during the line pickup.

If dry flies do not do the trick, try using single-hooked bucktails. Because of the many brook trout, an Edson tiger light is a good choice. Browns love this fly, too. If the water is high, use a sinking fly line. Otherwise, stick with a floating line. Cast quartering upstream and let the current take the fly down-

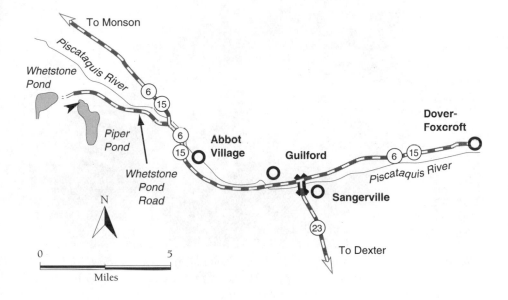

stream. Hesitate at the end of the drift. Let your fly hang in the water and give the rod a few twitches. This will sometimes spur a reluctant trout's aggressive tendencies. Use a weight-forward fly line here, since you may need to make long casts in order to reach fish out past the midpoint of the river.

Although local anglers fish here with small spinners and spoons, the author has seen few fish taken in this manner.

Directions: From Dover-Foxcroft, take Maine route 15 west toward Guilford. Turn left at the intersection with Maine Route 23 in Guilford, and park by the bridge. You can find fish both upstream and downstream from the bridge.

For more information: Call the Maine Department of Inland Fisheries & Wildlife Regional Headquarters in Greenville.

45. PIPER POND

> **Key Species:** *splake, brook trout possible, white perch, pickerel, landlocked salmon possible*
> **Best Way to Fish:** *boat, canoe*
> **Best Time to Fish:** *May through September, January through March*
> **MAG:** *31, B-3*

Description: Piper Pond, a specially managed splake water, is easily accessible. The shoreline has some development, in the form of seasonal cottages.

The Bridge Pool on the Piscataquis River. The glassy slick shown here is perfect for dry-fly fishing, while the riffles and fast water downstream are perfect spots to work a steamer or bucktail.

At 420 acres, the entire pond is easily fished from a boat or canoe, or through the ice. The deepest section (56 feet) is in the geographic center. There is little opportunity to fish from shore. Special regulations on splake and trout include a slot limit and a 2-fish daily bag limit. You can camp at nearby Peaks-Kenny State Park, and there are motels in Greenville, just north of Abbot.

Fishing index: Piper Pond receives annual stockings of splake, usually sometime in early May. Most anglers come here for the splake, and most splake are taken in winter. Small golden or silver shiners are the preferred bait. Using tip-ups, attach a leader of no more than 4-pound test to the end of the line and hook your shiner through both lips. Use only one small split shot for weight. Using a sounder to establish the depth, begin fishing in about 20 feet of water. When a splake bites, let it run with the bait before striking. Piper Pond splake are masters at stealing bait and will kill and drop your bait if they feel any resistance before they actually swallow it. Refer to the splake section of this book for detailed fishing techniques.

The best splake fishing, winter or summer, is found in about 20 feet of water, around points of land and near the mouths of coves. As you head south from the boat ramp, either side of the lake about halfway down is good for splake.

In May and June, anglers with ultralight spinning tackle can take splake by fishing near bottom with either earthworms or small minnows.

In summer, white perch can be taken in the middle of the lake with worms or live or dead minnows. Look for pickerel in weedy areas along the shores.

Directions: From Abbot Village, drive north on Maine Routes 6 and 15 and take the Whetstone Pond Road, which is the first road on the left. At about 4 miles, look for a public boat ramp on the left. Ample parking is available at the ramp.

For more information: Contact the Maine Department of Inland Fisheries & Wildlife Regional Fish and Wildlife Headquarters in Greenville.

46. Penobscot River, Lincoln to Costigan

Key Species: *smallmouth bass, pickerel*
Best Way to Fish: *boat, canoe*
Best Time to Fish: *May through September*
MAG: *43, E-4 and 33, B-4*

Description: This is a wide river with a moderate flow, a popular destination for float trips except during periods of high water when the river is powerful and can be dangerous for boating. There are plenty of access points and some opportunities to fish from shore. A special no-kill season is in place from October 1 to November 30. Campgrounds are located in Eddington and Enfield, and motels are scattered along U.S. Route 2.

Fishing index: Smallmouth bass are the main species on this section of the river. Fish average about 2 pounds, but 3- and 4-pound specimens are fairly common. It is possible to take dozens of fish in a day. Most anglers use spinning tackle. Small jigs, buzzbaits, Rapalas, Rebels, and small spinners are all effective. A few anglers use fly tackle and get tremendous action. Woolly buggers, leeches, and small poppers are favorite flies.

You can fish from shore from the various boat landings and at several access points along U.S. Route 2, but you will find that a canoe or small boat lets you enjoy the best fishing. If you have two vehicles, you can plan a day's float trip. Leave one vehicle at the take-out point and drive to the put-in point with the other vehicle. This will let you fish either side of the river at a leisurely pace. The Penobscot is one of the best smallmouth bass fisheries in the world; be prepared to take pictures of the action you are sure to enjoy. If you are not making a float trip, you may want to concentrate on the conglomeration of islands in Greenbush. There is a picnic table by the boat ramp.

Directions: From Milford take U.S. Route 2 north to Lincoln. Boat ramps are located along the road in the river towns of Milford, Costigan, Greenbush, Passadumkeag, West Enfield, and Lincoln.

For more information: Contact the Maine Department of Inland Fisheries & Wildlife Regional Fish and Wildlife Headquarters in Bangor.

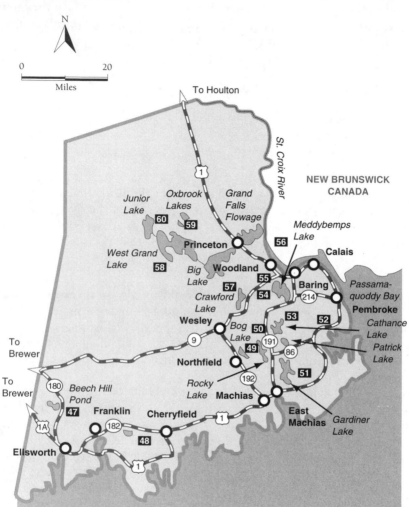

N

0 ——— 20
Miles

To Houlton

St. Croix River

NEW BRUNSWICK
CANADA

Junior
Lake

Oxbrook
Lakes

Grand
Falls
Flowage

[60] [59]

[56]

Meddybemps
Lake

Calais

Princeton

West Grand
Lake

[58]

Big
Lake

Woodland

[55]

[54]

Baring

Passama-
quoddy Bay

[57]

Crawford
Lake

(214)

Pembroke

Wesley

Bog
Lake

[50]

[53]

[52]

Cathance
Lake

To
Brewer

9

[49]

(191)

(86)

Patrick
Lake

Northfield

(192)

[51]

To
Brewer

(180)

Beech Hill
Pond

Rocky
Lake

Machias

**East
Machias**

Gardiner
Lake

[47]

Franklin

Cherryfield

1

(182)

Ellsworth

1A

[48]

1

Downeast Maine

Downeast Maine comprises Hancock and Washington counties, although there are no hard and fast boundaries to this region. What makes Downeast unique is the great number of lakes, rivers, and streams, along with the unspoiled nature of the region. There are plenty of places to camp and enjoy the outdoors.

Several species stand out in Downeast fishing. Native brook trout and landlocked salmon abound, and are the favorite species of Maine anglers. Additionally, Downeast Maine probably contains more high-quality smallmouth bass waters than any other part of the country.

47. Beech Hill Pond

Key Species: *lake trout, landlocked salmon and brook trout possible, white perch, pickerel*
Best Way to Fish: *boat, canoe*
Best Time to Fish: *June through September*
MAG: *24, C-1*

Description: This 1,351-acre pond has a deep trench running east to west down its center. The deepest point is 104 feet, perfect for huge lake trout. No practical opportunity exists for fishing from shore, but you can launch a boat at the private boat ramp. If you fish here in winter, be sure to get a copy of Maine's ice fishing regulations. Motels are available in Ellsworth, and you can camp at nearby Lamoine State Park.

Fishing index: A remnant population of landlocked salmon and some brook trout attract local anglers, but lake trout are the major species. Beech Hill Pond produces some of Maine's largest lake trout, and most are taken by ice fishing. If you come here in the winter, fish in the middle of the pond, where depths range from 90 to 104 feet. Use tip-ups and bait your hook with the largest golden shiners you can find. An 8-pound test leader is ideal. Suckers are productive here, too. You might want to kill your bait in order to ensure that it stays on the bottom where a lake trout can find it. Set your tip-ups far enough apart so that a fish, taking one hook, cannot easily get tangled in another line. Lake trout are often slow to bite, so you will need patience. As long as you are confident that your bait is on the bottom, you can do no more. Sometimes the fish will just turn on, and when that happens, you might get two or three bites at once.

Some anglers take lake trout by jigging with a large Swedish Pimple. A bit of minnow on the hook may bring more strikes. When jigging for lake trout, be sure that your reel has a functional drag and is loaded with least 100 yards of 8-pound test line. Lake trout bite best here around dawn, but fish are taken throughout the day. The chance to take huge lake trout attracts crowds of anglers, but despite the fishing pressure, the lake remains a steady producer.

In late April and May, you should concentrate on the areas closer to shore where the water is not so deep. Still-fish or troll with large shiners. Later on, use deep-trolling methods in the middle of the pond, either lead-core line and lake trolls with a minnow behind, or a minnow fished with a downrigger. You can also take lake trout with lead-core line, a large dodger, and a Jerry's smelt tied a few inches behind.

Directions: From Ellsworth, head west on U.S. Route 1A. At Ellsworth Falls, turn right on Maine Routes 179 and 180. Continue on Maine Routes 179 and 180, and bear left on Maine Route 180 where the combined roads separate. Continue north on Maine Route 180 and watch for signs for the Green Lake Fish Hatchery. Just past the hatchery sign, you will come to a fork in the road. Turn left at the fork onto the Gary Moore Road. At about 2.3 miles, you will cross a stream. Take the first left turn just past the stream. Follow this road to the private boat ramp.

For more information: Contact the Maine Department of Inland Fisheries & Wildlife Regional Fish and Wildlife Headquarters in Bangor.

48. Fox Pond

    Key Species: *brown trout, brook trout*
    Best Way to Fish: *canoe, bank*
    Best Time to Fish: *May through September*
    MAG: *24, D-5*

Description: This small, 77-acre pond is set in one of Downeast Maine's most scenic areas. It is a great spot to fish from shore, since one side of the pond is entirely bounded by Maine Route 182. If you are visiting any of the other sites in Downeast Maine, you might want to set aside a few hours to visit this beautiful spot as well. Special fishing regulations are a two-fish bag limit on trout and an artificials-only, no-kill season from October 1 through October 31.

Fox Pond is overlooked by most anglers because it is so small, yet it receives annual stockings of brook and brown trout. If you spend much time here, you can expect to catch some carry-over fish. The water remains fairly cool even in summer. As you drive by the pond, it is not unusual to see dozens of trout rising, a temptation to stop and have a go at them.

Maine Route 182 bounds the entire north side of the pond, allowing anglers to fish from any point on its rocky shores. This is a great spot to take children on their first trout-fishing trip because it is so easily fished and they will have a reasonable chance of catching something. An earthworm, fished on the bottom, is the easiest way to get a child tied onto a trout. Campgrounds are located in Orland, East Orland, Ellsworth, and East Sullivan.

Fishing index: Fly fishers can paddle this calm pond and troll for trout during the day in May and early June. Use Jerry's smelt, gray ghost, black-nosed dace, nine-three, and Barnes Special streamer flies. In the evening, dry-fly tactics will take fish. Carry an assortment of quill Gordons, red quills, Adams, and small dun variants. This is flatwater dry-fly fishing. Get as near as you can to where a trout is rising and try to anticipate its direction. Cast your fly ahead of the fish, taking care to make a delicate presentation, and be ready to strike should the trout hit. Most takes in flatwater situations are highly explosive.

During daytime in summer, use a canoe and troll with a sinking fly line.

Use a Jerry's smelt a few inches behind a dodger. A rod holder will come in handy here. Remember, you need not go fast when using a dodger. Go slowly and let the lure attract fish as it flutters and waves. Even in summer, you should see a few trout rising, especially toward evening. Unless caddis flies are on the water, these fish are difficult to take, because they feed primarily on midges. Use midge patterns in sizes 22, 24, and 26.

Directions: From Franklin, head east on Maine Route 182. At about 10 miles, look for Fox Pond at the bottom of a steep hill. There is a hand-carry boat ramp along Maine Route 182.

For more information: Call the Maine Department of Inland Fisheries & Wildlife Regional Headquarters in Bangor.

49. Bog Lake

Key Species: *landlocked salmon, brown trout, white perch, pickerel*
Best Way to Fish: *boat, canoe*
Best Time to Fish: *May through September*
MAG: *26, A-1*

Description: This easily accessible yet semi-remote 826-acre lake contains both coldwater and warmwater species. Small aluminum boats or canoes are perfect for fishing this small lake. Not much opportunity exists to fish from shore, and the boat ramp is not designed for large, heavy boats. There is a private campground in Alexander, and motels are available in Machias.

Fishing index: Local anglers hit Bog Lake for landlocked salmon early in the season, just after ice-out, which is usually in late April or early May. The lake receives annual stockings of salmon and is an unsung but steady producer. In May and June, troll around the shore of the single, large island at the north end of the lake, using tandem streamers. Gray ghost and Jerry's smelt are highly effective, as are orange and gold Flash Kings. Use a fly rod with sinking line and 20 feet of 6-pound test leader.

An initial stocking of brown trout took place at Bog Lake in 1995. Since the lake has a substantial smelt population, the brown trout should prosper and provide good fishing. Anglers trolling for landlocked salmon should pick up a few browns along with salmon during the 1997 season. Try dry-fly fishing for browns on still evenings in May and June. Use red quills, Adams, and small dun variants. Look for trout rising and get as close as you can without scaring them. You will need a 12-foot tapered leader with a 2-pound test tippet for wary flatwater browns. Look for brown trout around the mouth of Long Lake Cove, halfway up the eastern side of the lake.

Look for pickerel in Long Lake Cove and at the southern end of Bog Lake. For large pickerel, try drifting with live minnows in late April and May. You may want to use a short wire leader. Stick to shallow water. Night crawlers, fished slowly on bottom, will also take pickerel in early spring. September is another good month for pickerel. Cool water spurs these toothy predators to eat as much as possible before the lake is locked in with ice.

White perch fishing is excellent from mid-June through September. Try drifting north-south through the middle of the lake. Use worms, night crawlers, or small minnows, fished on the bottom while you drift. Small lead-head curlytail or sparkle-tail plastic-bodied jigs are good perch catchers, too.

Directions: From Machias, head north on Maine Route 192. Look for the boat ramp on the right side of the road in the town of Northfield, about 9 miles out of Machias.

For more information: Call the Maine Department of Inland Fisheries & Wildlife in Machias.

50. ROCKY LAKE

> **Key Species:** *smallmouth bass, pickerel, white perch, landlocked salmon and brook trout possible*
> **Best Way to Fish:** *canoe, boat*
> **Best Time to Fish:** *May through September*
> **MAG:** *26, A-3*

Description: This 1,555-acre lake is contained within the boundaries of the 10,904-acre Maine Public Reserve Land Rocky Lake Parcel. It is a wild and scenic natural area, with an abundance of wildlife. Campsites are available by the boat ramp at the mouth of the northern inlet, and on the southwest shore at Loose Rock. The latter is a water-accessed site, complete with Adirondack-style shelter. Rocky Lake is a great spot for families with children. From October 1 to November 30, all trout, landlocked salmon, lake trout, and bass must be released alive at once.

Fishing index: Smallmouth bass are the major species here, due to the dozens of rocky islands. Lead-head jigs and small plastic baits are top lures here. Paddle within casting distance of the shore and cast toward the island. If the water is calm, you may see a bulge in the water as a smallmouth bass dashes to intercept your lure. Carry a hook hone and use it often, because the hook point will be in constant contact with rocks. Fly fishers should use woolly buggers, black leech patterns with bead eyes, and small poppers.

White perch will be found in the deeper water at the lake's center. Use worms, night crawlers, or small lead-head jigs. Allow your boat to drift until you locate a school of perch. Action is good on these species all summer, but brook trout and landlocked salmon anglers do best in late May and early June. You should not come specifically for trout or landlocked salmon, since these species are not regularly stocked.

Directions: From U.S. Route 1 in East Machias, turn left on Maine Route 191 and head north. Drive 9.5 miles, and look for a gravel road on the left, at the beginning of a sharp right-hand turn. The gated, gravel road leads to a hand-carry boat ramp and primitive campsite. Another vehicle-accessible campsite is located on South Bay, along with a hand-carry boat ramp.

For more information: Contact the Maine Bureau of Public Lands.

51. GARDNER LAKE

Key Species: *landlocked salmon, smallmouth bass, pickerel, white perch*

Best Way to Fish: *boat, canoe*

Best Time to Fish: *May through September*

MAG: *26, B-4*

Description: Gardner Lake is only a few miles outside of East Machias and is easily accessible. Yet most of Gardner Lake and its companion lakes, Second Lake and Loon Lake, are in the undeveloped, semi-wild country so typical of Washington County. These three lakes, plus Harmon Stream, a long, narrow section of Second Lake, cover a huge area. You will need a boat or canoe to take advantage of these waters. There is little opportunity to fish from shore. You will find motels on U.S. Route 1 in Machias and campgrounds in Perry, Calais, and Alexander.

Fishing index: Gardner Lake is a popular spot for landlocked salmon right after ice-out, usually around the end of April. The entire eastern shore is good for salmon, including the islands at the north end of the lake. Troll here with streamer flies: gray ghost, nine-three, black ghost, pink lady, Jerry's smelt, and supervisor. Use a sinking fly line and about 20 feet of 6-pound test leader. Place a split shot on the leader, slightly above the fly. Dodgers, with single-hooked gray ghost or Jerry's smelt tagging behind, can bring strikes when action is slow. Some anglers troll with live smelt. Be sure to check the action of the smelt before beginning to troll. Hook the smelt and while going at a medium trolling speed, drop the bait in the water alongside the boat and check that it rides along without twisting. If it does spin, readjust the hook until the smelt rides straight. A slight twist back and forth is acceptable.

White perch can be found in any section of the lake in the summer. Begin fishing in about 20 feet of water. The lake's deepest spot, 56 feet, is just out from the boat ramp, but the water in the middle of the lake is of a uniform depth, between 30 and 50 feet. Fish on bottom with worms or small minnows. You can also take perch with small lead-head jigs, either curlytails or sparkle tails.

Look for pickerel near shore, in the coves where the water is shallow. Fly fishers take pickerel on poppers during morning and evening hours. Otherwise, use brightly colored bucktails. Medium-sized Dardevles work well on pickerel here. Cast the Dardevle, allow it to sink a bit, and reel it in slowly, applying additional action with the rod tip.

Since Gardner Lake is noted for fast salmon and pickerel fishing, few anglers bother with the resident smallmouth bass. Smallmouths are found along the rocky shores and around the islands at the north end of the lake. Lead-head jigs, the same kind you use for white perch, take smallmouth bass here. Cast the jig, let it sink to the rocky bottom, and raise the rod smartly. Reel in the slack and repeat the process. Smallmouth bass are masters at shaking off jigs when they jump. Most anglers like to give slack line when a big smallmouth jumps, but the author has found that keeping a moderately tight line makes it difficult for the fish to throw the jig.

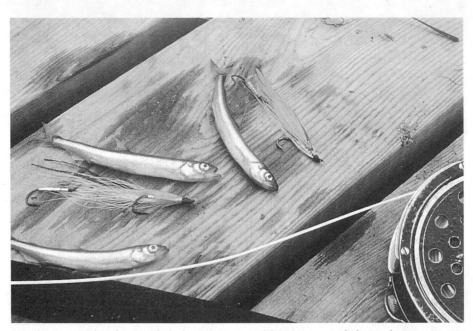

Smelt, a popular forage fish for Maine's coldwater gamefish, and streamer flies tied to mimic them. When wet, the flies will compress, creating a realistic imitation.

Directions: From East Machias, take U.S. Route 1 east and look for the first road on the left, about a mile out of town. Take this road to Chase Mills, where you will see the boat ramp. The road forks just past the boat ramp, and if you take the right-hand fork, you will come to a hand-carry boat ramp.

For more information: Contact the Maine Department of Inland Fisheries & Wildlife in Bangor or Machias.

52. PATRICK LAKE

Key Species: *brown trout, white perch, pickerel*
Best Way to Fish: *bank, canoe, boat*
Best Time to Fish: *May through September*
MAG: *26, A-4*

Description: Patrick Lake is really a 275-acre pond, typical of the little-known but productive small ponds found throughout Maine. The southwestern end of the lake is managed by the Maine Bureau of Public Lands and offers a beach, picnic tables, rest room, and boat ramp. Except for the occasional tourist stopping for a break, don't expect much company. You can fish from shore near the boat ramp, but a small boat or canoe will allow you to fully explore the lake. Lodging is available in Machias.

Fishing index: Patrick Lake is noted for white perch fishing. During the day in summer, you will take lots of perch by drifting with worms. Night crawlers will work, but the smaller earthworms are better for perch. If all you have are night crawlers, use only a small section, not a whole night crawler. Try fishing in about 30 feet of water in the area just south of a group of small islands in the center of the lake. Let your worm rest on the bottom for the most part, but raise and lower the rod every so often. Sometimes, perch will watch the worm and only bite when you impart action. If you find a spot where you get numbers of bites, you have found a school of perch. Try dropping the anchor and fishing the bottom with worms. The anchor may scare the fish away briefly, but they should return in a few minutes.

In recent years, brown trout have been stocked here, but except for some local anglers, few take advantage of their presence. In May and June, you should be able to take brown trout by daytime trolling with tandem streamers such as gray ghost or with a Jerry's smelt. Drizzly, dark days will bring more browns to your offerings. You can also take browns here by trolling with orange and gold Flash Kings and Mooselook Wobblers. Troll around the small islands in the middle and north end of the lake. In the evening, look for groups of trout rising. Use red quills, small dun variants, or Adams dry flies.

For pickerel, try small minnows fished off the islands. Hit the drop-off areas, where the water drops from 1 to 10 or 12 feet. Both white perch fishing and pickerel fishing remain good throughout the season.

Directions: From U.S. Route 1 in East Machias, take Maine 191 north to the intersection of Maine Route 86 on the right. Drive 1.75 miles on Maine Route 86 to the boat ramp at Patrick Lake.

For more information: Contact the Maine Bureau of Public Lands. You might also check with the Maine Department of Inland Fisheries & Wildlife in Machias.

53. CATHANCE LAKE

> **Key Species:** *landlocked salmon, pickerel, smallmouth bass, brook trout possible*
> **Best Way to Fish:** *canoe, boat*
> **Best Time to Fish:** *May through September*
> **MAG:** *36, E-4*

Description: Easy access and a good boat ramp make 2,905-acre Cathance (pronounced Cat-hance) Lake a popular spot for Washington County anglers. For the most part, the shoreline is wild, but the western shoreline does have some camps. Lots of islands, an irregular shoreline, and a long peninsula jutting out into the center of the lake make Cathance a favorite spot for trolling for landlocked salmon in early spring. The ice usually leaves by the first of May, and local anglers flock here for their first taste of open water fishing. Even then, you will not encounter long lines at the boat ramp and there is always plenty of open water for everyone to fish. Cathance Lake has a slot limit on bass and brook trout and a no-kill, artificial-lures-only season lasting from October 1 through October 31.

Fishing index: Most Maine anglers come here for the often fantastic, often slow landlocked salmon fishing. May is the best month for salmon. Try Gray Cove on the south end of the lake, and Sand Cove on the north end. Tandem streamer flies that imitate smelt are the preferred artificial lures. Using a sinking fly line and a 20-foot leader of 6-pound test, try gray ghost, supervisor, nine-three, pink lady, and red gray ghost. Jerry's smelt is also productive. Hardware addicts use Mooselook Wobblers and Flash Kings, fished on the same tackle used for streamer flies. Troll at a fast clip and you will get more hits. If you are going just a bit faster than other anglers, you should be just about right.

Come June, the smallmouth bass are so active that they interfere with the salmon fishing. While local anglers view the bass with scorn, you may feel differently. Fish the rocky shorelines, casting lead-head jigs trimmed with white or yellow bucktail, or lead-head jigs with plastic bodies. Mepps spinners are effective here too. Pickerel fishing is excellent as well, with plenty of larger-than-average individuals. Fish the shallow water near the shorelines, using large golden or silver shiners, orange Flash Kings, and brightly colored bucktails. Toward evening, you can take pickerel on fly-rod poppers.

Directions: From East Machias, take Maine Route 191 north toward Cooper. Just before the Cooper town line, look for a state boat ramp on the right side of the road.

For more information: Contact the Maine Department of Inland Fisheries & Wildlife in Bangor or Machias.

54. MEDDYBEMPS LAKE

Key Species: *smallmouth bass, white perch, pickerel*
Best Way to Fish: *boat, canoe*
Best Time to Fish: *May through September*
MAG: *36, D-4*

Description: This 6,765-acre lake is one of the reasons Maine's Washington County may rightly be called the smallmouth bass capital of the world. You will need a boat or canoe to fish this lake. Note that Meddybemps Lake is loaded with islands and rocky shoals, making it unwise for boaters to travel at other than slow speeds. The lake has no size or bag limits on bass, except that only one fish may exceed 14 inches. Lodging is available in nearby Baring, Calais, and Pembroke. Camping is available in Pembroke and at nearby Pleasant Lake.

Fishing index: Smallmouth bass fishing is fast and furious for fish weighing about one pound. You can catch them until your arms feel as though they will fall off. Because of the absolute certainty of success, this is an ideal spot to introduce children and beginners to bass fishing. A slot limit has been imposed in hopes of increasing the average size of bass in Meddybemps. Good fishing begins in late May, is best in June, and continues through September. Fish all around the rocky shore and islands. Cast lead-head jigs and plastic baits toward shore and slowly retrieve, giving plenty of action with your rod tip. Fly fishers can use poppers, woolly buggers, and leech patterns.

Look for pickerel in the shallow areas near shore and cast spinners, yellow bucktails, red plastic worms, or Dardevle spoons. In summer, white perch congregate in the deepest section of the lake, the 38-foot hole between Masters Island and Scott Arm. Use worms, small minnows, or lead-head plastic-bodied jigs while drifting in your boat or canoe. Do not be surprised if you take a few smallmouth bass along with the white perch; bass often accompany schools of perch, perhaps hoping to pick off any stragglers or small fish.

Directions: From U.S. Route 1 in Pembroke, head west on Maine Route 214 to Meddybemps Lake. A carry-in state boat ramp is located on the right of Maine Route 214.

For more information: Contact the Maine Department of Inland Fisheries & Wildlife in Bangor or Machias.

55. CRAWFORD LAKE

Key Species: *smallmouth bass, white and yellow perch, pickerel, brook trout possible*
Best Way to Fish: *boat, canoe*
Best Time to Fish: *May through September*
MAG: *36, D-1*

Description: This relatively shallow, 1,677-acre pond is set in a semi-remote part of Washington County. The East Machias River exits Crawford Lake at its south end. This lake sees little fishing pressure and fishing for the above-listed species is excellent. You will need a boat or canoe, since little opportunity exists for fishing from shore. Crawford Lake has a special fall fishing season from October 1 to November 30, during which all trout, landlocked salmon, lake trout, and bass must be released alive at once. Primitive campsites are located on an island in the northeast section of the lake and at the south end of the lake by the mouth of the Machias River. There is also a private campground in nearby Alexander. Motels are available in Baring.

Fishing index: Local anglers come to Crawford Lake for its exceptional pickerel fishing. Although you can take pickerel here throughout the season if you stick to the weedy areas, early spring is the best time to take large fish, those weighing 3 pounds or more. Why the biggest pickerel in the lake are on the prowl at this time is something of a mystery. Perhaps the sunlight is welcome after a long winter spent in diffused light under snow-covered ice. Interestingly, small pickerel are scarce at this time. Maybe because aquatic weeds have not yet begun to grow, the small fish have a difficult time finding cover and feel threatened. Old-timers used to take pickerel in the early season with a simple night crawler behind a Colorado spinner. You can have good luck with live minnows, spinners, and Dardevles.

White and yellow perch fishing is excellent. You can take these species all summer with ultralight spinning tackle and small jigs, live minnows, or earthworms. Drift about with your bait touching bottom, and when you find a concentration of fish, set your anchor. It is best to use bait to locate the fish, and cast spinners and small lead-head jigs after you have anchored.

Crawford Lake is dotted with islands, both large and small. The shorelines of these islands are prime places to cast for smallmouth bass. Use small lead-head jigs with plastic bodies, spinnerbaits, Dardevles, and Mepps spinners. Fly casters can take fish on woolly buggers, leech patterns, and small poppers.

Directions: From Wesley, head north on Maine Route 9, also called the Airline. After going by an extremely sharp curve in the town of Crawford, look for the first gravel road on the left. This road leads to the boat ramp. A hand-carry ramp is located just north of Great Pine Point, two roads up on the left from the first gravel road mentioned.

For more information: Call the Maine Department of Inland Fisheries & Wildlife in Machias.

56. St. Croix River

Key Species: *smallmouth bass, pickerel*
Best Way to Fish: *boat, canoe*
Best Time to Fish: *June through September*
MAG: *36, B-4*

Description: This wide river has a moderate flow, and is best fished from a small motorboat or canoe. The St. Croix is a boundary river with Canada and special boundary water regulations are in effect. These regulations are complex and vary considerably from Maine's General Law. Bag limits, open season dates, minimum length limits, equipment, legal hours, and bait types are all affected, so study the Open Water Fishing Regulations booklet carefully before fishing in this area. Campgrounds are located in Alexander, Calais, and Perry. Motels are available in Calais.

Fishing index: The St. Croix River, from Woodland to the dam at Grand Falls, is an ideal day-trip for boaters and canoeists looking for fast smallmouth bass action. In June, the spawning season, fly fishers and anglers using spinning gear take dozens of bass a day. Fly rodders should use woolly buggers, muddler minnows, Edson tiger light bucktails, and leech patterns. Spinning lures include small Dardevles, lead-head jigs, and spinnerbaits. Concentrate on the shorelines rather than the middle of the river. Position your boat or canoe so you can cast in toward shore as you float down the river.

When the water warms up in July and August, the best times are early or late in the day. You can still take bass in the daytime during the summer if you use a depth finder and locate the deep holes in the river. Bass will be holding in the cooler water here and you can take them by using deep-diving minnow imitations or by slowly fishing a plastic bait or plastic-bodied jig.

Directions: From Woodland, head north on North Main Street for 1.5 miles. The road turns to gravel and leads past a boat ramp on the right. Alternately, you can put a canoe in below the dam at Grand Falls.

For more information: Contact the Maine Department of Inland Fisheries & Wildlife in Bangor or Machias.

57. BIG LAKE

Key Species: *smallmouth bass, landlocked salmon, white perch, pickerel, cusk*
Best Way to Fish: *boat, canoe*
Best Time to Fish: *May through September*
MAG: *35, B-5 and C-5; 36, B-1*

Description: At 10,305 acres, Big Lake lives up to its name. If you combine Big Lake's acreage with the smaller lakes connecting to it, that figure nearly doubles. It is best to fish here with a boat. Big Lake is connected to the St. Croix River, Maine's border with Canada, by a massive body of water called Grand Falls Flowage. Although the flowage is shallow and has a considerable current, it offers excellent smallmouth bass fishing. Special regulations include a slot limit on bass.

Big Lake is a perfect location for the angler who has plenty of time and wants a quality backwoods experience. This lake is much too large to be thoroughly explored in one day. Lodging is available in Calais, and there are primitive campsites on Buckman Island and Little Pine Island in Big Lake.

Fishing index: Big Lake is a top-notch smallmouth bass water throughout the season. June and early July are probably the best times, but September is almost as good. Look for bass around Big Lake's numerous islands and points. Keep your hooks sharp, and make sure your line is in good condition, since it will get a real workout. You can take dozens of fish in a day with little effort. Use lead-head jigs with either bucktail or plastic bodies, black or purple plastic worms, plastic salamanders, and small Slug-Go lures.

In early spring, Big Lake is also a popular landlocked salmon water. Salmon fishers prefer tandem streamers such as gray ghost, black ghost, supervisor, and nine-three. Fish your streamers on a sinking fly line with at least 20 feet of 6-pound test leader.

Look for white perch in about 20 feet of water in the main section of the lake. Fish for them with worms, night crawlers, small minnows, or small lead-head plastic-bodied jigs. You might find perch near the surface in the evening, especially near the Long Lake outlet. For surface-feeding perch, use any dry fly pattern. White perch have small mouths, and you will probably miss the first few takes until you learn to hesitate a moment before lifting your rod. The eastern end at Long Lake is also the best bet for pickerel. It is relatively shallow and quite weedy. Use orange Flash Kings, red plastic worms, or brightly colored bucktails.

Directions: From Calais, take U.S. Route 1 north to Princeton. In Princeton, you can launch your boat at the state ramp on U.S. Route 1, or turn left on West Street and take the first gravel road to the right. Follow this road to its end at the ramp at Greenland Cove.

For more information: Contact the Maine Department of Inland Fisheries & Wildlife in Machias.

57-59 Big Lake/West Grand Lake/Lower Oxbrook Lake

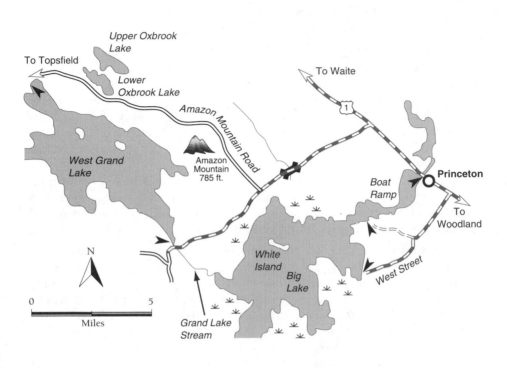

Upper Oxbrook Lake

To Topsfield

Lower Oxbrook Lake

To Waite

Amazon Mountain Road

1

West Grand Lake

Amazon Mountain 785 ft.

Boat Ramp

Princeton

To Woodland

N

White Island

Big Lake

West Street

0   5

Miles

Grand Lake Stream

58. West Grand Lake

Key Species: *landlocked salmon, lake trout, smallmouth bass, white perch, whitefish, pickerel*
Best Way to Fish: *boat, canoe, ramp*
Best Time to Fish: *May through September*
MAG: *35, B-3*

Description: West Grand Lake is big and deep, covering 14,340 acres, with depths up to 128 feet. It is connected to Junior Lake (Site 60) by a water thoroughfare—a waterway, without flowage, that connects two bodies of water. The famous Grand Laker canoe, a specialized fishing craft made to accept an outboard motor on its square stern, was designed for use on this lake; modern versions as well as venerable specimens can be seen here.

There is little opportunity to fish from shore. Boats should be at least 14 feet long, with lengths of 16 feet or more preferred for safety. West Grand Lake can become a raging sea during windstorms. Special regulations include a slot limit on bass and a no-kill, artificials-only season from October 1 through October 15. Lodging is available in Grand Lake Stream. Marks, Hardwood, and Kole Kill islands offer primitive campsites.

Fishing index: As soon as the ice leaves, usually sometime in late April or early May, West Grand Lake comes alive with anglers seeking landlocked salmon. Trolling, either with streamer flies or live smelt, is the most common method. When the water warms up, usually sometime in June, anglers use deep-trolling tactics for landlocked salmon and lake trout, although it is possible to take the occasional fish near the surface at any time. These tactics include smelt fished with downriggers, and lake trolls or dodgers fished with a lead-core line, with a smelt, minnow, or small fly such as Jerry's smelt for bait. Popular spots for landlocked salmon include Whitney Cove, Bear Island, The Narrows, Norway Point, and Marks and Hardwood islands.

Lake trout sometimes offer trollers an unexpected bonus. The water in the middle of West Grand Lake is uniformly deep (generally more than 60 feet), perfect for summertime lake trout fishing.

Smallmouth bass, until recently a universally ignored species, are on the spawning beds in June and offer fantastic fishing. When fishing for smallmouths, ultralight spinning tackle fans use Mepps spinners, small lead-head jigs (yellow and chartreuse are the best colors for the jig bodies), tiny Rapalas, and small casting spoons such as the Dardevle. Fly rodders use small poppers and deer-hair bugs, woolly buggers, and leech patterns. With a rocky shoreline, plus many points, coves, and islands, the entire lake offers good smallmouth bass fishing. Pug Lake, a narrow finger of Junior Bay in the northwest part of West Grand Lake, is a favorite spot.

In summer, look for white perch near the shore in relatively shallow water. Daytime fishing with small rubber-bodied jigs and live bait gets results, as does evening fishing with dry flies.

Directions: From Princeton, drive north on U.S. Route 1 and take the first left. Follow this road to the village of Grand Lake Stream. The boat landing is at the foot of the lake, right in the village. An alternate landing is located in Whitney Cove, accessible by Amazon Mountain Road, the same road used to get to Lower Oxbrook Lake (Site 59).

For more information: Call the Maine Department of Inland Fisheries & Wildlife in Machias.

Lower Oxbrook Lake is best fished by canoe. White perch, salmon, and brook trout provide plenty of sport on this wilderness lake.

59. LOWER OXBROOK LAKE

Key Species: *white perch, landlocked salmon, brook trout possible*
Best Way to Fish: *canoe*
Best Time to Fish: *June through September*
MAG: *35, A-3*

Description: Lower Oxbrook Lake is a small wilderness lake, offering complete solitude for those seeking a quiet outdoor experience. Except for a few seasonal cottages along the southeast end of the lake, the area is uninhabited. You will see no water skiers or jet ski watercraft here, since motorboats are prohibited. You will see loons, perhaps a deer or moose, and maybe even a black bear.

Lower Oxbrook is one of a set of twin lakes, attached by a thoroughfare (a waterway, without flowage, that connects two bodies of water). At only 365 acres, Lower Oxbrook Lake is really a pond. You will need a canoe to fish here, since the shoreline is studded with huge boulders, making bank fishing a hard task. Few anglers fish here in summer, so you can count on little competition. Lodging can be found in the village of Grand Lake Stream; there is also a primitive campsite at Upper Oxbrook Lake, the twin of Lower Oxbrook.

Fishing index: The remnant population of brook trout and the stocked landlocked salmon are not the main attraction here. Lower Oxbrook Lake offers some of the finest white perch fishing in Maine. Individuals often reach 2 pounds and occasional specimens weigh much more, a white perch angler's dream.

The lake's maximum depth is only 30 feet, with the deepest water in the center of the lake. Paddle your canoe into the wind and drift across the middle. You can catch white perch here on small spoons or lead-head jigs, but the largest fish will be taken on bait, either worms or minnows. If you decide to catch your own bait fish here, remember that smelt cannot be taken except by hook and line.

You can also take landlocked salmon by paddling against the wind (you can pretty much depend on afternoon breezes here) and using the wind for extra speed while you troll back.

Directions: From the village of Grand Lake Stream, take the main road north toward Princeton. Drive 5 miles to a gravel road on the left, known locally as the Amazon Mountain Road. Follow the Amazon Mountain Road for 8.75 miles and look for a small lake on the right, slightly downhill from the road. Pull well off the road and carry your canoe to the lake. To reach the primitive campsite on the north shore of Upper Oxbrook Lake, take the thoroughfare, which enters Lower Oxbrook Lake at the midpoint of its northern shore.

For more information: Call the Maine Department of Inland Fisheries & Wildlife in Machias.

60. JUNIOR LAKE

Key Species: *landlocked salmon, lake trout, smallmouth bass, white perch, whitefish*

Best Way to Fish: *boat, canoe*

Best Time to Fish: *May and June, January through March*

MAG: *35, A-1*

Description: This 3,866-acre, 70-foot-deep lake is part of a large chain of wilderness lakes. It is possible to go by boat from Junior Lake all the way to the village of Grand Lake Stream on West Grand Lake. Until recent years, Junior Lake had few cottages, but progress has taken its toll as lakeside lots have been sold off. However, the lake still retains its wilderness aspect in spite of the recent development. It is almost impossible to fish this semi-remote lake without a boat. Special fishing regulations permit the taking of cusk at night while ice fishing with no more than 5 lines. Junior Lake offers island campsites, and lodging is available in Lincoln.

Fishing index: Junior Lake is known primarily for its excellent early-season landlocked salmon fishing. May is the top month for landlocks here, and anglers take fish by trolling tandem streamer flies from 10 to 100 feet out from the rocky shorelines and off the group of islands known as the Big Islands. Any pattern that imitates a smelt will do. The author has had good luck with the nine-three, gray ghost, and Jerry's smelt. Orange and gold Flash Kings, fished on a sinking line with a 20-foot leader of 6-pound test, are another favorite. The occasional whitefish will sometimes hit a Flash King, a dividend for salmon anglers. The southeastern and southwestern shorelines are not as heavily fished and are good salmon spots. Landlocked salmon fishing picks up again in September, but fall is not as productive as spring.

Smallmouth bass fishing is excellent all through the open water season, and September is a top month. Look for smallmouths close to the rocky shores. You can take smallmouths by trolling with diving minnow imitations, or casting Dardevles, Mepps spinners, woolly buggers, black leech patterns, or topwater lures and poppers.

Ice fishers reach Junior Lake on snowmobiles and take lake trout, landlocked salmon, and cusk. Whitefish can be taken through the ice with a small hook and a tiny bit of cut-up minnow or a worm. The area between Bottle Island and the south end of the lake near the outlet of Junior Stream is a popular ice fishing spot. Lake trout and salmon are taken here on minnows and live smelt fished with tip-ups. You might want to set at least one tip-up near the shore. A friend of the author's once caught a 5-pound lake trout in 5 feet of water, just a few feet from shore. Cusk fishing through the ice at night can be productive. Using tip-ups baited with dead minnows, set the bait on the bottom. Stay near your tip-ups and have a flashlight ready at all times, to warn away snowmobiles that might not see the tip-ups.

Directions: From Lincoln, take Maine Route 6 east to Springfield, a distance of 20 miles. Continue east on Maine Route 6, and at 0.4 mile past Springfield, look for South Springfield Road on the right. Take South Springfield Road for 6 miles to its end at a gravel boat landing at Bottle Lake. Park off the road and take your boat across Bottle Lake to Bottle Lake Stream, the wide, slow-mov-

Junior Lake is famous for its rocky shores and fighting smallmouth bass. Here, an angler holds tight as an angry smallmouth makes a last-ditch attempt at freedom.

154

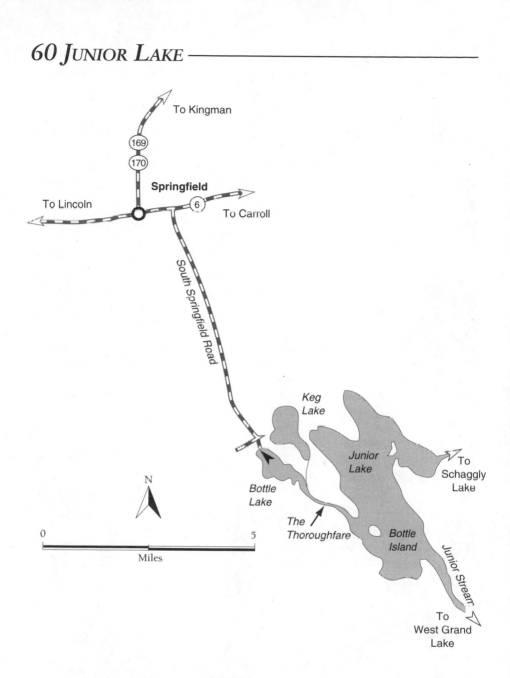

To Kingman

169
170

Springfield

To Lincoln

6 To Carroll

South Springfield Road

N

0   5
Miles

Keg Lake

Junior Lake

To Schaggly Lake

Bottle Lake

The Thoroughfare

Bottle Island

Junior Stream

To West Grand Lake

ing outlet. Follow Bottle Lake Stream to Junior Lake. If you have a deep-draft boat, be careful about hitting dead snags with your propeller. The stream is wide, but very shallow, except for the channel. You will enter Junior Lake near Bottle Island, a rocky island on the southwest end of the lake.

For more information: Call the Maine Department of Inland Fisheries & Wildlife Regional Fish and Wildlife Headquarters in Bangor.

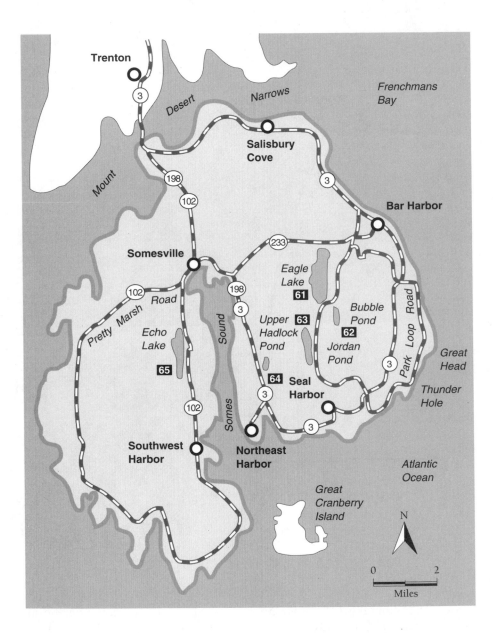

Trenton

③

Desert   Narrows

Frenchmans
Bay

Salisbury
Cove

Mount

⑲⑧

⑩②

③

Bar Harbor

②③③

Somesville

Eagle
Lake

⑥①

⑩②

Pretty Marsh   Road

⑲⑧

③

Upper ⑥③
Hadlock
Pond

Bubble
Pond

⑥②

Park Loop   Road

Great
Head

Echo
Lake

Sound

Jordan
Pond

③

⑥⑤

⑥④ Seal
Harbor

Thunder
Hole

⑩②

③

Southwest
Harbor

Somes

③

Northeast
Harbor

③

Atlantic
Ocean

Great
Cranberry
Island

N

0   2

Miles

MOUNT DESERT ISLAND

Mount Desert Island, site of Acadia National Park, is known throughout the world as a place of startling natural beauty. This largest of Maine's islands offers swimming, hiking, camping, bicycling, horseback riding on well-kept carriage roads, whale watching, and just leisurely vacationing. It also offers excellent fishing.

Few visitors take advantage of the island's varied angling opportunities, ensuring that those who do come here to cast a line can do so in comparative solitude. The waters of Mount Desert Island offer a rare opportunity for the serious angler who seeks good fishing amid incomparable scenery.

Mount Desert Island offers one more bonus for anglers. Even in summer, the cool waters of its lakes and ponds provide good brook trout fishing. You can fish here for brook trout throughout the open water season with a reasonable expectation of success.

Water quality in the lakes and ponds of Mount Desert Island is some of the best this nation has to offer. Sadly, clean, pure water has become something of a rarity in many parts of the country, but Mount Desert Island has more than its share.

61. EAGLE LAKE

Key Species: *brook trout, landlocked salmon, lake trout*
Best Way to Fish: *canoe, boat*
Best Time to Fish: *May through September*
MAG: *16, D-3*

Description: Eagle Lake is a pure, coldwater lake of 436 acres, with a maximum depth of 110 feet. It supplies drinking water to Bar Harbor. Special regulations include a ban on boats with motors of more than 10 horsepower. Part of the northeast corner of the lake is closed to all activity and is clearly marked with white buoys. Many of Mount Desert Island's most scenic mountains are visible from Eagle Lake, including Cadillac and Pemetic mountains.

Fishing index: This lake's great depth, cool temperatures, vast amounts of dissolved oxygen, and high water quality make it a premiere spot for trophy coldwater game fish. Try fishing for brook trout along the rocky shores in spring, early summer, and cool midsummer days. Fly fishers should use smelt imitations such as Jerry's smelt in sizes 8 and 10. Brook trout will average around 12 inches, but trophy fish are a distinct possibility here.

Try landlocked salmon fishing a bit further out in the lake, but do your best to follow the contour of the shoreline. Metal wobblers and streamer flies will do the trick when salmon are holding near the surface. In summer, try deep-trolling techniques for landlocked salmon and lake trout.

Directions: From Bar Harbor, drive west on Maine Route 233 for about 2.7 miles. Look for a boat ramp on the left, at the north end of the lake.

62. BUBBLE POND

> **Key Species:** *brook trout*
> **Best Way to Fish:** *canoe, shore*
> **Best Time to Fish:** *May through September*
> **MAG:** *16, B-4*

Description: Bubble Pond is a small, coldwater pond that receives annual
stockings of brook trout. Maximum depth is 39 feet, in the middle of the
pond. Shoreline depths run from 5 to 15 feet. There is no launch site at Bubble
Pond, but you can easily carry a canoe the short distance from the parking
area to the water. This site has a minimum length limit of 8 inches and a 2-fish
daily limit on brook trout.

Bubble Pond is easily fished from shore, as well. One of Acadia's famous
carriage roads bounds the entire western side of the pond. This easy access
makes Bubble Pond a great family destination.

Fishing index: Brook trout are the only fish in Bubble Pond. Water temperatures stay on the cool side, even in summer, because this little gem of a pond is
situated between two mountains, Cadillac to the north and Pemetic to the
south. The cool temperatures mean that brook trout can be in a biting mood
almost any month of the open water season.

Worms are a common bait but fly tackle can be effective, especially in early
morning and evening. Caddis flies, small bucktails, and colorful attractor patterns will take trout here.

Directions: From Maine Route 3 in Bar Harbor, take the Park Loop Road to
the intersection with the one-way road. Instead of turning left on the one-way
road, continue straight for about 2 miles and look for a parking lot on the left,
at the north end of Bubble Pond.

For more information: Call the Maine Department of Inland Fisheries &
Wildlife in Bangor, or Acadia National Park.

63. JORDAN POND

> **Key Species:** *landlocked salmon, brook trout, lake trout*
> **Best Way to Fish:** *canoe, boat*
> **Best Time to Fish:** *May through September*
> **MAG:** *16, C-3*

Description: Jordan Pond covers only 187 acres but is amazingly deep. Most
of the pond, including shoreline areas, is well over 100 feet deep. Because
Jordan Pond is a local water supply, the south end is marked as off limits to
swimmers. The boat ramp is located in this zone and boaters are advised to
travel past the white buoys before starting to fish. Boats with motors over 10

horsepower are prohibited. The daily bag limit on salmon, brook trout, and lake trout is two fish in the aggregate.

Fishing index: Although Jordan Pond contains brook trout and lake trout, landlocked salmon are most numerous and command the most attention. Regular stockings ensure a steady supply of the silver leapers. Traditional ice-out trolling methods can be employed in early spring and even on cool days in the summer. Use sparsely dressed single-hooked streamer flies: gray ghost, red ghost, nine-three, supervisor, and Jerry's smelt. You can also take fish with metal spoons such as Mooselook Wobblers and Flash Kings. During the hottest weather, deep-trolling tactics will be most effective.

Because of the uniformly deep water, almost any place on the pond is good for salmon. If you are trolling with lead-core line in summer, be sure to go as slowly as possible. Use a set of lake trolls with chrome-colored blades, with a small minnow or smelt trailing about 3 feet behind. You can also get good results by trolling with a fly rod and reel loaded with a fast-sinking fly line and a small dodger at the end of at least a 6-pound test leader. Use a single-hooked streamer such as Jerry's smelt or Joe's smelt on a short line at the end of the dodger. Be sure to carry a large landing net because the deep, cold waters of Jordan Pond are capable of producing huge salmon. Some anglers forego the dodger and simply troll with a live minnow or smelt, using a 25-foot leader tied to a lead-core line. However, the author believes that a dodger or set of lake trolls will attract fish from greater distances, thus bringing more strikes.

Directions: Take the Park Loop Road from Maine Route 3 in Bar Harbor. Follow the Loop Road and look for a sign for the Jordan Pond House on the right. About 0.2 mile before the Jordan Pond House, look for the parking area and boat ramp.

For more information: Call the Maine Department of Inland Fisheries & Wildlife in Bangor, or Acadia National Park.

64. UPPER HADLOCK POND

Key Species: *brook trout, brown trout possible*
Best Way to Fish: *canoe, bank*
Best Time to Fish: *May through September*
MAG: *16, C-3*

Description: This scenic 35-acre pond is situated along Maine Route 3. The deepest part, 37 feet, is slightly south of the center of the pond, and shoreline depths range from 5 to 17 feet, perfect for shore-based anglers. Special regulations include artificial lures only (except for children 12 years and under, who may use dead fish, salmon eggs, or worms), a daily bag limit on brook trout of two fish, a slot limit on brook trout, and a no-kill, artificials-only season from October 1 through October 31.

Fishing index: Easy access and plenty of fish make Upper Hadlock Pond the perfect spot to teach a young child about trout fishing. If the child is old enough to handle a fly rod, try to get here in the early evening, when trout are feeding on the surface. Otherwise, supply the child with an ultralight spinning outfit and have him or her fish with a single worm on the bottom. The pond is regularly stocked with brook trout.

You really do not need a boat here, since the entire west side of the pond is bounded by the main road. Fly fishers can easily launch a canoe along the road if they wish.

The high-quality brook trout fishing here is due to strict length, bag, and slot limits. This means that trout more than 12 inches long are a distinct possibility. If you fish here in daylight during summer, try a sinking line and a yellow bucktail such as Edson tiger light. On dark days, use a woolly bugger or leech pattern fished slowly near the bottom. If you hit the pond in early morning or evening, small dry flies will work, as will slowly fished nymphs.

Directions: From the intersection of Maine Routes 3 and 233 in Mount Desert, drive south toward Northeast Harbor for 4 miles. Look for Upper Hadlock Pond on the left, next to the road.

For more information: Contact the Maine Department of Inland Fisheries & Wildlife in Bangor, or Acadia National Park.

65. Echo Lake

Key Species: *brook trout, landlocked salmon, white perch*
Best Way to Fish: *canoe, boat*
Best Time to Fish: *May through September*
MAG: *16, B-2*

Description: This is a scenic 237-acre coldwater lake, specially managed for brook trout and landlocked salmon. The western side is lined by rugged cliffs. Boats with motors larger than 10 horsepower are prohibited. Special fishing regulations include a slot limit on brook trout, fishing restricted to one line only, and a no-kill, artificials-only season from October 1 through October 31.

Fishing index: Brook trout can be taken near the shoreline in spring. If you are fishing from a boat or canoe, you should cast to within one foot of shore, since brook trout often chase smelt into extremely shallow water. Try small Jerry's smelt, Edson tiger light bucktails, and Mickey Finn bucktails. Some anglers use night crawlers, casting toward shore, letting the crawler settle to the bottom, and slowly working it back.

Later in the summer, a deep trough extending from the center of the lake down to the southern end is a popular spot for brook trout weighing up to 2 pounds. A few garden worms or a small shiner fished near the bottom are good choices, as is a woolly bugger fished deep with a quick-sinking fly line.

The south end of the lake holds the deepest water and is a good spot for salmon during the summer months. A fast-sinking fly line and a Jerry's smelt behind a dodger will take salmon in summer. In spring, troll along the entire shoreline using live smelts, streamer flies, Flash Kings, or Mooselook Wobblers. Evening fishing with dry flies is productive during the summer months. Bring caddis flies, dun variants, Adams, and some hairwing royal coachmen.

Flatwater fly-fishing requires patience. Here, an angler gently works into position to cast to a rising trout.

Look for white perch in the upper and eastern sections of the lake. Summer is the best time to locate schools of perch. Use worms, night crawlers, small minnows fished on the bottom, or plastic-bodied lead-head jigs.

Directions: Driving south from Somesville on Maine Route 102, look for the intersection of Pretty Marsh Road on the right. Drive 2 miles past Pretty Marsh Road and look for a sign for Ike's Point on the right. Follow the sign to a parking lot and boat ramp.

For more information: Call the Maine Department of Inland Fisheries & Wildlife in Bangor.

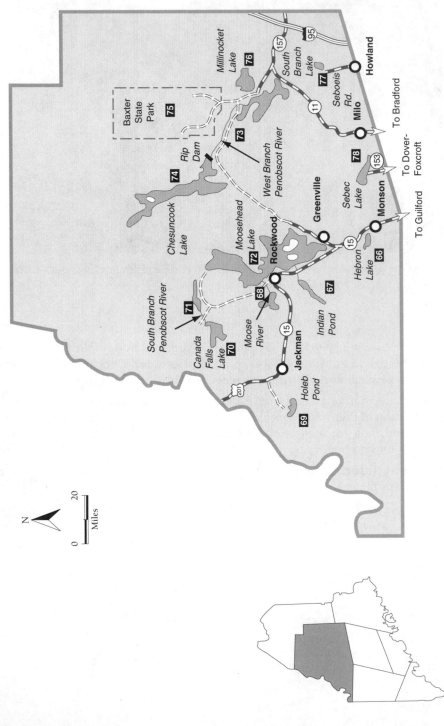

Millinocket Lake

95

157

76

Howland

South Branch Lake

77

Seboeis Rd.

Milo

To Bradford

Baxter State Park

75

11

73

West Branch Penobscot River

78

153

To Dover-Foxcroft

Rip Dam

74

Chesuncook Lake

Greenville

Sebec Lake

Monson

To Guilford

Moosehead Lake

72

Rockwood

15

Hebron Lake

66

67

South Branch Penobscot River

71

68

Indian Pond

Canada Falls Lake

70

Moose River

15

Jackman

201

Holeb Pond

69

N

20

Miles

0

NORTHERN MAINE

Northern Maine is a vast woodland region with mile-high Mount Katahdin at its center. Paper companies control a large percentage of this eastern wilderness. Working in partnership with recreational users of the north woods, these companies provide roads, campsites, and boat ramps.

Ice-out comes late to this region, as much as a month later than in Midcoast and Southern Maine. The dedicated angler can follow the seasons, beginning in the south and following the prime fishing north as spring progresses. Likewise, autumn comes early, providing the cool water temperatures needed for fall trout and landlocked salmon fishing.

Whenever you visit this wild and scenic region, be prepared. Always bring plenty of warm clothes and, in spring and summer, some sort of protection from biting insects.

66. LAKE HEBRON

Key Species: *brook trout, landlocked salmon, lake trout, white perch*
Best Way to Fish: *canoe*
Best Time to Fish: *May through September*
MAG: *31, A-3*

Description: This deepwater pond is managed for coldwater gamefish. Easy access and good fishing make Lake Hebron a popular spot for local anglers. The Appalachian Trail follows the northwest corner of the pond, and Monson Village is nestled around its eastern end. Monson was once famous for its slate industry, and examples of native slate may be seen along Maine Routes 6 and 15. This 525-acre lake receives huge annual stockings of brook trout. In 1994, 4,300 trout were stocked here; in 1995, another 4,300 brook trout were stocked, along with 250 landlocked salmon. There is a campground in Abbot, just south of Monson. Motels are available in Greenville.

Fishing index: Brook trout and landlocked salmon are the main attractions right after ice-out, in late April or early May. Look for salmon to be near the islands off the mouth of Towne Cove. Try trolling with live smelt or tandem streamer flies such as gray ghost, black ghost, nine-three, or supervisor. Using a sinking fly line and a 20-foot leader of 6-pound test, troll along the shorelines. You can also take salmon by trolling with Mooselook Wobblers and Flash Kings, using a fly rod and sinking line. In early spring, depths from 10 to 30 feet hold brook trout in the western end of the lake. You should also try Whiting Cove, in the southeast corner of the lake, and the area just in front of the boat ramp in Monson. Try trolling a Jerry's smelt or Edson tiger light along the shoreline, using a sinking fly line and a 12-foot tapered leader with a 3-pound test tippet. Go slowly and follow an erratic pattern. It helps if you work your rod, making the fly dart ahead just like a real bait fish.

The deepest water, from 80 to 102 feet, is in the middle of the lake, straight out from the boat ramp in Monson. Look for lake trout and landlocked salmon to congregate here in July and August. Use a live smelt or shiner, trolled behind a set of lake trolls with a lead-core line. Or use a live smelt or minnow trolled deep by means of a downrigger. Begin trolling slowly on the edge of the deep water, in depths of 40 feet. If you do not find fish, keep widening your trolling pattern to include deeper water. Remember, when slow-trolling, go as slowly as possible. If your motor does not idle as slowly as you like, try pulling a sea anchor made of a plastic 5-gallon pail tied to the back of your boat. The sea anchor should slow you down enough to reach the correct speed.

In the summer, you will find white perch in the narrows around the mid-point of the lake. Fish for them by drifting with worms, night crawlers, or small minnows. Small lead-head plastic-bodied jigs work well, too.

Directions: Drive north on Maine Routes 6 and 15 to Monson. As you get into town, look for the Bray Road on the left, just after passing a narrow part of the lake. The boat ramp is on the left off the Bray Road.

For more information: Contact the Maine Department of Inland Fisheries & Wildlife Regional Fish and Wildlife Headquarters in Greenville.

67. INDIAN POND

> **Key Species:** *landlocked salmon, lake trout, brook trout, splake, smallmouth bass, whitefish, cusk*
>
> **Best Way to Fish:** *boat, canoe*
>
> **Best Time to Fish:** *May through September*
>
> **MAG:** *40, C-5*

Description: This 3,746-acre impoundment was created by Harris Dam, on the Kennebec River. Water levels at Indian Pond are constantly changing because of drawdowns at the dam. You will need a boat or canoe to fish here. Special regulations include a daily limit on brook trout, lake trout, and landlocked salmon of two fish in the aggregate, a slot limit on trout and splake, and an artificials-only no-kill season from October 1 through October 31. Camping is available.

Fishing index: The East and West Outlets enter Indian Pond in its upper end. This area is full of little islands, coves, and points, and probably gets the most attention from anglers. Nevertheless, the fishing remains excellent. Look for brook trout, splake, salmon, and smallmouth bass in this part of the lake. For brook trout, try drifting with worms or night crawlers at any time of the year. In May and early June, you might find red quills or caddis flies hatching. Use red quills, Hendricksons, small dun variants, and any caddis pattern. You can also take brook trout here by fishing a small woolly bugger on the bottom. Use a fast-sinking fly line and let the fly hit bottom as you slowly drift along.

Smallmouth bass can be found all around the lake. Most anglers come to Indian Pond for the lake trout and landlocked salmon, but smallmouth bass fishing here is as good as it gets anywhere. For smallmouths, try lead-head jigs with plastic curlytail bodies, Mepps spinners, black plastic worms, and Dardevles. On calm days, try for topwater action with poppers. Cast toward the shore and cover as much water as possible before moving on.

The best way to take splake here is to still-fish on the bottom with worms, nightcrawlers, or small minnows. For landlocked salmon in May and early June, troll with tandem streamers, live smelt or minnows, or metal spoons. Use a sinking fly line and a 20-foot section of 6-pound test leader. Landlocked salmon will also take a single-hooked gray ghost or Jerry's smelt trolled behind a dodger. Chrome-and-brass colored dodgers seem to work best.

The deepest part of Indian Pond, 118 feet, is at the south end. In summer, this is where you should concentrate on trolling for lake trout of 10 pounds or more. Use a downrigger or lead-core line and troll with a large minnow or small sucker. Suckers, if you can find them, are a top lake trout bait. Troll slowly and be ready to strike hard and fast when a lake trout bites. Indian Stream enters the pond about halfway down on the right. This is a good spot for lake trout and salmon as well as brook trout.

Directions: From Rockwood, drive south on Maine Routes 6 and 15 and look for the Burnham Pond Road on the right, about 3.5 miles south of the bridge over the East Outlet of the Kennebec River. Follow this gravel road to a boat ramp on Indian Pond. An alternate boat ramp is located at the extreme south end of the pond. This is somewhat more difficult to get to. Take the unpaved road from The Forks east to Lake Moxie and follow the same road north to the boat ramp and campsite at Indian Pond.

For more information: See Moosehead Lake (Site 72).

68. MOOSE RIVER

Key Species: *brook trout, landlocked salmon*
Best Way to Fish: *wading, boat*
Best Time to Fish: *May through September*
MAG: *40, A-5*

Description: This is a freestone river with lots of deep pools and riffles. Water levels are controlled by the dam at Brassua Lake. The dam also ensures that river temperatures are always cold, a plus for coldwater species. Moose River residents include a population of larger than average crayfish, some with tails 3 or 4 inches long. These are known locally as "Moosehead Lobsters."

Special fishing regulations include a closed section of river, a 12-inch minimum length limit on brook trout, an 18-inch minimum length limit on lake trout, and special artificial-lures-only and fly-fishing-only seasons. Read the Open Water Fishing Regulations booklet carefully before fishing. Rockwood offers a number of private campgrounds.

Fishing index: This tributary of Moosehead Lake is a favorite spot for native brook trout and landlocked salmon fishing. The upper reaches are full of fast-water sections and large pools, and are best fished by wading. The lower section is deep and slow-moving. If you want to troll here, put in at the boat ramp in Rockwood on Moosehead Lake.

The area below Brassua Lake Dam offers excellent early-season landlocked

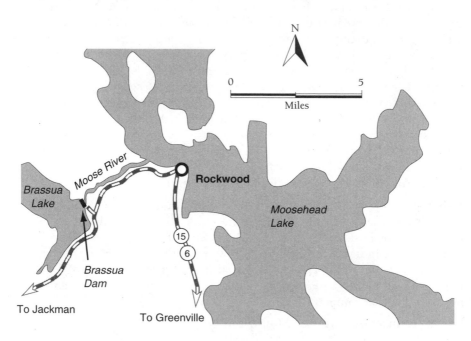

salmon fishing. Watch for red markers indicating a closed section immediately below the dam. While May and June are also productive, September is the best. Fly fishers prefer streamers and bucktails. Large, bushy dry flies work well too, although few use them. Be sure to bring a selection of caddis flies in the summer, when these insects appear in huge numbers. Evenings are the best time to fish to the caddis hatch. Interestingly, the brook trout taken from Moose River are, on average, slightly larger than those taken from Moosehead Lake.

Directions: From Rockwood on Moosehead Lake, take Maine Routes 15 and 6 west toward Jackman. After 4.5 miles, look for a gravel road on the right. Park along Maine Routes 15 and 6 and walk down the gravel road, which leads to the dam at Brassua Lake.

For more information: Contact the Moosehead Lake Vacation and Sportsmen's Association or the Moosehead Lake Region Chamber of Commerce.

69 HOLEB POND

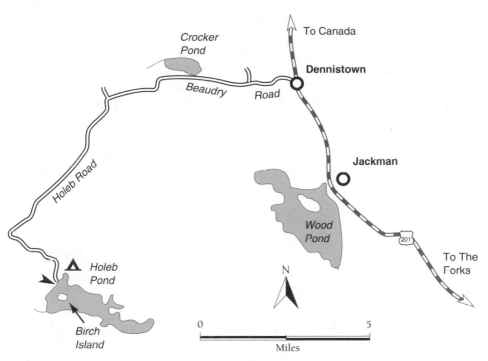

69. HOLEB POND

Key Species: *brook trout, landlocked salmon, splake, cusk, lake trout possible*

Best Way to Fish: *boat, canoe, bank*

Best Time to Fish: *May and June, January through March*

MAG: *39, C-3*

Description: Holeb Pond is a 1,055-acre pond located in the middle of the Holeb Parcel of the Maine Bureau of Public Lands. Attean Mountain and Sally Mountain provide a scenic background. This wild area is just west of Jackman, known as "the Switzerland of Maine." In 1995, Holeb Pond was stocked with 9,300 brook trout and 1,000 splake. There is a slot limit on brook trout and splake. A primitive campsite is available.

Fishing index: The maximum depth of Holeb Pond is only 52 feet, perfect for brook trout and splake. Beginning in mid-May, slowly troll the entire shoreline, using night crawlers, small smelt or minnows, or Jerry's smelt. Use a fly rod and sinking fly line. Anglers using spinning gear sometimes take brook trout on small spoons and spinners by fishing from a boat or canoe and casting in toward shore. The area just off the boat ramp is a good spot for brook trout and splake, as are the several small islands in the south end of the pond. Many anglers like to drift slowly with a lively worm, hooked once so that it retains a

167

natural appearance. Do this in 10 or 20 feet of water and you should take both brookies and splake. Lake trout can be found near the deepest section of the pond, just off the south end of the big island at the north end of the pond.

In May and June, try for landlocked salmon along the north end of the pond, between the mainland and the one large island. Troll at a fast clip, using tandem streamer flies, Mooselook Wobblers, and Flash Kings.

If you come here to camp, you may want to cast a line for cusk from the shore near your campsite. Use a night crawler or dead minnow and let it sit on the bottom. With your rod secured so that a fish cannot pull it into the water, you can watch the stars while you wait for a cusk to bite.

Directions: From Jackman, head north toward Dennistown on U.S. Route 201, and turn left on the Beaudry Road. Continue on the Beaudry Road until it becomes the Holeb Road. Follow the Holeb Road to the boat landing and primitive campsite, a distance of 13 miles from U.S. Route 201.

For more information: Contact the Jackman-Moose River Region Chamber of Commerce.

70-71 CANADA FALLS LAKE/SOUTH BRANCH PENOBSCOT RIVER

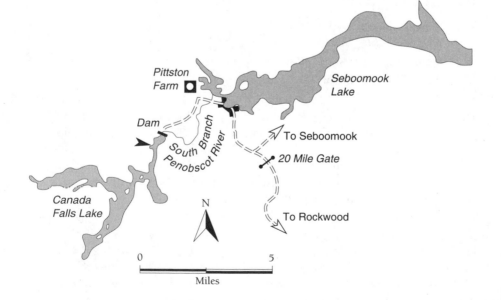

70. CANADA FALLS LAKE

Key Species: *brook trout*
Best Way to Fish: *canoe*
Best Time to Fish: *May and June*
MAG: *48, D-2 and D-3*

Description: Canada Falls Lake is a sprawling, shallow 2,627-acre impoundment. A canoe is the most practical way to fish here, because of the proliferation of dead stumps and tree trunks known in Maine as "dri-ki." Small motorboats are workable, but you must keep a sharp eye out for snags. A maintained campsite is located near the dam at the south end of the lake, close to the boat ramp. There are several special fishing regulations. From April 1 through August 15, the daily limit on trout is two fish, with a minimum length of 6 inches; only one trout may be longer than 12 inches. From August 16 through September 30, artificial lures only may be used, and the daily limit is one fish.

Fishing index: This remote lake is home to native brook trout and nothing else. Anglers here use bait and spinning gear, but fly fishing is the most productive method. The shallow, twisting nature of this lake makes it look like a huge beaver flowage. Dry flies and small bucktails work well here. Trout are pretty evenly spread out, but you should concentrate on the many points and on the mouths of small coves.

The best fishing is from late May through mid-June. After that, the shallow water becomes too warm for good fishing. The action can pick up again in September, during the artificials-only season. The huge area covered by this impoundment cannot be fished in one day, so you should plan to camp out for at least one night.

Directions: From Rockwood, on Moosehead Lake, head west on Maine Routes 15 and 6. Cross the Moose River in the Rockwood Strip. Follow the main road (unpaved) to the 20 Mile Gate. Watch for signs for 20 Mile Gate. Stop at 20 Mile Gate, register, and follow the signs to Canada Falls Lake. The road leads you to the campground and boat ramp.

For more information: Contact the Moosehead Lake Vacation and Sportsmen's Association, or the Maine Department of Inland Fisheries & Wildlife Regional Office in Greenville.

71. SOUTH BRANCH PENOBSCOT RIVER

Key Species: *brook trout*
Best Way to Fish: *wading*
Best Time to Fish: *May and June*
MAG: *48, D-3*

Description: This remote branch of the Penobscot River is largely overshadowed by the better-known sections. Thus, you can count on quality fishing with little competition. The stretch of river below Canada Falls Lake flows through a small but scenic gorge. A maintained campsite is located at Canada Falls Lake (Site 70).

Canoeing is not practical, but it is easy to fish the river from the bank or by wading. Note that some spots are too dangerous to wade when the water is high. There are several special fishing regulations. From April 1 through August 15, the daily limit on trout is two fish, and the minimum length is 6 inches; only one trout may be longer than 12 inches. From August 16 through September 30, artificial lures only may be used, and the daily limit is one fish.

Fishing index: The river is crooked and has many small islands, each offering choice spots to cast for brook trout. The water immediately below the dam is fast, but brook trout are common on the edges and in the few eddies. Farther down the stream, the river quickly drops through a series of deep pools and swift runs. Streamer flies and bucktails, especially Edson tiger light bucktails, are highly effective when fished on a sinking line. This river is usually too swift for effective nymph fishing, but if you hit a hatch of red quills toward the end of May, you might take fish on red quills, Hendricksons, or small dun variants.

The average brook trout here will measure 10 to 12 inches, but much larger specimens are present. The author once hooked a 4-pound brook trout that he had to chase downstream for a considerable distance. Nevertheless, this is not a large river when compared to the West Branch of the Penobscot or the Kennebec River. You will get the most pleasure if you use relatively light tackle. Use at least a 3-pound test leader.

Directions: From Rockwood, on Moosehead Lake, head west on Maine Routes 15 and 6. Cross the Moose River in the Rockwood Strip. Follow the main road (unpaved) to the 20 Mile Gate. Watch for signs for the 20 Mile Gate. Stop at 20 Mile Gate, register, and follow the signs to Canada Falls Lake. The road takes you to a campground just above the dam. Begin fishing downstream, on the left side of the river as you view it from the dam.

For more information: Contact the Moosehead Lake Vacation and Sportsmen's Association or the Maine Department of Inland Fisheries & Wildlife Regional Office in Greenville.

72. MOOSEHEAD LAKE

Key Species: *lake trout, landlocked salmon, brook trout*
Best Way to Fish: *boat, canoe, shore*
Best Time to Fish: *May through June*
MAG: *41 and 49*

Description: Moosehead Lake, 30 miles long by 20 miles wide, is the largest lake contained in any one state east of the Mississippi. Here the mighty Kennebec River begins its journey to the sea. Moosehead Lake's deep, pure water is ideal for coldwater species, which is why Maine's three native salmonids are found here in such abundance.

You can fish from shore in many areas, but will need a boat to thoroughly explore this huge body of water. The fishing and hunting opportunities on and

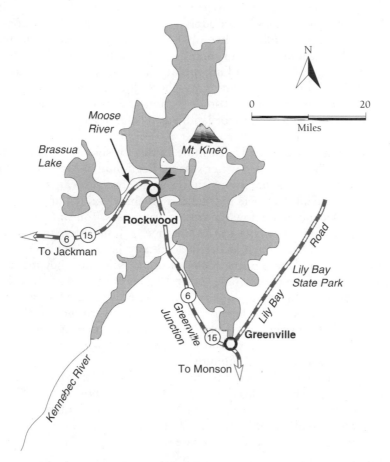

around Moosehead Lake have spawned a local service industry. Guide services, campgrounds, and boat and airplane trips are all available at the lake. Special fishing regulations include a slot limit on lake trout. There is camping at Lily Bay State Park and in Rockwood.

Fishing index: Anglers fishing from the pier in Greenville Junction catch landlocked salmon on spinning tackle using live bait. This is pretty much limited to the month of May. Later than May, a boat is needed because the salmon move to deeper, cooler water. It is possible to take landlocked salmon and brook trout from shore at the state boat ramp in Rockwood.

The liberal regulations on lake trout in Moosehead Lake are of special interest. The lake has so many lake trout of 18 inches and under, that they compete for food with the more popular landlocked salmon. In an attempt to rid Moosehead Lake of some of the smaller lake trout and thus balance the food chain, anglers are allowed to keep up to three lake trout a day. Only one of these lake trout may be longer than 18 inches, and all three may be between

14 and 18 inches. While you may not catch one of the 15-pound specimens for which the lake is famous, you have an excellent chance of catching good numbers of the smaller variety. If you have never taken a lake trout, a trip to Moosehead Lake is probably the easiest way to do it. The deep hole by Mount Kineo, across the lake from Rockwood, is a popular spot for lake trout as well as landlocked salmon. Troll with live smelts and a downrigger. Some anglers prefer lead-core line and a smelt or minnow fished behind a set of lake trolls. Go as slowly as possible while trolling for lake trout. It is possible to take lake trout here in May on streamer flies: gray ghost, Joe's smelt, or Jerry's smelt. Use a fast-sinking fly line and a 20-foot section of 8-pound test leader. Troll slowly. This is a popular method for landlocked salmon as well, so you might pick up a salmon along the way.

Landlocked salmon are evenly distributed along the shorelines and are taken by trolling throughout the open water season. Beginning in May, local anglers prefer to troll along the shorelines with live smelt, but you can also take fish with standard tandem streamers that imitate smelt. Metal trolling spoons are also effective. Depending on how the season progresses, you should be able to pick up salmon along the shore until sometime in June. After that, you will need to fish deep, using downriggers or lead-core line, as explained earlier. Brook trout are found close to the rocky shores in May, but they move out a little deeper toward the end of June, when the water warms up. In the early season, try drifting with a night crawler, small minnow or smelt, or a Jerry's or Joe's smelt. You can also work the shoreline and cast toward shore with Mickey Finn bucktails, Edson tiger light bucktails, or small spinners. When the water warms and drives brook trout to deeper water, try fishing on the bottom with worms, night crawlers, or small minnows.

Although few anglers bother with them, Moosehead Lake has a huge cusk population. Most cusk are taken by ice fishers at night, but in early May, you can take pails of them near the mouth of Moose River. Use a large ice fishing jig topped with a small bit of bait, and fish it near the bottom. Sometimes big lake trout hit these cusk jigs, so be prepared.

Directions: From Monson take Maine Routes 6 and 15 north to Greenville, at the south end of Moosehead Lake. In Greenville, you have several options. Lily Bay State Park offers two boat ramps and camping. To get to Lily Bay, go straight ahead at the 4-way intersection in Greenville and follow the Lily Bay Road north. Watch for signs for Lily Bay State Park on the left. A new state boat ramp at Rockwood offers access to the upper reaches of the lake. To get to Rockwood, turn left at the 4-way intersection in Greenville and follow Maine Routes 6 and 15 north to Rockwood. The boat ramp is on the left.

For more information: Contact the Moosehead Lake Vacation and Sportsmen's Association; the Greenville Chamber of Commerce; or the Maine Department of Inland Fisheries & Wildlife Regional Office in Greenville.

A public boat launch at Rockwood, on Moosehead Lake, with the sheer cliffs of Mt. Kineo in the background. Such facilities provide access to dozens of Maine's fabled fishing waters.

73. West Branch Penobscot River, Ripogenus Dam to Abol Falls

Key Species: *landlocked salmon, brook trout*
Best Way to Fish: *canoe, wading*
Best Time to Fish: *June*
MAG: *50, D-3*

Description: The West Branch of the Penobscot is a brawling river with falls, whitewater, and deep pools. Roads and paths border the river. This is Maine's premier trophy landlocked salmon river. Fishing regulations vary on different sections of the river, so check the Open Water Fishing Regulations booklet before fishing. Wading and bank fishing are both possible at this site. You can easily launch a canoe at Nesowadnchunk Deadwater, a wide and calm section of the river. There are campsites at Big Eddy, Nesowadnehunk Deadwater, and Abol Falls. You can find motels in Millinocket, a 45-minute drive from the river.

Fishing index: The West Branch of the Penobscot River below Ripogenus Dam contains bigger landlocked salmon than any other river in the country. June is the best month for fishing, but the always-cool water keeps salmon active throughout the open water season. Smelt imitations are most effective in May and June. The gray ghost, Maine's old standard streamer fly, is effective here, as are all the standard bucktails and streamers. You should have a 9-

73-74 West Branch Penobscot River, Ripogenus Dam to Abol Falls/Chesuncook Lake

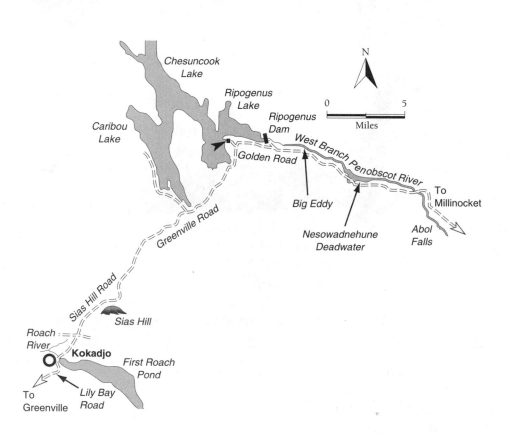

foot fly rod of at least 6-weight. Fill your reel with plenty of backing, since it is possible to hook a landlocked salmon of up to 8 pounds. If the water is at all high, you can get by with a 3-pound tippet.

Dry-fly anglers should use large attractor patterns when no insects are showing. In summer, caddis hatches are the key to success, so bring plenty of caddis imitations. Soft-hackle flies are often killers on this river. Always keep a few soft-hackles in your fly box. The West Branch special is a popular Maine pattern and is highly effective on the West Branch. The dressing for a West Branch special, to be fished wet, is as follows: size 12 hook, dark brown dubbing, wing of reddish-tinted mallard body feather, tied sparse, and a few winds of a soft, brown hackle from a hen neck.

When wading this brawling river, be especially careful of rising water. Always keep an avenue of escape open. Felts and grippers will be a great help.

Big and wild, the West Branch of the Penobscot River lies in the heart of Maine's unspoiled north country. This classic water holds trophy-sized brook trout and landlocked salmon, and is a prime destination for fly-fishers from around the country.

Directions: Roads leading to the West Branch of the Penobscot River are part of the North Maine Woods Multiple Ownership-Multiple Use Management Area. From Maine Route 15 and 6, in Greenville, take the Lily Bay Road north to Kokadjo. From there, head north on the Sias Hill Road, to the Sias Hill Checkpoint, where you must stop and register. Continue north, following signs for Ripogenus Dam and go straight to the Greenville Road. Follow the Greenville Road to the intersection of the Golden Road and turn right, at the south end of Caribou Lake. Continue on the Golden Road and turn left at the checkpoint for Ripogenus Lake, where you will find a boat ramp and campsite. It is 42 miles from Greenville to Ripogenus Dam. The river, from below the dam to Abol Falls, a distance of about 10 miles, is bounded by the Golden Road, which provides almost unlimited access. An alternative route would be to take Interstate 95 to Exit 56 in Medway and from there, take Maine Routes 157 and 11 west to Millinocket. From Millinocket, take the Golden Road to the West Branch.

For more information: For a campsite reservation, contact the North Maine Woods office. You should request one of their pamphlets. It is strongly recommended that you purchase a map of the area. Great Northern Paper publishes a detailed map of the region, cost $3. You can pick one up at the checkpoint or contact Great Northern Paper. If you plan to stay at different sites in the general area, call the Northern Region Headquarters in Island Falls for fire permit information 7 days a week. Many campsites along the West Branch of the Penobscot River are under the jurisdiction of the Maine Bureau of Parks and Recreation.

74. Chesuncook Lake

Key Species: *Lake trout, landlocked salmon, brook trout, white perch, cusk*
Best Way to Fish: *boat*
Best Time to Fish: *May and September*
MAG: *50, D-1*

Description: Chesuncook Lake, formed by Ripogenus Dam, is Maine's third largest body of fresh water. Three distinct sections of the lake are connected. The main stem is known as Chesuncook Lake, the lower body as Caribou Lake, and a third appendage as Ripogenus Lake. The total acreage is 26,200, with a maximum depth of 150 feet. Chesuncook Lake runs in a northwest-southeast direction and prevailing winds can cause large waves and whitecaps. Do not stray far from shore unless you have a large boat (16 feet minimum) and a dependable motor.

This is a semi-remote lake, with a few cottages at the southern end. Marine fossils can be found along the shore near Ripogenus Dam, at the extreme southeast end of the lake. Gero Island, at the head of Chesuncook Lake, is maintained by the Maine Bureau of Public Lands. The daily bag limit on landlocked salmon is one fish, with a minimum length limit of 16 inches. Camping is available.

Fishing index: Try for brook trout in May, in the north and south ends of the Caribou Lake section. Troll slowly near shore, using Jerry's smelt, Edson tiger light, red gray ghost, or black ghost. Anglers using bait take trout by drifting with worms or night crawlers. Salmon fishers do well around Sandy Point, on the west side of the Chesuncook Lake section, and around the mouths of the many brooks and streams that enter the lake. Large tandem streamers are effective here. Use any pattern that represents a smelt, especially gray ghost, red-gray ghost, supervisor, and nine-three. Joe's smelt and Jerry's smelt are also productive when trolled.

White perch can be found in all parts of the lake, especially the south end and at the north end around Gero Island. For perch, begin in about 30 feet of water and drift, with a worm or night crawler on bottom. You can also take perch with rubber-bodied lead-head jigs and small Swedish Pimples. If you want to take an occasional whitefish while white perch fishing, stick to the small Swedish Pimples. You may want to put a bit of worm on the treble hook of the Swedish Pimple as an incentive. In summer, lake trout will hold in and along the deep north-south trench that extends the length of Chesuncook Lake. Using a downrigger or lead-core line and a set of lake trolls, slowly troll with a large shiner, smelt, or small sucker riding just off the bottom.

For cusk, try night fishing in any shallow area. Use a dead minnow, a night crawler, or a gob of worms. Prop your rod securely to prevent a large cusk from pulling it into the water.

Directions: Roads to Chesuncook Lake are part of the North Maine Woods Multiple Ownership-Multiple Use Management Area. From Maine Routes 15 and 6 in Greenville, take the Lily Bay Road north to Kokadjo. From there, head north on the Sias Hill Road to the Sias Hill Checkpoint, where you must

Rising nearly 100 feet from its base, Rip Dam holds back the waters of Chesuncook Lake, Maine's third largest lake. Below the dam is a wild and scenic gorge formed by the West Branch of the Penobscot River.

stop and register. Continue north, following the signs for Ripogenus Dam, and go straight to the Greenville Road. Follow the Greenville Road to the intersection of the Golden Road, and turn right at the south end of Caribou Lake. Continue on the Golden Road and turn left at the checkpoint for Ripogenus Lake, where you will find a boat ramp and campsite. It is 42 miles from Greenville to Ripogenus Dam. You can also take Interstate 95 to Millinocket. From Millinocket, take the Golden Road to the West Branch.

For more information: To reserve a campsite, contact the North Maine Woods office. You should also request one of their pamphlets, and you are strongly advised to purchase a map of the area, obtainable at the checkpoint or from Great Northern Paper. The map will show all authorized campsites where no fire permit is required, as well as campsites where a fire permit is required. If you plan to stay at different sites in the area, contact the Northern Region Headquarters of Great Northern Paper in Island Falls seven days a week.

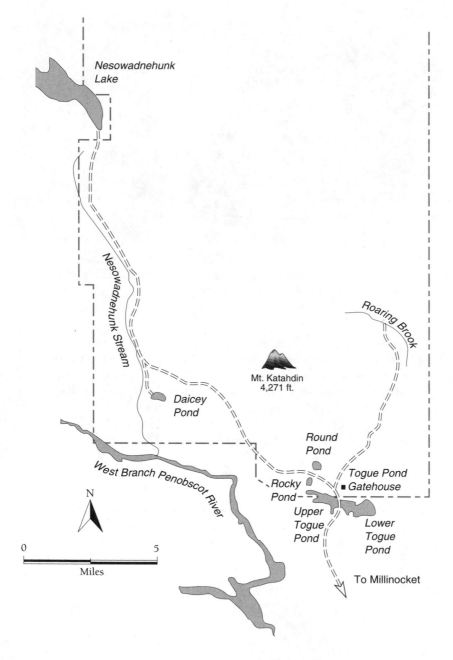

Nesowadnehunk
Lake

Nesowadnehunk Stream

Roaring Brook

Mt. Katahdin
4,271 ft.

Daicey
Pond

Round
Pond

West Branch Penobscot River

Rocky
Pond

Togue Pond
■ Gatehouse

Upper
Togue
Pond

Lower
Togue
Pond

N

0   5

Miles

To Millinocket

75. BAXTER STATE PARK

Key Species: *brook trout*
Best Way to Fish: *wading, bank, canoe*
Best Time to Fish: *May through September*
MAG: *50 and 51*

Description: 202,539-acre Baxter State Park is sometimes called the last stronghold for native eastern brook trout, although the same could be said about the entire state of Maine. Former Maine governor Percival P. Baxter purchased this land and gave it to the people of Maine, as a part of their heritage to be kept forever wild. Baxter gets crowded in summer and campgrounds are often packed, so you should reserve a campsite well in advance.

In spite of the large number of visitors, Baxter State Park is still truly wild. Roads, trails, and campgrounds cover only a small percentage of this vast area, and all of Maine's wildlife species are found in profusion. Moose, white-tailed deer, black bear, and eagles thrive in the remote splendor of the park. Since hunting is barred in most of the park, the animals are not particularly afraid of humans. Because of this, be sure to respect the animals' right to peace and tranquillity and do not attempt to come in close contact with any wildlife.

The speed limit on the park's unpaved roads is 20 miles per hour. No gasoline or other amenities are available within the park. You should write to the park authorities and request maps of the area. Special fishing regulations include a ban on motorboats except on Matagamon or Webster lakes and a prohibition on the use of live fish as bait. Dead fish, worms, and salmon eggs are permitted.

Fishing index: Brook trout anglers will enjoy the great fishing and wilderness atmosphere of Rocky and Round Ponds. Rocky and Round Pounds are easily accessible and hold plenty of brook trout. Fishing from shore or wading is productive. Fly-fishers can take brookies on dry flies, including hairwing royal coachman, Adams, Mosquito, caddis patterns, and small dun variants. Nymphs, small woolly buggers, and small leech patterns are also effective, as are size 10 bucktails such as Edson tiger light, black-nosed dace, and red-and-white. Small spinners can be used effectively here and non-fly fishers take trout on worms. May, June, and early July offer the best fishing in these ponds. Rocky and Round Ponds are perfect choices to take children fishing.

Next, you can take fish all summer in Nesowadnehunk Stream, a fly-fishing-only water. The lower reaches of this stream contain landlocked salmon as well as brook trout, so carry a few Jerry's smelt for the salmon. Daicey Pond, along the Appalachian Trail, is another fly-fishing-only water. You can rent cabins on this beautiful pond if you contact the park authorities. July sees some of the best dry-fly fishing of the year on Daicey Pond.

Directions: From Millinocket, follow signs for Baxter State Park. This leads you to the park entrance at Togue Pond. Bear left after passing the checkpoint and at about 1 mile, you will see Round Pond on the right and Rocky Pond on the left. At about 8 miles up the road you will cross the Appalachian Trail, leading into Daicey Pond. About 3 miles after that, Nesowadnehunk Stream bounds the road on the left.

76. MILLINOCKET LAKE ───────────────────

Key Species: *brook trout, lake trout, landlocked salmon, white-fish, white perch, pickerel, cusk*

Best Way to Fish: *boat, canoe*

Best Time to Fish: *May through September*

MAG: *43, A-2 and 51, E-2*

Description: This rocky, 8,960-acre coldwater lake lies within sight of Mount Katahdin, Maine's highest mountain. Millinocket Lake is noted for landlocked salmon and lake trout fishing, but to the delight of white perch fans, it is also one of Maine's best producers of bragging-size white perch. Local anglers often catch a winter's supply of perch in only a few days' time. Little opportunity for fishing from shore exists. Millinocket Lake is big and mostly open, and winds can whip the surface to a froth. On windy days, do not venture far from shore in a boat less than 16 feet long. Medway offers several campgrounds, and there are motels in Millinocket.

Fishing index: Try trolling for landlocked salmon just after ice-out, in late April or early May. Anywhere along the irregular shoreline of the lake has potential, but the stream mouths in the northwest corner and the area near the mouth of Millinocket Stream deserve special attention. Topwater action can be had through May and June. Using a 9-foot fly rod of at least 6-weight, a sinking fly line, and 20 feet of 6-pound test leader, troll with tandem streamers such as nine-three, gray ghost, red gray ghost, black ghost, supervisor, and pink lady. Joe's smelt is effective, as are large Jerry's smelt, Mooselook Wobblers, and Flash Kings. Local anglers often take good catches by slowly trolling with live smelt. You can use either spinning rods or fly rods to troll with live smelt, but a fly rod gives you more leverage and, in the author's opinion, is more effective at keeping a tight connection between you and the fish, especially when the fish jumps.

At the same time of year, brook trout will be found even closer to shore, in shallow water. Drifting with small minnows, smelt, or worms will take brook trout. You can also cast toward shore with small metal spoons and spinners. By July, both brook trout and salmon will seek cooler, deeper water, but will still approach shore during the early morning and evening hours and on cool, overcast days.

You will find the deepest water and consequently the best lake trout fishing in the northwest section of the lake. Use live smelt, small suckers, or large minnows, fished near the bottom by slow trolling with a downrigger, or lead-core line and a set of lake trolls, in at least 50 feet of water. Deep trolling is best done when the water is calm, so try to get out early before the wind picks up. You can also drift over the deep areas and jig for lake trout with a large Swedish Pimple or strip of sucker belly. A fish locator will help you find where the lakers are holding. The lake trout here can weigh more than 10 pounds.

Millinocket Lake is justifiably famous for its excellent white perch fishing. Fish weighing up to 2 pounds are common. Using worms, night crawlers, small minnows, small Swedish Pimples, or lead-head, plastic-bodied jigs, try fishing in about 20 feet of water in the rocky section of the lake just off the boat ramp. You will catch plenty of perch here from June through September. Since the perch bite so well and are so large, this would be a great place to introduce children to the joys of fishing. Watch for submerged boulders in this area.

Pickerel fishing is best in the northeast section of the lake, near a large group of islands where the water is shallow and weedy. Try drift-fishing here for pickerel. Use a medium-size golden or silver shiner, hooked through both lips. Use enough split shot to keep the shiner at least 10 feet beneath the surface. If you use spinning gear, be ready to open the bail when a pickerel strikes, so you can let it run before it swallows the bait. The author has taken 3-pound pickerel here on chrome Mooselook Wobblers. You can either troll with a Mooselook Wobbler as you would when using bait, or you can drift along and cast as you go.

Directions: From points south, take Interstate 95 north to exit 56 in Medway. From Medway, take Maine Route 157 west to Millinocket. In Millinocket, follow signs for Baxter State Park for about 10 miles until you see Millinocket Lake and the boat ramp on the right.

For more information: Call the Maine Department of Inland Fisheries & Wildlife Regional Office in Greenville.

77. SOUTH BRANCH LAKE

Key Species: *smallmouth bass, white perch, pickerel*
Best Way to Fish: *boat, canoe*
Best Time to Fish: *May through September*
MAG: *43, E-4*

Description: This 2,035-acre, semi-remote lake is known for its warmwater species. It is a prime destination for the serious smallmouth bass angler because the lake contains no coldwater game fish. Many Maine anglers prefer to fish for trout, landlocked salmon, or lake trout, and regard smallmouth bass as trash fish. Consequently, fishing pressure is light, except for local anglers in search of white perch for the frying pan. South Branch Lake has a special fall fishing season from October 1 through November 30, during which all trout, landlocked salmon, and lake trout must be released alive (but note that the lake actually contains no trout, salmon, or lake trout). The largest island in the center of the lake offers a primitive campsite.

Fishing index: Concentrate on the middle and southwest sections of the lake, which are dotted with islands. Using small casting spoons, black plastic worms, lead-head jigs, muddler minnows, small poppers, woolly buggers, or leech patterns, fish around the islands. The areas between the islands offer varying depths, so by fishing the drop-offs, you can easily locate where smallmouth bass are holding.

For white perch, try the 28-foot-deep hole north of the largest island, slightly above the lake's center. Local anglers take good catches of perch by fishing with worms on the bottom. Small minnows or night crawlers will also take perch, as will small lead-head jigs with plastic bodies. On calm days, drift along with your bait or jig bouncing bottom; when you locate a school of perch, keep drifting over it. On windy days, you might need to anchor your boat in order to maintain contact with the perch.

For pickerel, try the mouths of the small streams at the north and south ends of the lake. Try still-fishing with a minnow and bobber, or cast Mepps spinners, Dardevles, or yellow bucktails.

Directions: From Bangor, take Interstate 95 north to Howland, and get off at exit 54. Head east toward West Enfield and turn left on Maine Route 116, also called the Edinburg Road. Heading north on 116, turn left on the North Howland Road. Follow the North Howland Road over the Interstate 95 over-pass and turn right on the Seboeis Road. Follow the Seboeis Road to Seboeis Village, where you will find a boat ramp at the end of the main street.

For more information: Contact the Maine Department of Inland Fisheries & Wildlife Regional Fish and Wildlife Headquarters in Bangor.

78. SEBEC LAKE

> **Key Species:** *lake trout, landlocked salmon, smallmouth bass, white perch, pickerel, cusk, brook trout possible*
> **Best Way to Fish:** *boat, canoe*
> **Best Time to Fish:** *May through September*
> **MAG:** *32, A-1*

Description: This deep, easily accessible, 6,803-acre lake is best fished by boat. Some bank fishing is possible at nearby Peaks-Kenny State Park, but as with most of Maine's large lakes, it is generally impractical and usually not very productive. The daily limit on landlocked salmon is one fish. Peaks-Kenny State Park offers lakeside camping amid great scenery. This park is never crowded, and in September it may be nearly deserted. Motels and other lodgings are available in Greenville.

Fishing index: Although this site is noted for excellent lake trout and land-locked salmon fishing, it does not receive undue fishing pressure. Traditional early-season landlocked salmon fishing methods work well here, and May is a top month for landlocks. Using a fly rod and sinking fly line, troll with tandem streamer flies, live smelt, Mooselook Wobblers, or Flash Kings. Work the shore-line areas around South Cove Point, Deer Point, Green Point, and Jordan Island at the west end of the lake.

In summer, deep-trolling for lake trout is productive at either end of the lake, where depths range from 70 to 155 feet. However, you will have diffi-culty trolling effectively in depths of more than 100 feet. Use live smelt fished with a downrigger, or lead-core line and lake trolls. Troll as slowly as possible.

Smallmouth bass fishing and white perch fishing remain good from June through September. South Cove Point, just off Peaks-Kenny State Park, is good for both species. For smallmouth bass, use Mepps spinners, small Dardevles, lead-head jigs trimmed with bucktail, or lead-head jigs with soft, plastic bodies; curlytail bodies are especially effective. For white perch, fish in about 20 feet of water, using worms, night crawlers, or small plastic-bodied jigs.

Directions: From Dover-Foxcroft, head north on Maine Route 153, also known as the Greeleys Landing Road. This road terminates at the state boat ramp, at the eastern end of the lake.

For more information: Contact the Maine Guide Fly Shop and Guide Service.

AROOSTOOK COUNTY

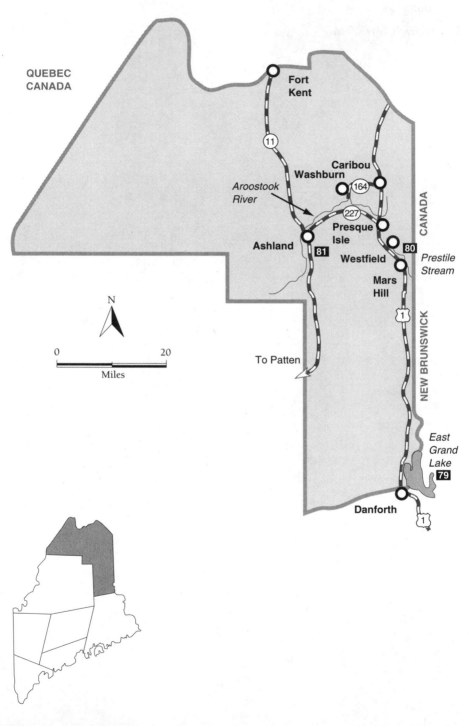

QUEBEC
CANADA

Fort
Kent

11

Caribou
Washburn

164

Aroostook
River

227

Ashland

Presque
Isle

81

Westfield

Mars
Hill

80

Prestile
Stream

1

CANADA

NEW BRUNSWICK

To Patten

N

0   20
Miles

East
Grand
Lake

79

Danforth

1

AROOSTOOK COUNTY

Aroostook County borders Canada to the north, east, and west. The largest county in Maine, it is called simply "The County" by state residents. If true wilderness still exists in the East, it must be here, in Aroostook County.

Native brook trout are the number one fish in Aroostook County. This area may be one of the last and best places to encounter these speckled symbols of young America.

Aroostook County sees the coldest temperatures in Maine and sometimes in the country. Perhaps that is one of the reasons this area remains wild and free, a haven for those who seek outdoor recreation in a pristine setting.

79. EAST GRAND LAKE

Key Species: *landlocked salmon, lake trout, brook trout, smallmouth bass, white perch, pickerel*
Best Way to Fish: *boat*
Best Time to Fish: *May and June*
MAG: *45, A-4 and 53, E-4*

Description: East Grand Lake, at 16,070 acres, is located in Washington and Aroostook counties in Maine. You will need a boat to fish at this site. Anglers in boats less than 14 feet long should stay relatively close to shore, since the lake can become dangerous quickly when the wind comes up. Camping is available at Greenland Point.

Since East Grand Lake is a boundary water with Canada, special regulations apply. Additionally, regulations for the Canadian side of the lake differ greatly from Maine regulations, and Canadian officials are quick to write summonses for any transgressions. Do not stray into any coves on the Canadian side unless you have a valid Canadian fishing license.

Fishing index: East Grand Lake is one of Maine's top landlocked salmon lakes. Anglers trolling for salmon can find fish anywhere, but good choices include the waters near Greenland Island and near Five Islands, the group of islands just north of the lake's center. Live smelt and tandem streamers are the standard fare for springtime salmon trolling, but you can also get good results drifting with live smelt when the salmon are deep.

Smallmouth bass fishing, which has only recently become popular, is excellent. Smallmouths can be found anywhere along the lake's rocky shoreline. Follow the shore and cast Mepps spinners, Dardevles, and lead-head curlytail jigs toward the shore. Fly fishers take bass on small poppers and deer-hair bugs, as well as black-nosed dace bucktails, muddler minnows, leech patterns, and woolly buggers.

Lake trout fishing is excellent as well. In summer, lake trout will be found in the deep water at the center of the lake. Troll slowly, using smelt or small suckers behind a set of lake trolls and lead-core line, or use a downrigger. Make sure your bait is on or near the bottom.

A calm morning on East Grand Lake. The anglers in boats to the middle right of photo have discovered a concentration of landlocked salmon and are slowly trolling with live smelt.

Directions: From Calais, take U.S. Route 1 north to the Danforth town line. After crossing the line, go 6 miles and look for a road to the right, just before a long curve. Follow this road to Greenland Point, where there is a boat ramp and private campground.

For more information: Contact the Danforth Chamber of Commerce or the Maine Department of Inland Fisheries & Wildlife in Machias.

80. PRESTILE STREAM

> **Key Species:** *brook trout, rainbow trout possible*
> **Best Way to Fish:** *wading*
> **Best Time to Fish:** *May through August*
> **MAG:** *59, A-2*

Description: Like the famed trout waters of Pennsylvania, Prestile Stream is a limestone stream, a rarity in Maine except for a few spots in Aroostook County. The countryside here consists of woods, fields, and rolling hills. Some bank fishing is possible, but wading is the best method when the water is low. Canoes can be used early in the season. Aroostook State Park, just across the Westfield town line in Presque Isle, offers camping.

Fishing index: Unlike their brethren in the rest of the state, the brook trout in this incredibly fertile stream are often quite selective, forcing you to become proficient at matching the hatch. This is a perfect fly fishing water. The stream is easily waded. Use sparsely dressed dry flies; flick-style dries are perfect. Carry a selection of small dun variants, Hendricksons, creme variants, and blue-winged olives. You should also bring a selection of midges, as well as some ant patterns. In summer, ants become a favorite trout food. On dark days when no flies are hatching, try slack-line fishing with red-and-white bucktails, Edson tiger light, and purple and green-bodied soft-hackle flies. Presentation is important here, so take pains to approach the fish from downstream, getting as close as possible before casting. Try not to let the fish see your shadow. The native brook trout here are very dark, with brilliant markings. Fishing is excellent through August. Brook trout average a bit less than 12 inches, so use light tackle; a 4- or 5-weight outfit is perfect. Long, thin leaders are a help.

Directions: Take U.S. Route 1 to Mars Hill and continue on U.S. Route 1 (also known as the Presque Isle Road) to the intersection of the Shorey Road on the left and the Westfield Road on the right. Turn right onto the Westfield Road and follow it to town. Look for the Egypt Road on the left. Access to Prestile Stream is from the Egypt Road, heading north. This road borders the stream, allowing plenty of access. Fishing is good at all points.

For more information: Call the Maine Department of Inland Fisheries & Wildlife Regional Office in Ashland.

81. AROOSTOOK RIVER

Key Species: *brook trout*
Best Way to Fish: *canoe, wading*
Best Time to Fish: *May through July*
MAG: *64, E-2*

Description: This fertile, gravel-bottomed river flows through the woods and potato fields of Aroostook County. The sections of river in Ashland and Washburn are easily accessible. The river can be waded or fished from the bank in most sections, but a canoe is useful during periods of high water. Wood ticks are prevalent in this area, so try not to come in contact with the brush.

Fishing index: The Aroostook River contains a sizeable population of native brook trout. While the average length is less than 12 inches, the sheer numbers make for fast action. This is prime water for fly fishers. May and June are best for dry-fly techniques. Use hairwing royal coachman, Adams, red quills, Hendricksons, mosquitos, any caddis patterns, and creme variants. Small bucktails such as red-and-white, black-nosed dace, and Edson tiger light will take fish almost anytime. Anglers using bait sometimes take large brook trout by fishing a night crawler on the bottom. Fish weighing up to 4 pounds sometimes fall to this method.

The mouths of feeder brooks are good places to try for brook trout and landlocked salmon. Search for these areas with a canoe and fish them thoroughly. You might even leave your canoe on the shore while you fish up these streams. This is a good practice in summer, since the cooler water of the small streams attracts trout.

Low water on the Aroostook River. Angler is casting a fly to one of the river's brilliantly colored native brook trout.

Directions: From Ashland, take Maine Route 11 north. Look for a bridge over the Aroostook River, just outside of town. A canoe launching area is on the right, just before the bridge. You can fish downstream from this point. An alternate site is located at Pudding Rock. To get there, take Maine Route 227 east from Ashland, then take the second road to the left. This road ends at the river, near another canoe launching area. You can fish either upstream or downstream from here. Another canoe launching area is located about a mile south of Washburn on Maine Route 164. You can fish upstream or downstream from that spot.

For more information: Call the Maine Department of Inland Fisheries & Wildlife Regional Office in Ashland.

Savoring the Results

Catch and release is a discipline that will not only save our precious angling resources but increase them for the benefit of future generations. You cannot have your cake and eat it too; neither can you kill everything you catch and expect the resource to last.

Still, some fish species are so prolific that killing a limited number has no effect on the population. Harvesting a small percentage of some species actually increases average size by reducing the number of individuals competing for limited food.

Panfish represent a nearly unlimited resource. Some saltwater species, such as mackerel, are underutilized (according to the 1992 report on the status of U.S. living marine resources put out by the National Oceanic and Atmospheric Administration of the U.S. Department of Commerce). These species are here for us to catch . . . and eat, if we wish. Some remote areas have tremendous populations of stunted brook trout. If you find such a place, nobody will fault you for killing a few for the pan. To that end, here are some classic Maine fish recipes.

Brook trout

Brook trout should be eaten the same day they are taken. Trout and other oily fish lose their quality in storage. Many fancy recipes exist for preparing trout, but the traditional, albeit simple Maine trout fry cannot be topped.

Use only trout that fit conveniently in the pan. Larger specimens are often strong. For the best flavor, stick to small or medium fish. As soon as you catch the trout, kill it and remove the guts and gills, leaving the head in place. Keep the trout moist and cold. If that means dunking it in the pond or stream every few minutes, then so be it. A handful of damp ferns in a wicker creel is the time-honored way Mainers keep trout fresh during the transition from stream to plate. Never put your trout in a plastic bag because the heat build-up can turn the fish rancid.

Now that you have taken exquisite care of your trout, rinse the fish in fresh, cold water and remove the blood line that lies at the top of the rib cage, along the backbone. Roll the trout in flour and fry in clarified butter (margarine will do) until the flour is golden brown. Remove from the pan and drain on a paper towel.

You will notice that the fish curl as they are being cooked. This is the mark of fresh fish. It in no way affects the delicate flavor of the finished product. Serve the trout with fresh greens. Most Mainers also like a pot of black tea with this meal.

White perch

Old-time Mainers naturally equate white perch with fish chowder. While a chowder made from freshwater fish may seem a contradiction in terms, perch make the best chowder going.

Skin and gut at least 12 white perch. Remove the heads and rinse clean. Steam the perch in a small amount of water, just until the flesh turns white.

Remove the fish and allow to cool. Pick the meat from the bones and place back in the water. In a separate frying pan, render 6 or 8 small bits of salt pork. Add the salt pork (or omit, if you are cholesterol-conscious). Boil 2 potatoes and 1 medium onion for 5 minutes, making sure they are not completely cooked. Dice the potatoes and onion and add to the liquid in which the fish was cooked. Add 1 quart of milk and a pat of butter. Salt has been provided by the salt pork, but freshly ground pepper can be added. Simmer the chowder until the potatoes are completely cooked. Be careful not to let the mixture boil. Just before serving, drop a few springs of parsley in the chowder and serve piping hot.

You can vary this recipe to your tastes. After all, a chowder is an ever-changing entity and great chowders are often composed on the spur of the moment. The most important factor in a good chowder is the white perch.

You can also have a more fat- and cholesterol-free perch meal that will have guests begging for more. Skin and fillet all the white perch you care to deal with. Wash the fillets carefully to remove any loose scales. Roll in flour, corn meal, or a combination of the two and fry in safflower oil until golden brown. Drain cooked fillets on a paper towel before serving. Salt and pepper to taste.

Pickerel

Although bony, the flesh is sweet and flaky. When coated with cornmeal and fried to a golden brown, they make excellent table fare. Because of the bones, pickerel are often ground and used in fishcakes. Here is a recipe for pickerel cakes:

1 cup skinned pickerel fillets

1/3 cup bread crumbs

1 teaspoon dried parsley

1/4 teaspoon basil

1/4 teaspoon thyme

salt and pepper to taste

juice of 1/2 lemon

1 green pepper

1 small onion

Grind the pickerel, green pepper, and onion. Place in bowl and mix in remaining ingredients. Form into patties and dredge with flour and fry until golden brown or save in freezer by separating cakes between strips of waxed paper.

Mackerel

Mackerel, like trout, must be kept absolutely cold until cooked. While it is unrealistic to expect anyone to carry an ice cooler on the trout stream, it is no problem to keep a cooler on a boat, dock, or bridge. The first step in preparing a memorable mackerel feed is to take the fish from the hook and place it on ice.

Clean the fish like this: remove the head and place the mackerel on its belly. Make a cut down through the back, from end to end along either side of the backbone, being careful not to cut through the belly. Open the fish and remove the insides. The end result will be a flat mackerel. Ocean fish were once prepared for drying in this manner.

Don't fry mackerel. They are too oily and you will not appreciate their delicate flavor. Instead, broil the fish in the oven or better yet, outdoors on the grill. You can broil mackerel as is, but the author likes to make a marinade. Italian salad dressing is a quick and easy marinade but almost anything will work; use your imagination. You can also squeeze lemon juice over each mackerel and coat with freshly ground black pepper.

Watch the mackerel closely as you cook them. Don't let them dry out. The oil will drip into the fire, fanning the flames while at the same time basting the fish in flavorful smoke. Keep checking for doneness by separating the flesh with a fork. When it is pure white, with no trace of red, the mackerel is done. The final product is an epicurean delight, fit for royalty.

Bluefish

Bluefish, like mackerel, are oily and must be broiled. It is interesting to note that fish oil is rich in Omega-3 acids, which are beneficial to human health. Skin and fillet your bluefish. Some people like to remove the dark strip of meat found in the middle, but that is a matter of personal taste. Prepare as you would mackerel. Or, you could try this more elaborate recipe:

Planked bluefish

Fillet the fish, leaving the skin on. Nail the fillet, skin side down (use only bright nails, not galvanized) to a 1-inch-thick board. Cut up 12, 1-inch sections of salt pork and enough similar-sized onions to accompany each piece of pork. On a nail, skewer a section of salt pork and a bit of onion. Do this with all the salt pork and onions. Lightly nail the salt pork-onion kebabs to the bluefish, being careful to distribute them evenly.

Prop the board straight up next to a thick bed of hardwood coals. Don't place the fish so close to the coals that it begins to cook immediately; the idea is to slow cook, so that the oil drips out of the fish and is replaced with the onion/salt pork mixture. When the flesh is yellow but not golden brown, pull off a bit and sample. Cooking time is usually two hours or more, depending on the size of the fillet. Planked bluefish can be the crowning achievement of a shore picnic. Once you try it, you will certainly agree that it was more than worth the effort.

APPENDIX: SOURCES FOR MORE INFORMATION

Maine Department of Inland Fisheries & Wildlife Offices

Information Division
Maine Department of Inland Fisheries and Wildlife
284 State Street, Station 41
Augusta, ME 04333-0041
207-287-2871

Regional Fish and Wildlife Headquarters (game wardens and biologists). Phone calls only to these offices, please:

Gray Headquarters
207-657-2345
1-800-295-2345

Sidney Headquarters
207-547-4145
1-800-292-7346

Strong Headquarters
207-778-3322

Bangor Headquarters
207-941-4440
1-800-624-2498

Greenville Headquarters
207-695-3756
1-800-624-2538

Machias Headquarters
207-255-3772

Maine Department of Inland Fisheries and Wildlife Automated Telephone Service:

Information and Education, Licensing and registration, Commissioner's Office or Business Office:
207-287-8000

Wildlife, Fisheries, Hatcheries, Warden Service, and ATV and Hunter Saftey:
207-287-8002

Recorded Seasonal Information:
207-287-8003

Other State Agencies

Maine Bureau of Parks and Recreation
Department of Conservation
State House Station 22
Augusta, ME 04333-0022
207-287-3821

Maine Bureau of Public Lands
State House Station 22
Augusta, ME 04333
(207) 287-3061

Federal Agencies

U.S. Forest Service
Northeast Forest Experimental Station
Concord-Mast Road
PO Box 640
Durham, NH 03824
603-868-7600

Acadia National Park
PO Box 177
Bar Harbor, ME 04609
207-288-3338

Private Contacts

Dag's Bait Shop
Corner of Minot and Towle Street
Auburn, ME 04210
(207) 783-0388

Ed's Bait Shop
Maine Route 141
Belfast, ME 04915
(207) 338-3927

Elma's Tackle Shop, Inc.,
Route 3
Augusta, ME 04330
(207) 626-7033
1-800-719-2221

Great Northern Paper Company
Northern Region Headquarters
Island Falls, ME 04747
(207) 463-2214

Great Northern Paper Company
Attn: Recreation Forester
1024 Central Street
Millinocket, ME 04462-2100

Harpo's Emporium, Inc.,
Route 133
Wayne, ME 04284
(207) 685-4697

Jackman-Moose River Region
Chamber of Commerce
PO Box 368M
Jackson, ME 04945-0368
(207) 668-4171

Kittery Trading Post
U.S. Route 1
Kittery, ME 03904
(207) 439-2700

L.L. Bean Fly Fishing Hotline
(800) 347-4552

Maine Guide Fly Shop
and Guide Service
PO Box 1202
Main Street
Greenville, ME 04441
(207) 695-2266

Moosehead Lake Region
Chamber of Commerce
PO Box 581
Greenville, ME 04441
(207) 695-2702

Moosehead Lake Vacation and
Sportsmens Association of Rockwood
Box TP
Rockwood, ME 04478
(207) 534-7300

North Maine Woods Office
PO Box 421
Ashland, ME 04732
(207) 435-6213

Rangeley Region Chamber of
Commerce
P.O. Box 317TP
Rangeley, ME 04970
207-864-5364

Sebago Lake Marina
(phone calls only please)
(207) 787-2444

The Outdoor Sportsman
U.S. Route 1
Northport, ME 04915
(207) 338-4141

FALCONGUIDES

FISHING GUIDES
Fishing Alaska
Fishing the Beartooths
Fishing Florida
Fishing Montana

HIKER'S GUIDES
Hiker's Guide to Alaska
Hiking Alberta
Hiking Arizona
Hiking Arizona's Cactus Country
Hiking the Beartooths
Hiking Big Bend National Park
Hiking California
Hiking Carlsbad Caverns
    and Guadalupe National Parks
Hiking Colorado
Hiking Florida
Hiking Georgia
Hiking Glacier/Waterton Lakes National Park
Hiking Hot Springs
    in the Pacific Northwest
Hiking Idaho
Hiking Maine
Hiking Michigan
Hiking Montana
Hiker's Guide to Montana's
    Continental Divide Trail
Hiking Nevada
Hiking New Hampshire
Hiking New Mexico
Hiking New York
Hiking North Carolina
Hiking Oregon
Hiking Oregon's Eagle Cap Wilderness
Hiking Olympic National Park
Hiking Tennessee
Hiking Texas
Hiking Utah

Hiking Vermont
Hiking Virginia
Hiking Washington
Hiking Wyoming
Hiking Wyoming's Wind River Range
Hiking Northern Arizona
Trail Guide to Bob Marshall Country
Wild Montana

ROCK CLIMBER'S GUIDES
Rock Climbing Colorado
Rock Climbing Montana
Rock Climbing New Mexico & Texas

DENNIS COELLO'S
AMERICA BY MOUNTAIN BIKE SERIES
Mountain Biking Arizona
Mountain Biker's Guide to Central Appalachia
Mountain Biker's Guide to Colorado
Mountain Biking the Great Lake States
Mountain Biking the Great Plains States
Mountain Biking the Midwest
Mountain Biking New Mexico
Mountain Biker's Guide to
    Northern California/Nevada
Mountain Biking Northern New England
Mountain Biker's Guide to Ozarks
Mountain Biking the Pacific Northwest
Mountain Biking the Southeast
Mountain Biker's Guide to Southern California
Mountain Biking Southern New England
Mountain Biking Texas and Oklahoma
Mountain Biker's Guide to Utah
Mountain Biking the Midwest

FALCON
1-800-582-2665
P.O. BOX 1718
HELENA, MT 59624